IMPLIED NOWHERE

IMPLIED
NOWHERE
ABSENCE IN
FOLKLORE
STUDIES

SHELLEY INGRAM
WILLOW G. MULLINS
TODD RICHARDSON

FOREWORD BY ANAND PRAHLAD

UNIVERSITY PRESS OF MISSISSIPPI / JACKSON

The University Press of Mississippi is the scholarly publishing agency of the Mississippi Institutions of Higher Learning: Alcorn State University, Delta State University, Jackson State University, Mississippi State University, Mississippi University for Women, Mississippi Valley State University, University of Mississippi, and University of Southern Mississippi.

www.upress.state.ms.us

The University Press of Mississippi is a member of the Association of University Presses.

Copyright © 2019 by University Press of Mississippi
All rights reserved

First printing 2019
∞

Library of Congress Cataloging-in-Publication Data

Names: Ingram, Shelley, 1979– author. | Mullins, Willow (Willow G.), author. | Richardson, Todd, 1975– author. | Prahlad, Anand, author of foreword.
Title: Implied nowhere : absence in folklore studies / Shelley Ingram, Willow G. Mullins, and Todd Richardson ; foreword by Anand Prahlad.
Description: Jackson : University Press of Mississippi, [2019] | Includes bibliographical references and index. |
Identifiers: LCCN 2018049263 (print) | LCCN 2019012677 (ebook) | ISBN 9781496822970 (epub single) | ISBN 9781496822987 (epub institutional) | ISBN 9781496822994 (pdf single) | ISBN 9781496823007 (pdf institutional) | ISBN 9781496822956 (cloth : alk. paper) | ISBN 9781496822963 (pbk. : alk. paper)
Subjects: LCSH: Folklore in popular culture. | LCGFT: Essays. | Informational works.
Classification: LCC GR41.7 (ebook) | LCC GR41.7 .I64 2019 (print) | DDC 398—dc23
LC record available at https://lccn.loc.gov/2018049263

British Library Cataloging-in-Publication Data available

Dedicated to Elaine J. Lawless and Anand Prahlad

CONTENTS

ix **FOREWORD**
The Goose Is Out: Toward New Paradigms in Folklore Studies
Anand Prahlad

xv **ACKNOWLEDGMENTS**

3 **INTRODUCTION**
Shelley Ingram, Willow G. Mullins, and Todd Richardson

19 **ONE**
Our Lady of Authenticity: Folklore's Articles of Faith
Willow G. Mullins

38 Email from Nebraska
Todd Richardson

44 On Fanfiction and the Amateur/Professional Divide
Shelley Ingram

55 **TWO**
Misanthropelore
Todd Richardson

85 Revelry: Shirley Jackson and Stanley Edgar Hyman
Shelley Ingram

viii CONTENTS

THREE
95 The Footprints of Ghosts: Fictional Folklorists in the Work of Gloria Naylor, Lee Smith, Randall Kenan, and Colson Whitehead
Shelley Ingram

118 The Folklore of Small Things
Willow G. Mullins

125 The #Landmass between New Orleans and Mobile: Neglect, Race, and the Cost of Invisibility
Shelley Ingram

FOUR
135 A Folkloristics of Death: Absence, Sustainability, and Ghosts in the Film *Welcome to Pine Point*
Willow G. Mullins

157 Check Snopes: Cyborg Folklore in the Internet Age
Willow G. Mullins

163 "Judas!"
Todd Richardson

FIVE
169 White Folks: Literature's Uncanny, Unhomely Folklore of Whiteness
Shelley Ingram

191 Where Have All the Hoaxes Gone?
Willow G. Mullins

SIX
201 Folklore in Vacuo (and Other Disciplinary Predicaments)
Todd Richardson

215 **INDEX**

FOREWORD

The Goose Is Out: Toward New Paradigms in Folklore Studies

Anand Prahlad

After forty-some years of reading folklore texts, I've settled into a kind of ennui approaching new publications. While there have been many advances in the field, too much is fundamentally the same as it might have been a century ago. Many of the same questions that have preoccupied folklorists for over a hundred years are still major concerns. All too often, texts reflect a field that imagines itself in a vacuum, disconnected from disciplines whose materials, upon close inspection, overlap that of folkloristics, and whose theoretical depth and longstanding histories highlight the voyeuristic appropriation that one could argue forms the foundation of folklore studies. Indeed, folklore studies continues to suffer the curse of its colonialist heritage, chugging steadily forward in one direction, like a train that occasionally poses important critical questions about possibilities "out there" in some other direction, but invariably stays on the "track" of its own traditions, beliefs, ideologies, and practices.

The almost dizzying pace of modern technological advancement makes this dilemma more acute, as each day, the boundaries of any known social, academic, or semantic category become more porous, often disintegrating before our eyes. Undeniably, the pervading momentum in the late 20th and early 21st centuries is toward the new and innovative, driven by relentless forces of new age capitalism and technological visions of a plugged-in, global, post-human sensibility. While folklorists may romanticize the folk, basking in the nostalgia of the "old-timey," remote, "authentic" village, enclave, or barrio, the "folk" certainly do not romanticize themselves, or the material conditions of their lives that might give rise to the cultural nuggets that we fetishize. Beyond surviving, most folk are concerned with economic, political, educational, and social advancement, and understand that modern life inherently involves ongoing cultural compromises, hybridity, masking, mutations, and often, metamorphosis. Most people are seldom afforded the luxury of holding onto rigid notions of cultural identities or expressive forms, even when their rhetoric suggests otherwise.

Such rigidity in an academic field leaves the discipline in a position oddly similar to ones taken by political conservatives and nationalist reactionaries— defending some imagined cultural purity from an earlier historical period. In a fashion not too dissimilar from some other academic fields, folklore first invented its materials, and then its vocabulary. It has basically spent much of the last one hundred and fifty or so years debating the semantics of that jargon. What are genres? Who are the folk? What is folklore? Besides issues of lexicon, the field has continued to grapple with its academic identity, but always relative to and in the shadows of other disciplines. Since the late 19th century, the field has taken occasional flurries into identifying itself as a science. For the sake of comparison, imagine if fields of plant and animal biology, to which folklore studies has looked for organizational and research models, had not by the 21st century moved beyond debates about terminology and vocabulary, organizational principles, or which materials fell within its purview and which ones did not.

So, what does this mean for the contemporary field of folklore, a discipline deeply invested in the celebration, documentation, and analysis of cultural "authenticity?" While this inquiry serves as a starting point for this collection of essays, the authors' critical reach extends far beyond an academic engagement with this question. In fact, the myriad threads of this extension are a part of what makes this such a valuable text. The collection of essays begins by identifying and then interrogating some of the key, but often unspoken, assumptions and beliefs that are foundational to the field, at times referring to them as "articles of faith" and framing them as a part of the folklore of folklorists, comparable to religious beliefs within groups such as those we are accustomed to writing about. This critical interrogation is a thread that connects essays focusing on topics as diverse as the songs of Bob Dylan; cyborgs on the Snopes.com website; folklore and representations of folklorists in novels; and the uncanny absences in the film *Welcome to Pine Point*.

The major concepts addressed in this work include "folklore," "folk groups," "authenticity," "genres," and "vernacular," all terms whose resonance for folklorists is comparable to that of "Eucharist," "communion," or "the Trinity" for devout Catholics. As such, some may consider the discussions in this text sacrilegious, to which I would respond, "Hooray for sacrilege!" In fact, the authors are only making explicit many shadowed realities that have haunted us all along, but that for many various reasons, we have kept at the margins. For example, the boundaries between the "popular" and the "folk" are largely ones that we have constructed and that fly in the face of most people's everyday realities. Individuals can have folklore apart from groups. Most communities in the modern world do not consist of groups that interact face to face, or necessarily exist over extended periods of time. The cultural lives of modern communities are inextricably bound to forces of commerce and technology. "Authenticity" is more about our fetishistic desires than about any essential or inherent quality that exists in cultures or in forms of cultural expressions.

At the same time that the authors remind us that it is we who construct and need the folk, and not the other way around, they also reaffirm the relevance of the field. Not only are folklorists uniquely attuned to elements and dynamics of culture that are commonly underappreciated by other fields, but we have vital communities of scholars, public sector professionals, and enthusiasts who make significant contributions to broad spheres of American society, including educational and cultural institutions and public life. And our traditions are meaningful for us, and as such, just as important as those of any other group. The beliefs of folklorists give structure and meaning to our lives. They facilitate the organization of our research, the tenor of our social lives, the focus of our writing, and the system in which our publications thrive and matter. The authors readily acknowledge that these are all matters of importance. They contend, however, that they could matter even more, across more disciplines and in ways we may not have up to now conceived of, given some fundamental shifts in our approaches.

The suggestions made in this group of essays are sound and often subtle, to the point that some of them may go unrecognized to readers being introduced to them for the first time, or to readers without exposure to some of the other disciplines or theoretical frameworks the authors implicitly draw from. The style of the writing, for example, is a conscious move away from the commonly dense and jargon-filled folklore articles that populate journals or book chapters. They are often a nod to the essay form familiar to creative nonfiction, in which metaphor, imagery, irony, and humor are at home.

There is also a refreshing philosophical bent to this text, which, without ever explicitly stating the case, points to the potentially rich, hybrid discourse that could emerge from dialogue between folklore and philosophy. This is evident throughout the book, in the authors' willingness to consistently question every aspect of how we envision our field, from the materials that we study, to the ways in which we conceptualize them, and equally important, how we imagine who *we* are. They insist that nothing we do or think should be a given. But this is philosophy with an edge, with both feet firmly planted in social and political reality, and in the corporeal and material worlds. Discussions drawing from critical race theory and studies of post-humanism amply demonstrate this, indicating how profoundly some of our practices might shift if such discourses were more integral components of our field. At the core of folklore study are basic assumptions about what it means to be human, and any radical change in these age-old ways of imagining our species could create a ripple effect in how we "do" folklore. It so happens that the nature of the human is a core concern in fields such as black studies, post-humanism, neuroscience, and disability studies. Certainly, in an age in which large populations across the globe are transitioning from the human to the post-human, it is incumbent on scholars in any field with people as its main focus to be invested in the developments in this area of theory.

Studies in fields concerned with social identity, communication, and the nature of the human also invariably lead to considerations of race, and by extension, to critical race theory and black studies. How can folklorists not be attuned to discourses in black studies when race continues to be among the most critical signs of identity in American society, shaping our public and institutional conversations and defining our body politic? Although no other social reality has had more impact on folklore studies than race, folklorists continue to avoid direct engagement with the theories and fields that focus specifically on the racial history and ideology. To do so, would, of course, involve a critical engagement with white identity and privilege, and the overwhelming influence of these on our field. It would furthermore transform assumptions we make about who we are and what we are doing, and why we are doing it.

This groundbreaking book goes beyond the identification of problems in the discipline to crafting essays out of intellectually fresh perspectives, and in doing so, offers a tremendous leap forward for the field. While grounded in folklore research, it insists on an uncommonly rigorous interrogation of folklore ideology and practices that are "traditional" within the field and that are commonly the foundations of our pedagogical and research agendas.

I was delighted and proud to read this collaborative work by three of my former students, which offered that "spark" that Emily Dickinson suggested was the sign of a good poem and that I have found to be the hallmark of any good piece of scholarship or creative writing. I have no doubt that some of these chapters will become seminal essays in the field and I look forward to being able to assign this as a text in my folklore courses. This book reminds me of the story of the Zen master who poses the koan to his disciples, "How do you get the goose out of the bottle?" After months of wracking their brains, throwing guesses in the master's direction, only to have him shake his head and send them back to continue their meditations and pondering, one of the disciples claps his hands and excitedly exclaims, "Master, the goose is out!" After only 160 years, the folklore goose is out.

ACKNOWLEDGMENTS

This book found an initial form as we walked through the streets one night during the moveable nowhere that is the annual meeting of the American Folklore Society, but we began the journey of jumping from one glimmering idea to the next and staring at the dark spaces between years before. The authors are indebted to all those who have helped guide us through this ongoing process of becoming folklorists, including Elaine J. Lawless and Anand Prahlad, to whom this book is dedicated. We would also like to thank Craig Gill, Katie Keene, and the whole editing team of the University Press of Mississippi for their faith in this project and thoughtful comments along the way. Finally, much gratitude is due to our families, friends, and colleagues, who have never (as of this printing) failed to put up with us.

IMPLIED NOWHERE

INTRODUCTION

Shelley Ingram, Willow G. Mullins, and Todd Richardson

But it was fitting like a tight chemise. I couldn't see it for wearing it.
—Zora Neale Hurston, Mules and Men (1935)

Although we do not sign formal contracts when we become folklorists, there seems to be a traditional and often unspoken assumption that it is our obligation to perform certain types of cultural work directed toward implicitly sanctioned goals. This implied contract, like all contracts, also has implied terms. In law, implied contractual terms are those terms that are not explicitly stated but assumed to exist by tradition. Implied terms cover a lot of ground, from the presumption that the seller of an object has the legal right to sell to the belief that part of the secretary's job is to get his boss coffee. Implied terms are where law and culture come together, opening a space to work *within* the rules, not just *by* the rules. They can be the cause of legal snarls, as litigants and judges try to discern just how much can or cannot be inferred from the contract itself, but they can also create productive spaces that allow the parties of the contract to dive deep into or push against the limits of the explicit terms (Cohen 2000: 80).

Folklore studies has its own implied terms within its unwritten contract: there are things that folklorists have implied to mean nothing and things that are nowhere implied, and both of these absences exert pressure on the field, determining whom, how, and to what ends we study. *Implied Nowhere: Absence in Folklore Studies* is a collection of essays that explores such absences in an effort to trouble some of the tacit assumptions that determine scholarly authority and worthiness within the field.[1]

Having long been invested in the "representation of underrepresented peoples in powerless positions," our contractual obligation assumes that folklorists will devote their attention to cultures and expressions either imperiled or underappreciated, to bring to light those traditions and cultures often unseen or, paradoxically, deemed in danger of disappearing, the "poetics of disappearance," as Barbara Kirshenblatt-Gimblett has said (1998: 300). While most folklorists no longer endorse the paradigm of "survivals"—the belief that folklore exists only as a remnant of a disappearing or bygone era—the spirit of survivals, manifest in the demand that certain folklore needs protection and/or advocacy, continues to animate folkloristic work in both the academy and the public sector. As Kirshenblatt-Gimblett argues, the concept of survivals "continues to shape folklore's disciplinary subject" even if it has gone "under other names" and been "purged of explicit evolutionary explanation" (1998: 300).

Many of us, then, understand that as a field folklore studies still struggles with its lingering "romantic nationalism," with its historical investment in a rhetoric that locates purity and authenticity on a colonial scale: in the not-white, the not-urban, the not-wealthy.[2] Perhaps most trenchant is the criticism laid out by John Roberts in his 1998 American Folklore Society presidential address, during which he assessed the apparent invisibility of folklore as a scholarly discipline. Roberts suggested that "our origins in romantic nationalism are not what threatens our visibility but, rather, our refusal to expel the phantoms, to engage the politics of romantic nationalism by challenging those discourses and practices that we have embraced in our efforts to make our work conform to its silent dictates" (1999: 123). Amy Shuman calls this silence a "legacy of romantic advocacy" that often works, despite our best intentions, to reinscribe the marginalization and exoticization of others (2015: 23). So how do we not only continue our commitment to imperiled folklore, but also work in a way that directly engages the "silent dictates" that Roberts, Shuman, Kirshenblatt-Gimblett, and others point out?

Perhaps we push the bounds of our implicit contract through an active pursuit of perilous folklore, those traditions and customs commonly cited as the problem. Or we give scholarly attention to non-canonical, improper, or even fraudulent theories, methods, and subjects—things that are either absent or that we *wish* were absent. We can question implicitly sanctioned beliefs, what Michael Ann Williams has termed our "shared values," about academic professionalism, responsible disciplinary practices, and "proper" folkloric subjects (2017: 138). We can interrogate the very nature of these often unspoken obligations and beliefs that continue, for better and worse, to structure our field. Perhaps we reframe our obligations in less rigid terms, less like law and more like trust. After all, if anyone can appreciate that unspoken, informal arrangements like trust shape a worldview more powerfully than formalized contracts, it is folklorists.

INTRODUCTION

We intend the essays in *Implied Nowhere* to be a meditation on what appears absent from folklore studies and on the absent but implied terms that, whether consciously constructed or implicitly sanctioned, direct our current practices. In doing so, we take the opportunity to put into practice an interrogation of absence by offering a way to think a little differently about folklore, literature, film, popular culture, popular scholarship, and the stories we tell ourselves about who we are and what it is that we do. We endeavor, in short, to render visible some of the unarticulated boundaries of folkloristic inquiry.

This kind of work has been undertaken at various points in the field's history. In folklore scholarship, though, such critiques have tended to center on particular concepts rather than the larger conglomerate that makes up our contractual obligations. Américo Paredes and Richard Bauman's edited collection *Towards New Perspectives in Folklore* (1972) and Regina Bendix's *In Search of Authenticity* (1997) both sought to trouble fundamental concepts of the study of folklore—tradition and authenticity, respectively. *Towards New Perspectives in Folklore* redefined folklore as not so much something that is (a text, whether the text is a tale or a quilt), but as something that is done at a particular time in a particular place. *Towards New Perspectives* radically altered the trajectory of folklore studies. But the retrospective critics of *Towards New Perspectives* noted that the shift toward viewing folklore as an emergent element of culture also invited the re-essentializing of the people who were deemed "the folk."[3]

Bendix takes up this questioning of the field's reliance on antiquated notions of the folk by arguing that the "search for authenticity" has emerged as one of folklore's most questionable legacies, one that continues to shape the field and its subjects. She argues that the turn toward performance simply moved authenticity from a material dimension to an experiential one, and suggests that understanding the field's history of constructing authenticity can and will be liberating because once we are free of that central dichotomy, of authentic versus inauthentic, we can begin to look at that dichotomy itself as an object of study (1997: 156). Additional disciplinary re-visioning has taken place within the pages of our academic journals: *Theorizing Folklore*, a special issue of *Western Folklore* (Shuman and Briggs 1993), and *What's in a Name*, a special issue of the *Journal of American Folklore* (1998), perhaps being the most well-known. But even the essays in these forward-thinking collections tended to focus on groups or texts firmly within the bounds of a folklorist's contract, appropriate subjects like Moroccan markets and western rodeos.

Then the internet happened, and the clear contract between folklore studies and orality was shredded into digital bits. The internet has been around for decades, but it has only been in the last fifteen years or so that the *study* of it has been relatively mainstreamed in the humanities and social sciences. There has been hesitation, like Bill Ivey's when he suggested that "we know, deep down, that these virtual communities—the nights spent staring at a screen navigating YouTube, MySpace, or SecondLife—are not the same, and not even decent substitutes for, the kind of communities where neighbors and families see and talk to one another" (2011: 15). Or when a well-known folklorist recently told one of the authors that it was acceptable to use popular culture as a lure to reel students in, but that once we had them in our classroom it was essential to teach them of more important matters, of *real* folklore. Nonetheless, we have seen a slow and steady increase in works of folklore that consider both the folk and the lore in new ways: including Bill Ellis's *Making a Big Apple Crumble* (2002) and *Aliens, Ghosts, and Cults* (2003), Rosemary Hathaway's "Life in the TV" (2005), Mikel Koven's work on *The X-Files* (2009), Robert Glen Howard's *Digital Jesus* (2011), Darcy Holtgrave's work on YouTube narratives (2015), and the summer 2015 special issue of the *Journal of American Folklore* focused on "Digital Network Hybridity." These texts reflect a growing body of work within folklore studies that firmly positions folklore as contemporary, immanent, and technological.

This is all important and vital work. However, John Dorst anticipated the allure that the internet would have for folklorists twenty-five years ago, and he cautioned that the biggest stumbling block for folklorists in the telectronic age would be a desire to search for "covert thematics." Covert thematics, he argued, would allow us to dismiss how advancing technological means of mass communication do not just give us new fields in which to go collect lore, they also "epitomize the forces and relations of production through which such lore is constituted" and "inform and inhabit the lore from within, structurally and ideologically" (1990: 184, 181). That is, he calls to mind Alan Dundes's explicit caution against "motif spotting" and "genre hunting," lest we, as Hermann Bausinger warned in 1961, proceed to simply "match new objects and population groups with the old concepts."[4] Are the advances in folklore studies systemic, then, or are they primarily about locating "new objects?" Is the field adapting to change or simply enduring it?

To be sure, it is not by technological changes alone that we are compelled. The change in technology revealed gaps and fault lines in how folkloristics has historically been structured, but those gaps have long been present. Indeed, our interest here is better exemplified by Dorst's opening salvo, what he calls the "ghost joke." This is a joke that was erased from a story about the censorship of that joke. The story then passed around the HUMANIST bulletin board in the early days of the internet, and all that was left of the joke was its trace, one that at the time of his essay's publication still "haunt[ed] . . . telectronic labyrinths." Dorst uses this "ghost joke" as the central metaphor of the "boundary-less, dematerialized space" of mass culture, one that uses folklore to replicate its own hegemonic means of production, its meaning residing in its possibility of reproduction (1990: 183). We want to avoid suggesting that online fieldwork or the study of memes or the spreading of urban legends through social media is the only new, forward-looking folkloristics. So we take up the mantle of those before who urged us not to "miss a great deal of what is going on" by looking at how absences, as physical, metaphysical, and disciplinary siblings of Dorst's ghost joke, can, to use the words of the writer Shirley Jackson, "Only be trusted through its manifestation, the actual shape of the god perceived, however dimly, against the solidity he displaces" (2014: 34).

Thus absence is a dominant subject that drives this book—the things that have been implied to be nothing and the things that are nowhere implied. In particular, we engage absence as a critical discourse that shapes both ideology and actuality. We are interested in the construction and performance of absence in contemporary American cultures, as, along with the affiliated forces of modernity, industrialization, and mass-mediated communication, absence has long acted as one of the centers against which marginality is determined. We endeavor to understand how absence shapes what it is we do as folklorists and how it can be a productive site of analysis and interpretation. Mark Workman once argued that folklorists "can be accused of recording those things which seem almost to be marked *a priori* for recognition," leading us to "construct accounts which instill additional order and consequence" (1995: 29). Workman was talking here about the "literature of exile," asking those who study folklore and literature to think beyond community, or rather, *outside* community, to see how folklore is used in literature to disrupt order in service of representing life for those who have been, either through choice or by force, pushed out to nowhere. What is of interest to us, though, is the idea that there could exist a folklore that is *not* marked *a priori* for recognition. That there is folklore not, indeed, always already present. That there is folklore that remains "outside the realm of notice and narrative" (Workman 1995: 29).

In practice, that which is "outside of narrative" has received a bit of notice. Most prominently perhaps is the attention that has been paid to "untellable" narratives. Folklorists such as David Hufford (1982), Diane Goldstein (2009, 2016), Elaine Lawless (2001), and Amy Shuman (2005, 2016), among others, often take Labov and Waletzky's (1967) notion of "tellability" as a starting point: if some narratives are tellable, then there must also be narratives "that resist representation, resist reading, and resist hearing" (Goldstein and Shuman 2016: 2). This strand of scholarship urges us to think about what is not said and what *cannot* be said. In some cases, it is because the narrative is ungrammatical, to use Bill Ellis's term. A society has a "belief language," a culturally derived vocabulary that shapes both how and what experiences can be shared with a larger public.

Thus stories that do not speak in their native language of belief—for example, narratives about alien abductions in our own society—either remain unarticulated or are transformed into acceptable, grammatical utterances (2003: 95).

In other cases, the untellability of the narrative is rooted in trauma, because "language disintegrates in the face of trauma," as "memory sometimes fails protectively" (Goldstein 2012: 189). In such an essay about trauma, untellability, and the absence of "near miss" narratives in 9/11 legends, Diane Goldstein argues that we know to look for such absent legends because other storytelling cycles about mass tragedies include them. In this case, constructing absence is a simple methodological issue, "essentially comparative," she argues, a sifting through of "a variety of seemingly relevant texts and contexts; focusing on recurrent patterns in the initial corpus compared to recurrent patterns in other extant corpuses hypothesized to be similar" (2009: 250).

Implied Nowhere, however, considers that which remains *outside* of "extant corpuses." Workman's argument that folklorists only mark as folklore that which has already been marked as folklore should have far-reaching implications for the ways we study it, because, as Roger Abrahams points out, "Particular groups are designated as *folk* under specific social and political conditions," which leads to "certain genres becom[ing] marked as important forms of *lore*" (1993a: 389). Past "social and political" dimensions of folkloric analysis worked to articulate a particular kind of text as present—the rural, the subordinate, the oral, the ethnic. Because of the well-known influences of romantic nationalism and the impact of theories of cultural evolution on the field, we have received, as Charles Briggs argues, folklore that is always "part of a strange world that is radically Other" (1993: 403).

This book is indebted to the work of all of the scholars above and more who take absence, in some form, as an object of study. We find inspiration in works like Dorst's essay and his monograph *The Written Suburb* (1989), which turns a critical eye toward texts that are deemed inauthentic and thus meaningless, absent texts presumably washed clean by postmodern consumerism. And in Susan Stewart's *On Longing* ([1983] 1993), with its evaluation of the objects that help us make meaning of our daily lives both by their persistent and unquestioned presence or by their oddity, demarking the limits of the real and present through the unreal, the virtual, and the absent. In Anand Prahlad's essay "Guess Who's Coming to Dinner" (1999), in which he probes the absence of folklore in African American literary studies in order to make trenchant claims about racism and the academy. In Kimberley Lau's *New Age Capitalism* (2000), which troubles both folk and authenticity, layering the real and fake in her analysis of new age practices, and in Bauman and Briggs's *Voices of Modernity* (2003), which argues that "modernist metadiscursive practices produce intertextual links and gaps" (314) that help uphold systems of inequality through the construction of a purified, and ideological, language.

We hope to add to this small but important tracing of the absences, gaps, and silences in folklore studies. We take as our subjects the loner, mass media, popular music, the dandy collector, the white middle-class—but we are not approaching these subjects as simply either vessels for or destroyers of "real" folklore. We instead take as a tenet that all elements of expressive culture are authentic somethings. We acknowledge them as part and parcel of the expressive cultures of a vast number of people who live in the world, emergent and heterogeneous traditions that do not always conform to our discipline's framework. We choose to see them as present rather than absent.

Implied Nowhere considers some of the particular absences by which our implied contract, emerging as it does out of what Bill Ivey called folklore's "settled" laws, has been constructed, how it became and remains disarticulated, and for what ends it continues to be invoked. In this vein, the essays here simultaneously engage competing discourses—historical and contemporary, academic and public—of who a folklorist is, of what we are supposed to be, and of what we are supposed to study. These discourses are informed by the unarticulated implied terms that give shape to our field, and we want to take an opportunity to, as Zora Neale Hurston said, stand off and consider our garment. We offer this consideration with the full understanding that in limning the absences and presences of the field, we necessarily both fill gaps and open new ones.

WHAT WE WRITE

The difficulty with defining absence, as many a dictionary writer has discovered, is that it implies a binary—absence is always defined by a lack of presence. Absence always points to that which has never been or is no longer there. Thus taken as guiding conceits, absence and presence are almost laughably arbitrary, as marking an absence necessarily entails the acknowledgement of a presence—and vice versa. Furthermore, absence is a continuum, and what is absent for one group can be outstandingly present for another. However, the essays that follow bring into focus slightly different negotiations of our imaginary contract, with its absent but always present implied terms. These differences arise according to the multiple inflections possible with our title. As such, *Implied Nowhere* works in two ways. It calls attention to the force that absence, whether of group or space or text, inevitably exerts, that which is nowhere implied. It also marks presence, asking: what do we note as meaning *less*? What do we see but assign no value? What do we imply is nowhere?

Willow Mullins thus begins by considering some keywords of folklore studies as articulations of faith, that substance which is so commonly construed as the evidence of things not seen. In "Our Lady of Authenticity: Folklore's Articles of Faith," she questions the folklorist's investment in the tenets of folklore studies by looking behind the curtain of academic discourse to consider our belief in the language we use. Her argument rests on the seemingly simple claim that every mode of thought contains an element of faith. Beginning with some of our keywords—authenticity, vernacular, and genre—and one folklorist's crisis of belief, this chapter seeks to peek behind the veil of our articles of faith. What are they? How do they influence our practices and products? Bendix claimed that the authenticity of the subject gave legitimacy to the field, but in doing so created a troubling gap between self and Other: a gap around which we have continued to form our field, even as we have questioned and laid bare its problems (1997: 7, 17). Like most humans faced with unknowable spaces, however, we have sought to fill that gap with something—our theories of folkloristics. To think in terms of faith gives us space to doubt, to question, and critically, to disagree. Mullins explores the implications of a shaken faith to ask, if you challenge the articles of faith or find them lacking, can you still call yourself folklorist?

We then move to explore specific absences, and their coproduced presences, in the study of folklore+: folklore in literature, film, history, on the internet, and in culture at large. We are so used to folklore being "marked *a priori* for recognition" that often we fail to notice the conspicuous construction of its (seeming) absence. In writing about exclusions and invisibilities, we take a different approach to folklore, one that does not identify expressive culture so much as it traces the shape of its absence. In this way, the following chapters demonstrate a recalibration of the folkloristic gaze, one that shifts focus away from what is apparent and toward the patterns implied by what isn't, and taken as a whole, they strive toward a methodology that can put theories of absence into practice.

In chapter two, "Misanthropelore," Todd Richardson considers the roots, manifestations, and expressive dimensions of disaffiliation, the absence of group, as represented in the comic books of Daniel Clowes. Focused as it is on the shared aspects of expressive culture, mainstream conceptualizations of folklore struggle to assess how individuals creatively convey the absence of belonging. Richardson introduces the idea of misanthropelore as a way of assessing such performances of disaffiliation, connecting the notion to William Hugh Jansen's discussion of emic and etic folklore and Richard Bauman's consideration of the role of differential identity in folk performances. Throughout the chapter, Richardson looks at how Clowes's protagonists use gainsaying, nostalgia and awkwardness to disaffiliate from their communities, always striving to assert their autonomy. In each instance, misanthropelore is not necessarily about a lack or loss of shared identity, which is how conventional folklore scholarship approaches it; misanthropelore, rather, is a refusal of shared identity through the creative expression of absence.

Chapter three, Shelley Ingram's "Footprints of Ghosts: Fictional Folklorists in the Work of Gloria Naylor, Lee Smith, Randall Kenan, and Colson Whitehead," looks at the fictional folklorists who appear in the work of four writers, arguing that the character of the folklorist serves as a metonymic signifier of the absence always present in the representation of cultures. It would be easy to dismiss these fictional representations of folklorists simply as caricatures, particularly since they are often bumbling and always wrong. But because the fictions of Naylor, Smith, Kenan, and Whitehead are in part about the epistemologies at work in contemporary American society, this chapter strives to take the characters a bit more seriously. So while the academic folklorist is used in various ways for various reasons in these fictions, an interesting pattern emerges when you consider the works side by side: each of the stories are structured through a metafictive, self-conscious framework, each ask the reader to think critically about notions of authenticity, and each are haunted by ghosts, both figurative and literal. The ghostly is not an arbitrary signifier. It figures an absence that has something to do with knowledge and text, with literary tourism, and with the inability to ever know, really, the shape of a community's past, present, or future.

In our fourth chapter, "The Folkloristics of Death: Absence, Sustainability, and Ghosts in the Film *Welcome to Pine Point*," Mullins looks closely at *Welcome to Pine Point*, a 2011 interactive web documentary about a Canadian town that was physically demolished when the mine closed and residents dispersed. As folklorists, we tend to seek continuation, preservation, and sustainability, and we see in stories like Pine Point the demise of a folk group in the face of class struggle. "Pine Point" the web video, however, suggests a story and a folk group may be more important in their absence than in their continuation. *Welcome to Pine Point* questions the preservationism inherent in not only folklore but in much of the arts and humanities: as the filmmakers ask, "Imagine your hometown never changed . . . would it be so bad?" What does sustainability look like for such a community? Or, by contrast, does death itself have something important, perhaps even redemptive, to offer in the form of a ghost? Like Derrida's hauntology, it might be that Pine Point offers more having been and now being gone than it would if it still was.

In chapter five, "White Folks: Literature's Uncanny, Unhomely Folklore of Whiteness," Ingram suggests that the tendency to exempt the literature of white writers and the folkloric nature of whiteness from dominant conversations about folklore and literature helps reaffirm a dangerous hierarchical system of power in which whiteness is marked as absence. In this essay, she focuses on the ways in which whiteness is not, in fact, absent—instead, it is an identity that is guarded and negotiated. This chapter uses critical race theory in an examination of moments in literature when the boundaries of folk groups are constructed through negotiations of whiteness and made visible where absence "begins its presencing" (Bhabha 1994: 7). She pushes back against a critical narrative of whiteness as absence by bringing whiteness into focus as an identity that is guarded and negotiated, present in its absence, and critical to the making of meaning and folklore in American literature. The chapter looks at moments of constructed uncanniness and unhomeliness in Russell Banks's *Affliction* and Eudora Welty's *Delta Wedding*, two American novels in which whiteness is inextricably linked to the creation, through acceptance or rejection, of folk groups. Banks and Welty both construct a whiteness that has stability and variation, that reacts to the presence of a folk Other, and that becomes part of a vernacular language of identity for those inside, outside, and on the borders of their groups. It is a construct, paradoxically absent and unquestionably present.

The last chapter of *Implied Nowhere* is Richardson's "Folklore in Vacuo (and Other Disciplinary Predicaments)," a conclusion of sorts. Richardson uses the lyric essay form to interrogate the motives and methods of mainstream folklore scholarship. He identifies a variety of factors that discourage folklorists from taking more expressive chances, everything from the intellectual legacy of the discipline's early architects to the ironic ontology of folklore's ghostly subject, in order to understand the specialized style that has come to dominate folklore scholarship. This hyper-professionalization of folkloristic writing has, Richardson argues, led to what Benjamin Botkin once called "folklorists talking to themselves or *folklore in vacuo*." In order to make folklore studies resonate with a broader audience, Richardson calls for folkloristic writing that is more imaginative and less thesis-driven, writing that invites the curious in rather than excluding them in the name of scholarly prestige. Doing so, he suggests, can reestablish folklore studies' broad appeal, which was once a unique strength of the field, as well as make the actual practice of folklore studies more playful and enjoyable.

FRAUDS, QUACKS, AND DILETTANTES

Our main chapters, written in a more traditional scholarly vein, are balanced with a series of short interstitial chapters, informally known to us as "Frauds,

INTRODUCTION

Quacks, and Dilettantes." The name comes from Roger Welsch's comment to the authors that "folklore has traditionally provided a home for frauds, quacks, and dilettantes," making it clear that by folklore he meant both the stuff that is studied as well as the study of it. Recently, Michael Ann Williams called for a more serious appraisal of those folklore enthusiasts and scholars who have been so dismissed and discredited. Williams asks, "Why were we so intent on seeking out the evil that lurked in the hearts of our predecessors, at the same time leaving a few sacred individuals untouched?" (2017: 133–34).

So in these études, we take as our subjects thinkers and writers and spaces and texts that tend to be on the edges of folklore for a variety of reasons. Giving attention to folklore recently created and folklore forgotten, neglected, mislaid, or left behind, these short in-betweens function interstitially, bridging between and marking the frayed edges of our chapters and the field itself. Like notes in an academic journal, these explorations allow us to dip our analytical toes into the interstitials of the field in short form. We see these pieces as places primarily of play, as a process to spark new ideas and forge new pathways—as folklorists know well, play can be deadly serious—yet they also contribute to the book's theme in that all three designations are defined through absence: a fraud lacks accuracy, a quack lacks rigor, and a dilettante lacks focus.

Taken together, they collectively represent a lack of discipline, a dangerous trait within a field that has vigorously defended its disciplinary legitimacy. Nevertheless, the figures and practices considered have shaped the authors' thoughts about folklore, and we are making their influence explicit. In these interstitial chapters we take time to look at some of our favorite frauds, writers, and thinkers who are in tenuous possession of folkloristic "authenticity" and who, in one way or another, have either ignored or outright refused to acknowledge our contract—writers like Bob Dylan and Roger Welsch. We focus on the folklore of hoaxes and the way that invisibility shapes an internet meme, on the dyad of writer Shirley Jackson and her husband, the literary critic and folklorist Stanley Edgar Hyman, and on the non-marked, ever-present small things of life. We write on David and Barbara Mikkelson as cyborgs and on fanfiction writers as studied professionals. In these essays, we call attention to gaps in our studies of folklore: things that are nowhere implied.

CONCLUSION

We the authors inhabit a liminal generational space, between the older generations for whom culture ideally remains face bound and the younger with their Reddit and their Snapchat. Such liminal periods recur, they link, they provide the stuff of creative theory and leaps in the field, but they are populated by ghosts, like Dorst's ghost joke, and those ghosts demand their due. We do this in service of a larger goal: we argue that the field's preoccupation with boundary-work, with delineating folklore's presence and its absence, is a bit like a dog chasing its tail, so intent on its own game that it does not notice that the rest of the world has moved on, into the greener pastures of media and reception and cultural studies. And yet, we are committed enough to the field that we get frustrated—no, *angry*—when an essay about urban legends written by a children's literature scholar cites nary a folklorist.

The importance of folklore studies seems to be staggeringly clear in a world in which intersectional studies of cultures and texts are driving scholarship in the humanities and the social sciences. Yet we remain, as usual, frustratingly absent from these larger discussions. John Roberts was onto something important when he argued that the invisibility of folklore studies is attributable to a false notion of disciplinary coherence. "Our future health as a field," he suggested, "lies not in denying or even fighting against our fragmented identity but, rather, in learning to see ourselves in it, in accepting our essential dividedness, our diversity if you will, as our greatest virtue rather than the problem to be overcome" (1999: 138). Both this desire for a stringent disciplinary coherence and our "refusal to expel the phantoms" of romantic nationalism, then, arise from and help maintain our implied contract.

We have thus come to believe that the absences *in* folklore are connected to the absence *of* folklore, of the knowledge that it even exists as a field, from the broader academic landscape. Within our field are subjects, scholars, and spaces that are immensely valuable to larger academic and public discussions about authenticity, social isolation, and colonialism. One of the results of writing this book is that we have been reminded what is so great about the study of folklore: it gives us the framework to think about group and community and *communion* in a way that is unique amongst academic disciplines. Putting aside our shortsightedness and perceived inadequacies and thinking about these absences honestly, as we hope we show in this book, reveals a field of study endlessly relevant and full of vitality.

NOTES

1. As William Hugh Jansen argues, the folklore field worker "is tacitly assuming that the material being recorded or analyzed has peculiar virtues arising from its existence within a more or less peculiar group. This hazy, tacit assumption may be recognized as a truism, and, as with many truisms, deserves a full, careful definition and a systematic exploration of its actual and potential applicability" (1959: 45).

INTRODUCTION

2. Linda Dégh was pushing against this impulse in 1994 when she argued that the "phantoms" of romantic nationalism that Roger Abrahams had identified continued to be felt in the discipline, that they have "persisted" and "linger to the present day" in a way that obscures the deep interconnections between literary and folk, urban and rural, in an effort to retain a notion of the folk as a pure bulwark against modernity (1994: 20). There is a whole range of work that makes some form of this same argument, from Bausinger's *Folk Culture in a World of Technology* (1961) and Dundes and Pragter's *Urban Folklore from the Paperwork Empire* (1973) to Dégh's *American Folklore and the Mass Media* (1994) and Bauman and Briggs's *Voices of Modernity* (2003).

3. Cf. Abrahams (1993a); Bendix (1997); Shuman (2005); Briggs (2008); Mechling (1993)

4. Hermann Bausinger's *Folk Culture in a World of Technology*, first published in 1961, noted a contrast between the *theoretical* concern for urban folklore and the actual, published accounts of it. There was a lot of talk about studies in folklore that would question the "notion of the old village as a self-contained organism" remaining unsullied by the Industrial Revolution, but he argued that there was little action, other than to "match new objects and population groups with the old concepts" ([1961]1990: 33, 6). He believed that even the theoretical desire for studies of urban folklore reinforced, rather than destabilized, the rural/urban, folk/not-folk binary because it skipped those spaces in between, where so many people lived and worked.

REFERENCES CITED

Abrahams, Roger. 1993a. "After New Perspectives: Folklore Study in the Late Twentieth Century." In *Theorizing Folklore: Toward New Perspectives on the Politics of Culture*, edited by Amy Shuman and Charles Briggs, special issue, *Western Folklore* 52 (2/4): 379–400.

Abrahams, Roger. 1993b. "Phantoms of Romantic Nationalism in Folkloristics." *Journal of American Folklore* 106(419): 3–37.

Bhabha, Homi K. 1994. *The Location of Culture*. London: Routledge.

Bauman, Richard and Charles Briggs. 2003. *Voices of Modernity: Language Ideologies and the Politics of Inequality*. Cambridge: Cambridge University Press.

Bausinger, Hermann. [1961] 1990. *Folk Culture in a World of Technology*, translated by Elke Dettmer. Bloomington: Indiana University Press.

Bendix, Regina. 1997. *In Search of Authenticity: The Foundation of Folklore Studies*. Madison: University of Wisconsin Press.

Briggs, Charles. 1993. "Metadiscursive Practices and Scholarly Authority in Folkloristics." *Journal of American Folklore* 106(422): 387–434.

Briggs, Charles. 2008. "Disciplining Folkloristics." *Journal of Folklore Research* 45(1): 95–105.

Bronner, Simon J. 1986. *American Folklore Studies: An Intellectual History.* Lawrence: University Press of Kansas.

Cohen, George M. 2000. "Implied Terms and Interpretation in Contract Law." In *Encyclopedia of Law and Economics*, eds. B. Bouckeart and G. deGeest. Cheltenham, UK: Edward Elgar Publishing.

Dégh, Linda. 1994. *American Folklore and the Mass Media*. Bloomington: Indiana University Press.

Dorst, John. 1989. *The Written Suburb: An American Site, An Ethnographic Dilemma*. Philadelphia: University of Pennsylvania Press.

Dorst, John. 1990. "Tags and Burners, Cycles and Networks: Folklore in the Telectronic Age." *Journal of Folklore Research* 27(3): 179–90.

Dundes, Alan. 2005. "Folkloristics in the Twenty-First Century." *Journal of American Folklore* 118(470): 385–408.

Dundes, Alan, and Carl R. Pagter. 1975. *Urban Folklore from the Paperwork Empire*. Austin: The American Folklore Society.

Ellis, Bill. 2002. "Making a Big Apple Crumble: The Role of Humor in Constructing a Global Response to Disaster." In *New Directions in Folklore* 6.

Ellis, Bill. 2003. *Aliens, Ghosts, and Cults: Legends We Live*. Jackson: University Press of Mississippi.

Goldstein, Diane E. 2009. "The Sounds of Silence: Foreknowledge, Miracles, Suppressed Narratives, and Terrorism—What Not Telling Might Tell Us." *Western Folklore* 68(2/3): 235–55.

Goldstein, Diane E. 2012. "Rethinking Ventriloquism: Untellability, Chaotic Narratives, Social Justice, and the Choice to Speak For, About, and Without." *Journal of Folklore Research* 49(2): 179–98.

Goldstein, Diane E., and Amy Shuman. 2016. *The Stigmatized Vernacular: Where Reflexivity Meets Untellability*. Bloomington: Indiana University Press.

Hathaway, Rosemary V. 2005. "'Life in the TV': The Visual Nature of 9/11 Lore and Its Impact on Vernacular Response." *Journal of Folklore Research* 42(1): 33–56.

Holtgrave, Darcy. 2015. "Broadcasting the Stigmatized Self: Positioning Functions of YouTube Vlogs on Bipolar Disorder." In *Diagnosing Folklore: Perspectives on Disability, Health, and Trauma*, edited by Trevor Blank. Jackson: University of Mississippi.

Howard, Robert Glen. 2011. *Digital Jesus: The Making of a New Christian Fundamentalist Community on the Internet*. New York: NYU Press.

Hufford, David. 1982. *The Terror That Comes in the Night*. Philadelphia: University of Pennsylvania Press.

Ivey, Bill. 2011. Values and Value in Folklore (AFS Presidential Plenary Address, 2007). *Journal of American Folklore* 124(491): 6–18.

Jackson, Shirley. [1958] 2014. *The Sundial*. New York: Penguin.

Jansen, William Hugh. 1959. The Esoteric-Exoteric Factor in Folklore. In *The Study of Folklore*, edited by Alan Dundes, 43–51. Englewood Cliffs, NJ: Prentice-Hall, Inc.

Kirshenblatt-Gimblett, Barbara. 1998. "Folklore's Crisis." *Journal of American Folklore* 111(441): 281–327.

Koven, Mikel. 2009. "The X-Files." In *The Essential Cult TV Reader*, edited by David Lavery. Louisville: University of Kentucky Press.

Labov, William, and Joshua Waletzky. 1967. "Narrative Analysis: Oral Versions of Personal Experience." In *Essays on the Verbal and Visual Arts*, edited by June L. Helm, 12–44. Seattle: University of Washington Press.

Lau, Kimberly. 2000. *New Age Capitalism: Making Money East of Eden*. Philadelphia: University of Pennsylvania Press.

Lawless, Elaine. 2001. *Women Escaping Violence: Empowerment through Narrative*. Columbia: University of Missouri.

Mechling, Jay. 1993. "On Sharing Folklore and American Identity in a Multicultural Society." *Western Folklore*. 52 (2/4): 271–89.

INTRODUCTION

Paredes, Américo, and Bauman, Ricard, eds. 1972. *Towards New Perspectives in Folklore*. University of Texas Press: Austin.

Prahlad, Anand. 1999. "Guess Who's Coming to Dinner: Folklore, Folkloristics, and African American Literary Criticism." *African American Review* 33(4): 565–75.

Roberts, John. 1999. "'. . . Hidden Right out in the Open': The Field of Folklore and the Problem of Invisibility." *Journal of American Folklore* 112 (444): 119–39.

Rose, Tricia. 1994. *Black Noise: Rap Music and Black Culture in Contemporary America*. Middletown, CT.: Wesleyan University Press.

Shuman, Amy. 2005. *Other People's Stories: Entitlement Claims and the Critique of Empathy*. Urbana and Chicago: University of Illinois Press.

Shuman, Amy, and Charles Briggs, eds. 1993. *Theorizing Folklore: Toward New Perspectives on the Politics of Culture*. Special issue of *Western Folklore* 52 (2/4).

Shuman, Amy, and Charles Briggs, eds. 2015. "Disability, Narrative Normativity, and the Stigmatized Vernacular of Communicative (in)Competence." *In Diagnosing Folklore: Perspectives on Disability, Health, and Trauma*, eds. Trevor J. Blank and Andrea Kitta, 23–40. Jackson, MS: University Press of Mississippi.

Stewart, Susan. [1984] 1993. *On Longing: Narratives of the Miniature, the Gigantic, the Souvenir, the Collection*. Durham and London: Duke University Press.

Williams, Michael Ann. 2017. After the Revolution: Folklore, History, and the Future of Our Discipline (American Folklore Society Presidential Address, October 2016). *Journal of American Folklore* 130(516): 129–41.

Workman, Mark. 1995. "Folklore and the Literature of Exile." In *Folklore, Literature, and Cultural Theory*, ed. Cathy Lynn Preston, 29–42. New York: Garland Publishing.

ONE

Our Lady of Authenticity: Folklore's Articles of Faith

Willow G. Mullins

Every mode of thought contains an element of faith. As folklorists, we[1] accept this intrinsically when we talk about folk belief. We point it out to our students when we cover urban legends: they insist they do not believe there was ever a killer in the backseat of a car, but many check their cars before they get in at night, "just in case." As Kenneth Pimple says about washing our hands, we wash them and believe the washing will work, even if we know nothing about germ theory (1990: 52). In the West, we like to contrast faith with science, yet even our basic scientific assumptions often require leaps of faith. Marilyn Motz, in the "What's in a Name?" issue of *The Journal of American Folklore*, stated, "The concept of belief is so central to the discipline that it is hard to talk about folklore without talking about belief" (1998: 340). She was discussing the beliefs of our subjects of study and informants. She might have been talking about the field itself.

But if folklore studies has a set of beliefs, a faith, to which folklorists ascribe and on which our work is predicated, how do we know them? What are folklorists' articles of faith? And how do they influence our practices and products? Admittedly, we are unlikely to agree as a field on what constitutes folklore's articles of faith; few organized religions have such consistency even as their congregants recite their creeds. What brings each member regularly to church may vary widely. No doubt, each folklorist possesses their own articles of faith, but a few seem to exert a stronger hold on the field than others, weaving through writings, discussions, and presentations. In a pluralistic society, and folklore studies generally attempts pluralism, we need not agree with the faiths of others, only accept their and our right to believe them. Individually, we might not even know consciously what we believe, but we might have an idea of who our priests are. In a field heavily marked by boundary maintenance and concerns about institutional identity, our articles of faith can provide us with a sense of relative certainty. However, they can also become the deepest sources of our doubt.

This exploration focuses on only three articles of faith in folklore studies: authenticity, the vernacular, and genre. My faith in and doubt regarding authenticity, the vernacular, and genre have shaped my thinking on my work as a folklorist and my relationship to folklore as a field. My understanding of these three words has changed extensively in my academic career. Some I have questioned vigorously, others I have tended to accept at face value. To recast these concepts not as accepted truths or as words seeking greater definition or as cornerstones or even keywords of my field but as articles of faith, subject to negotiation and requiring active belief, has allowed me to work through that crisis, but it has also forced me to think more deeply about what it is we as folklorists do and do not do, what paradigms shape our practices, what we see and what seems absent.

It has become something of a commonplace for ethnographers and folklorists to acknowledge their own positionality and the hierarchies and biases incumbent therein. Awareness of power discrepancies (Clifford and Marcus 1986; Behar 1993) and of the limits of empathy (Shuman 2005), and the intent of reciprocity (Lawless 1992) and social consciousness (Gencarella 2009) have aided scholars in redefining their relationships with those they study. These approaches and shifts in praxis have been integral in working towards what Elaine Lawless calls "collectivity in interpretation and a new authentication of a multivocal kind of ethnography" (1992: 302). These discussions have brought to methodology and relational awareness what keyword study provided analysis, a sense of commonality of purpose and praxis. Such subjects, however, embed a set of ethics for not only how folklorists do their work in the field but also how they represent and discuss that work. If ethics describes how individuals act based on a set of beliefs, what are the beliefs that undergird those ethics?

I want to be cautious here, to write ethically, if possible. To suggest that we treat elements of folkloristics as though they were beliefs is not the same as to say that all things are "merely" matters of belief and therefore subject to contradiction by other systems of belief. This extreme relativism has led to no end of difficulties in the relationship between science and politics, as Adam Sokal among others have pointed out (2008: xv). And folklore studies could not have come so far without the contributions of the previous and current generations of scholars. I want to take a different tack. I want to add to our knowledge rather than reject or replace. I am interested in what we may discover not when we turn away from our articles of faith, but when we query what we might have neglected in the spaces between them. By looking at folkloristics as faith, I hope to reveal that these elements we have deemed important might not be the only ones worth our energies and to point towards those things that folklorists might have missed because we were busy looking elsewhere.

FROM KEYWORDS TO ARTICLES OF FAITH

Folklorists have invested critical research into our keywords, examining how certain ideas and terms have carried valences and been negotiated over the course of the field's history. Excellent definitions of each of the terms here and more have been written and refined. My interest in these terms, however, is not in how they help us cohere and articulate our field and our notoriously diverse subjects. In choosing some words as central to a discipline, we inevitably though often less consciously do not choose other words. I would like to pose about the terms the same questions that many folklorists pose in the course of our work about the various instances of folklore that we study: Why this thing? Why at this time? What is at stake for the people who say Appal-ay-cha and for those who say Appal-ah-cha? Why do so many Americans still check the backseat of the car for the killer that was likely never there? Why, as one senior folklorist asked after an American Folklore Society Annual Meeting panel on postcolonial theory in the study of folklore, are we still talking about authenticity after Regina Bendix (1997) and others so ably deconstructed it?

The 1990s were a period of definition and "boundary-work"[2] in folkloristics. Discussions abounded on where folklore studies was headed and where it had been, what held the field together, even whether it should continue to be called folklore. Burt Feintuch, as editor of the *Journal of American Folklore*, sought to describe some of the binding threads in the field with the 1995 special issue "Common Ground: Keywords for the Study of Expressive Culture." The group of eight authors each tackled a specific word: group, art, text, genre, performance, context, tradition, and identity.[3] In organizing this special issue and the 2003 book that followed, Feintuch referenced the work of Raymond Williams, whose book, *Keywords: A Vocabulary of Culture and Society*, had undertaken a similar project with a significantly broader scope in 1976. Feintuch's goal was more direct, to "examine a set of words that are at the heart of conversations about expressive culture" (2003: 1). The idea of "keywords," as Feintuch claims, draws attention to both the centrality of this specific set of words to the field and to how looking at these specific axes can help unlock the mysteries of culture (2003: 2). The specific list of words could have been expanded or changed. Certainly, it reflected the era in which it was written—after the 1970s turn towards performance, before the widespread use of the internet. Yet the journal special issue and the book have continued to carry weight in the field. These eight words remain integral to folklore study, even as scholars have suggested additions, amendments, and refinements. The keywords have continued to influence how folklorists define what we do. But keywords tell us something more, they sketch out who we, in our professional capacity as folklorists, believe ourselves to be. Genre is included in that book; authenticity and the vernacular are not.

Yet both authenticity and the vernacular have also been given their due. Intervening in this discussion of keywords and definitions, Regina Bendix published *In Search of Authenticity* in 1997, reframing the history of folklore as a field predicated on the notion of and search for authenticity. Authenticity of the subject gave legitimization to the field (1997: 7), Bendix claims, but in doing so created a troubling gap between self and Other (1997: 17), a gap around which we have continued to form our field, even as we have questioned and laid bare its problems. Similarly, we have toiled over the meanings of the vernacular. Gerald Pocius, in his chapter on "art" for *Eight Words*, examined the Kantian tradition of marking only those things without utilitarian purpose as art, thereby sidelining most of the material and oral culture that folklorists study (2003). Richard Bauman, too, tackled what folklorists deemed the vernacular and how our use of it defined the field (2008). Diane Goldstein and Amy Shuman dove into the tension created by the stigmatization of the vernacular that has seemed to undercut so much of folklore study and the problems for those who have been stigmatized in telling their stories (2012). These works provide a sampling of the depth of keyword discussions. Many more names could be added.

Such keyword study has provided us with important articulations of our commonalities and our field. I propose here to think of these words in the language of faith to expose the slippages within them. Keywords imply greater definition; faith suggests unknowability. Faith exposes gaps, and like most humans faced with unknowable spaces, we have sought to fill that gap with *something*—our theories of folkloristics. Yet as a result of these deep explorations, our keywords have become mantras and we have made them sacred, even as their definitions seem to shift and slip out of reach. As myths helped humanity order the cosmos and became faith, our theories have helped us order our subject, and they have also become faith.

Faith is important. We can offer a million examples of support for our theories of folklore, but they remain theories—we can never fully prove them, an ambiguity particularly dear to a more relativistic field such as folklore, but potentially anxiety producing all the same. At some point, a leap is required. These keywords may be hashed out but their importance to the field and its praxis is beyond the leap of faith. Within folkloristics, authenticity, the vernacular, and genre, amongst others, serve as articles of faith, beliefs so fundamental as to seem unquestionable. Are they non-negotiable though? To think in terms of keywords helps us to define our subject, but to think in terms of faith gives us space to doubt, to question, and critically, to disagree with our communities, our informants, and each other.

"SALVATION" OR HOW I LEARNED TO STOP WORRYING AND LOVE FOLKLORE

Langston Hughes' essay "Salvation" describes the moment he is saved in his aunt's evangelical church. Except that, the last child stuck sitting on the sinners' bench, he lies. He does not see Jesus, literally, as his childhood self had assumed that he would, or metaphorically, as his aunt assumes he has. Hughes stops believing that night, more ashamed of his lie in the face of his aunt's enthusiasm than that he has not been saved. Yet his choice of title suggests that Hughes found a kind of salvation, a clearer sense of himself and his place in the world, through his failure to be saved (1993). This is the story of my own academic crisis of faith and the salvation it provided.

I wrote the first version of this piece as a farewell to folklore studies, because I had lost faith in authenticity, rarely thought about genre except as somewhat archaic, and found the vernacular meaningless. These ideas seemed to me at the time a conservative force in the field to which I could not find a balancing dynamism. They seemed to be creating barriers and blocking important discussions. We were indeed still talking about authenticity, but not, I thought, as a question, rather as a foregone conclusion. How far, I wondered, had we advanced from Dorson's "fakelore." But then, returning to those texts, I found a kind of solace in the genre, with its ever expandable structure, and I never left. To echo Lawless, the point of this text is to explore how the folklorist's own belief system guides their work, and in order to talk about that, I must talk

AUTHENTICITY

Authenticity, as Bendix argues, may have shaped the field of folklore from its earliest conception, but it has also caused me as a folklorist the most qualms. Motz contrasts belief and authenticity: while belief cannot be proven, authenticity "assumes a central truth that can be verified or disproved" (1997: 349). To suggest, as I do here, that we believe in authenticity is to say that we have placed authenticity, as an essential and essentially unknowable characteristic, at the center of our system of belief, while at the same time assuming it a quality that can be measured. In other words, we can never prove definitely what is authentic, but we believe ardently that authenticity, as something quantifiable and recognizable, exists and is important to us and by extension to those whose folklore we study.

The importance of authenticity in folklore studies implies an adherence to Walter Benjamin's understanding of the aura (1955). The folk performance, like the work of art, seems to possess some unknowable value that is diminished with mechanical reproduction. Benjamin saw authenticity as one element within the aura of the work of art. Once that artwork was mechanically reproduced, however, its cultural context changed. While the artwork now became available to a wider audience, the thing that made it art in the first place was gone. Bendix's exploration of authenticity's value in folklore studies suggests that many folklorists would agree with Benjamin—the folk performance also has some inherent value that is lost in mechanical reproduction. However, the relationship between the authentic, reproduction, and the value placed on a work of art, folk or otherwise, might be much more complicated.

For me, it all started downhill in graduate school. In an early rendition of my dissertation topic, I was interested in exploring how Kyrgyz traditional feltmaking and felted objects have changed as they have gained greater attention in the global marketplace and adapted to western tastes and expectations. As I began my preliminary research, however, a series of problems presented themselves. The first was an issue of anthropological conceit: to look at how something has changed with contact assumes that there was a distinct moment of contact, a before and after. It assumes that there is such a thing as a culture that is not always already in conversation with the cultures around it. In retrospect, this notion strikes me as particularly ridiculous in my case, since the Kyrgyz reside along one of the longest and oldest trading routes in the world, the Silk Road. Market concerns and "inauthentic" influences have been changing the local products for millennia. Secondly and more interestingly, I found it impossible to describe my project without having to clarify, often multiple times, that I was not interested in making an argument of greater or lesser authenticity. I was interested in change, as an ongoing, dynamic, and necessary process, in which each step has value and meaning. But to describe a before and after in relation to tradition, I found, implied a value judgment in which the before, the authentic, was inherently positioned as superior to the after, the contaminated and inauthentic. One might think this to have been more of an issue among non-folklorists, but they were surprisingly easier to convince. Tellingly, it became apparent that folklore training itself appeared to create folklorists invested in authenticity, even a decade or more after we as a field critiqued and explored this investment.

My topic grew and changed, as topics do, and I began to focus on the newly opening marketplaces for these textiles in the United States. I no longer faced questions about the authenticity of the objects, though not because authenticity stop mattering in this new context. Instead, on some level, the felt seemed to be *assumed* authentic. This struck me as curious, since many of the Kyrgyz felt items sold in the United States are Christmas ornaments. I assure you, they are not generally produced by the approximately 0.1% of Kyrgyz Christians but by nominally Muslim Kyrgyz women, who often told me that they found the ornaments' intended use rather quaint. Further, I knew from fieldwork that Americans with the Peace Corps and other agencies were actively working with feltmakers to help them tailor their products for Western markets. Now I had what might be considered inauthentic objects, perceived and accordingly valued in the West as authentic. Instead of being questioned about the objects, however, I began to be asked why I was studying Kyrgyz textiles outside their natural habitat. "But how are they used in Kyrgyzstan?" some would ask. They aren't; no one has Christmas trees. "Marketplaces? What are the Kyrgyz marketplaces like?" Busy, just like here, but probably outside and with more mutton for sale. There's not a lot of felt in the bazaar; it's more of a specialty shop item. "Wouldn't it be better to study them there?" No, it wouldn't answer my question. I went through stages of grief. Denial. Surely, you aren't really asking me these questions after I just explained. Anger. Why can't you hear what I'm saying—textiles. From there. Sold here. Here, here, here! Bargaining. What if I did a comparison between there and here, would that help? Depression. Everyone hates my topic. Acceptance. I'm just going to write about this anyway, just wait and read it. It only occurred to me later that the conceptual problem was one of context and authenticity, the same issues, in other words, that have flowed through folklore studies from the start.

Kyrgyz textiles in America are inauthentic. I can study felt in Kyrgyzstan or quilts in America, not the other way around.[4] Authenticity, however, was a given. Something, somehow, had to be authentic. Without a location for authenticity, the objects effectively cease to exist for the folklorist, just like Anne Fausto-Sterling has claimed about a third sex between male and female (2000). If we scientifically cannot see it, it cannot be there. If the authenticity wasn't in the context, the felt was no longer in Kyrgyzstan, then it had to be the text, these must be what Kyrygz feltmakers have always made. If it wasn't the text, Muslim-made Christmas ornaments, then it had to be the performer, surely Kyrgyz women have always made felt this way. Even in Charles Briggs' *The Woodcarvers of Cordova, New Mexico*, authenticity can still be found in the woodcarvers themselves and the art they practice, even if they have retooled their artform to comment on the inauthentic white buyers (1980). The shifting burden of authenticity is reminiscent of Glassie's shifting location of tradition in maker, object, or process (1995). In the examples provided by Briggs and Glassie, authenticity lies in the performer, but even that failed to work out quite as expected in the case of the Kyrgyz felt. Feltmaking was suppressed under Soviet rule since it was connected to nomadism and traditional culture. Many of the feltmakers had learned to make felt to supplement family incomes following Kyrygz independence in 1991. As Deborah Kodish has pointed out, the shift of gaze from text to context, while widening the definition of what counted as folklore, did not dispose of the hierarchies of genre but rather "added additional requirements for virtuosity, leisure, and authority on the part of the performers" (1993: 200). Yet my experience with my dissertation research demonstrates the ultimate problem with the shifting location of authenticity: we still assume it has to be there somewhere.

Of greater concern than our objects of study, however, may be our subjects of study. If we believe in authenticity as an article of faith, and we become, at times against our wishes and better judgment, effectively priests at the altar by the positions we hold not only in academia but also in arts agencies and humanities councils, on grant panels and in advocacy groups, then do we gain the privilege of gatekeepers? I am less interested here in our role in determining what may or may not be authentic, but rather the privilege we have to declare the importance of authenticity in the first place. For the women making felt Christmas ornaments in Kyrgyzstan, the authenticity of their process and products was of significantly less importance than the money earned from selling those products to Westerners. I have met those, in the West, who see this state of affairs as sad, a testament to the women's poverty and desperation. But that judgment circumscribes the women in Western terms—what Westerners think the Kyrgyz women *should* think is important. The women themselves told me they were entrepreneurs. They were proud of their business acumen. The authentic, for them, was just as bound up with Otherness and nostalgia as it often is for Westerners. If I asked about authentic feltmaking, I was invariably told that there were probably some women in the villages who still practiced it and there were some excellent examples in the national museum, but you would never do it as a business, not in the old way. They often compared it to American quiltmaking, something old timey people used to do because they had to but now they do for other reasons, as a hobby or fine art. At the other end of the spectrum, authenticity may be of great importance to the people we choose to work with, marking their work as separate from and of higher value than competitors. Yet we must be cautious there, too, for authenticity may not be working in the ways we typically assume.

As Kodish questions what is neglected by the turn to context, I question what is neglected by our belief in authenticity. Partly, this is an issue of how we might be curtailing the *objects* of our study. What, for example, do we do with the simulacrum, the copy with no original? Do we as a field, with Baudrillard (1994), dismiss the postmodern, the suburban, and the mass or popular? In doing so, do we shut ourselves off to the potential for the hybrid, in Bhabha's terms the sign appropriated and turned to transgressive purposes (1994)? Or do we find ways to find the performative and the folkloric there, too? How do we describe voyeurism and spectacle? How does folklore speak to the experiences of virtual experience? What do we make of the cyborg? In terms of authenticity, how do we quantify the object that is both authentic and inauthentic simultaneously? I am reminded of a friend from Ireland's comment about a shop in the United States that specialized in Irish items. "It was great," she declared. It reminded her exactly of the shops that sell "tourist crap at home," and for her, an expat, there was a certain value in the authenticity of the inauthenticity.

VERNACULAR

I was teaching a graduate level course on folk music cultures, a course one of the students had redubbed "Keepin' It Real through Music and Storytelling" in deference to the quantity of class time ultimately spent discussing authenticity, even though it was only on the schedule for two class periods. We had covered the Lomaxes and Lead Belly, Child and Sharp, the Irish minstrel show, Juggalos and Dead Heads. We were at the end of the semester, when one student wondered aloud what "folk music" was anyway. She said that if you had asked her before the semester started, she would have known exactly what to say—Bob

Dylan, "stuff with banjos," and the performances of local ethnic musicians at the annual international festival. After a semester of folklore and music, she felt she no longer knew. The students were not "folklore students," this class was their introduction to the field.

Someone suggested that it might be easier to think about what was *not* folk music. Like Taylor Swift, said another, the epitome of "not folk." But why? Because Swift is pop and on the radio? Or because she appeals mostly to preteen girls? Are preteen girls not folk? What about Ryan Adams' remake of Taylor Swift's album *1989*? For some, Adams' remake felt closer to "folk" than the original album. Was folk a style? What about those preteen girls singing Swift's music on the school bus? Definitely folk. So in a spectrum between not folk to folk, the original music was somehow the least authentic and the least folk because it was the least vernacular.

In *Folk Groups and Folklore Genres*, Elliott Oring concludes his introduction with an assertion of folklore's specialness based neither on genre (despite being a book about genres) nor on authenticity but on the vernacular. Folklorists, Oring argues, "do not regard folklore as simply art, music, dance, medicine, or custom whenever or wherever found. . . . Folklore cannot be legislated, scripted, published, packaged, or marketed and still be folklore. In some sense, for something to be folklore in an urban society, it must be touched and transformed by common experience—ordinary humans living their everyday lives" (1986: 16). Oring is not alone in seeing folklore as first and foremost the study of the vernacular. Folklorists started out in the nineteenth century as vernacular's faithful, a faith that has held fairly true to this day, though it has become more nuanced in the face of genre-bending studies at the crossroads of folklore and pop culture and the internet, as the Taylor Swift example partly demonstrates. I tell the story of Taylor Swift's songs, however, not to reiterate the tension between pop and folk but to point towards something else—the commercial and the official. Looking at the vernacular can obscure how what is deemed commercial and what is deemed official continues to have influence outside the realms of pop and subtly works within the subjects of folklore, even when these genres are not the direct object of folklore. Underneath the designation of the vernacular lie at least two other commentaries: one about economics, folklore's relationship to the marketplace and the socio-economic status of those who have folklore; the other, related, about the relationship between the official and the unofficial.

The economics and economies of the vernacular may be related to how folklore has historically been configured as art and positioned in relation to other artforms. The separation of form from function, artistic merit from utility of purpose, as a defining characteristic of what makes something art, lies in the Enlightenment. Since Johann von Herder, folklorists have attempted to push back against the universality and implicit elitism implied by Kantian definitions of beauty (Bauman and Briggs 2003: 181). Yet, the genres folklorists have chosen have often reinscribed that very division; as Gerald Pocius has said, folklorists have tended to research "*their* versions of *our* art forms" (2003: 48). While this issue in part reveals a genre problem, it also points towards an economic one. Pocius points out that part of the division between art and craft in Western thinking came as a result of a rising middle class and the transformation of art into product (2004: 45). Commodification paved the way for the vernacular as a distinct form, yet commodification has also historically been what separates the folklorist's subjects of study from mass and popular culture, Swift's CD release from the girls on the bus. Yet this separation puts the productive folk in a double bind; to maintain status as folk, they must not be too commercially successful, but commercial success was often the goal of producing in the first place. When does a folk artist hit the "right" amount of commodification without crossing the line into the mass produced? When does vernacular, unofficial folklore become, for better or worse, the official?

In writing about the internet, Robert Glenn Howard has commented that "invoking the vernacular web necessarily also invokes that which is not vernacular: the institutional" (2008: 195). The same may be and has been said of the vernacular offline as well as on. One difficulty with this construction, however, is the tendency to always be defining our subjects, and as a result ourselves, in opposition to something else, which sets up the potential for stigmatization, real or claimed (Goldstein and Shuman 2012: 116–17). One might see in the folklorists' faith in the vernacular the legacy of what Alan Dundes (2005) and Charles Briggs (2008) have described as a focus within folkloristics on boundary work over theory. By worrying more about what folklore is or is not, folklorists have remade themselves into "provincial intellectuals," the vernacular scholars of the vernacular, while paradoxically trying to use that vernacularism to claim institutional legitimacy (Briggs 2008: 95). The dichotomy, however, may be a false one. The subjects of our study are rarely so clear cut—traditional or not traditional, vernacular or institutional. Why would we expect ourselves to be? Even the most crafted corporate message can have buried within it the hallmarks of a corporate folklore; even the most seemingly spontaneous folk performance, the girls on the bus, may still reveal commercialism, the learning of the song by some, at least, from the radio. What might be more useful is to question our faith in the vernacular.

I still believe there is something different and special about the girls singing on the bus, something that can be described through the lexicon and beliefs of folklorists that is more difficult to describe through other fields. I still have faith that what marks the study of folklore as distinct from our sister fields is our attention to the vernacular. My faith has faltered, however, in believing that the vernacular and the official are so distant. Rather they seem more like two sides of a coin. We cannot look at one side or the other without engaging with the alloy that binds the sides together, without producing absences. We would not have the girls on the bus without Taylor Swift or maybe Ryan Adams, but we also would not have Taylor Swift or Ryan Adams without the girls on the bus. As Howard has suggested in his study of the vernacular web, what we study is less one or the other, vernacular or official, but a hybrid, offering a critique of both.

GENRE

The evolution of my thinking on authenticity has been one of the main streams of my academic life, and the vernacular has not been far behind. I have read about it, written about it, presented on it, lost and regained faith in it, but in thinking about our articles of faith, those things so accepted they seem almost absent from our daily thought, I realized that a lot of people were thinking, writing, presenting, and believing in and facing down doubts about genre much as I did with authenticity. Yet genre, for me, was so accepted, so embedded within in the foundations of our field, that I had never questioned it. Because I never questioned it, I have no interesting generic story to tell. Indeed, that genre is important to folklore studies never seems to be questioned by many other folklorists either, even in all of those books about genre by those who have declared it central to their scholarship. One might question how something fits within the genres thus far enumerated, pushing the bounds of generic taxonomies, or one might explore ways to better delineate and define a known genre (cf. Ben-Amos 1976, Stewart 1991, Kapchan and Strong1999, Oring 1986, Bauman 2004, Schacker 2007). One does not, however, question genre itself.

I am not interested here in recapping the many excellent discussions of what genre means or contains. Folklorists have been hashing out the definition of genre generally and genres specifically since the beginnings of the field.[5] No doubt that essential work will continue. Rather, why do we believe genre to be so important? For one thing, genre serves an organizing and authenticating function, for both the text or context studied and the folklorist, "isolating distinctive forms and articulating how folklorists' training was essential in understanding them" (Harris-Lopez 2003: 101). Genre has been important in part because knowing folklore genres is part of what make a folklorist different from a literary scholar or anthropologist; genre performs boundary maintenance. Barre Toelken has also argued effectively that genre gives folklorists a way to talk to each other from across our wide range of subjects and cultural bases. Like theory, genre forms a common language and satiates a desire to find connections and similarities beyond and across both cultures and the genres themselves as well as a firm footing from which to dive into the meaning articulated by difference (Toelken in Sims and Stephens 2005: 12).

In the development and discussion of genre lies the nineteenth-century popular antiquities roots of the field and the Victorian fascination with categorization of all kinds (Bronner 1986: 20). It is a commonplace to say that genre is the cultural analog to biology's taxonomy. Yet genre has proven more slippery than those natural history taxonomies, as a text can appear in multiple places, bridge genres, or break off into something new. A folkloric text can have proverb, joke, and anecdotal versions or include all three. As Dan Ben-Amos pointed out, the work of Linnaeus differed from that of the early folklorists in direction—Linnaeus worked from what he saw and built categorical ideas, the folklorists created ideals and then divided up what they saw, or in Gerald Pocius's view, borrowed them from their own culture (2003: 48), and then tried to impose them on samples from the field (Ben-Amos 1976: xvi). Genre has also been more adaptable, however, taking in stride the field's widening focus from text to context to performance (Bronner 1986: 108–9, 120). Combined with a contextual and intertextual approach, looking at genre can draw attention to how power relations and agency interweave in a folkloric event (Gilman 2009: 357).

No doubt, not all is rosy for genre. Genre has its difficulties. As with any system of classification, absences are inherent. Dundes wondered what we missed in our adherence to genre (quoted in Ben-Amos 1976: xiv). Since, folklorists have long struggled with hybrid genres, distressed genres, and unruly genres (Kapchan and Strong 1999, Stewart 1991, Schacker 2007). The classification system itself can impose limits that create absences, items that do not conform and thus remain under-described. I do not know how I would begin to choose a genre for the song on the bus. The genres themselves can cause problems as well. There can be categories too broad to be entirely meaningful, such as the biological taxon of fish.[6] The genre of urban legends sometimes endures such critique, as the legends cross over into rumor, saying, and folk tale. There are difficulties of universality and emic versus etic categories. An over-adherence to the process of generification, too, risks suppressing deeper analysis, leaving the field stuck at formalism. Ben-Amos linked genre with the "first stage of research—the very act of collecting" (1976: xi). As he pointed out, what happens second also matters.

Nonetheless, genre has proven tenacious, and while I have wrestled with my faith in authenticity and the vernacular, I have tended to see genre as unshakeable. I simply never thought about it. The adherence to the importance of genre as a kind of undergirding to the field may be primarily a matter of sales and marketing. In part, genre lists offer an effective way to describe what it is folklorists study, especially to non-folklorists. Like most folklorists, I have told many people proudly that I am folklorist only to be met with the assumption that I tell fairy tales to schoolchildren, which I assure everyone the schoolchildren would not appreciate. In an elevator pitch for the field, the quickest way to expand that view is to list genres. Indeed, folklorists have been doing just that since the field was young. W. J. Thoms's definition of folklore includes "manners, customs, observances, superstitions, ballads, and proverbs, etc." (quoted in Oring 1986: 7). All manner of things might be contained in that "etc." but the genres seemed to Thoms to best explain what it was he was writing about. Later, Alan Dundes' lengthy but admittedly partial list of genres at the beginning of *The Study of Folklore* does much the same (1965: 2). While Dundes' list was not meant to be a definition, in a field where definitions of folklore itself have proven often just out of reach, the list of genres has served "to identify for the introductory student those forms that have traditionally interested the folklorist" (Oring 1986: 17). That student may be the most crucial link in uncovering the rationale for the field's faith in genre.

In 1976, Dan Ben-Amos briefly surveyed the extent to which folklorists have relied on genre as an organizing principle both in the classroom and on the page. Ben-Amos begins with Francis Child's lectures on balladry offered at Harvard in the 1890s and continues through to his own publication, citing that genre specific classes appeared on the books of folklore programs second in number only to introductory courses. Further, folklore publications adhered to generic divisions as well, focusing on one or two genres over more wide ranging paradigms (Ben-Amos 1976: x-xi). To see how much had not changed in forty years, I too looked up recent publication catalogues and journal contents and surveyed course syllabi. While journals have moved somewhat more towards conceptual concerns, many books and articles still favor genre as a situating device.

But the syllabi were most telling. My own introduction to folklore as a student had been generically based—an introduction to folklore through an introduction to a few of the genres of folklore. I teach as I was taught, I realized, and so do most of my colleagues. While not the only way, genre remains by far the most common way to organize introductory folklore courses in whole or in part. Even courses ostensibly organized by theory, approach, or chronology still tended to use genre as a secondary structure: for instance, psychoanalytic approaches *and* märchen. And why not? Students like the sense of structure it provides. Genre gives them a sense of familiarity, being similar enough to the breakdown of the university itself into field-based departments, and those departments into sub-specialties. Genre-based structures help the instructor, too. Because folklorists tend to publish on a specific genre, readings are easily found and easily placed within the syllabus. Genre does offer a kind of common language, as Toelken hoped, if for no other reason than that anyone who has ever taken or taught an introduction to folklore course most likely speaks it.

Our faith in genre, then, might not be about what folklore seems to be, authentic and vernacular, or who folklore is of and for, the folk group, or the performance of folklore itself. Rather, our faith in genre might be architectural and pedagogical. It offers us a scaffolding on which to hang our concepts, but more than that, it lets us speak to each other, across fields, and to our students. Categorization offers a useful tool both internally, as a way to subdivide a sometimes unwieldy field, and externally, as a sales technique to hook interested members of the public and students, to show them a slice of what folklore is about, and draw them in. Perhaps it is best to think of genre as Dan Ben-Amos does: a "means to an end which instrumentally satisfies social and spiritual needs" (1976: xxiv). However, we should keep in mind that those social and spiritual needs are often the folklorist's own—for a common ground, for a sense of institutional legitimacy, for a clear statement, a creed, about what folklore is (or may not be).

CONCLUSION

> Purity and authenticity are negotiable traits.
> (Harris Lopez 2003: 112)

While doing fieldwork in the late 2000s, I was riding the bus back into town from the Santa Fe International Folk Art Market. The passengers were eager to chat about their purchases. One woman had bought an African drum, which was attracting considerable attention. A second woman asked her if she intended to play it. "No," replied the first, looking slightly aghast. The second woman said that she thought maybe someone in Albuquerque might be able to give lessons. A man sitting nearby jumped in, asking to see the drum. "It's easy!" he declared as he started to play. He encouraged the buyer to try. She would not. After some back and forth, the man finally asked, with a tone of exasperation, "Well, what ARE you going to use it for?"

"A coffee table," the buyer replied.

There were audible gasps. The second woman suggested that this was possibly insulting to the drum maker, who took such time to craft an instrument that worked, a drum with a nice sound. At first, I, too, was shocked. I still believed in authenticity then. How could this woman take this handmade, authentic thing from one genre (musical instruments) and turn it into something so decontextualized and bourgeois as a coffee table (household furnishings), a different genre altogether? Shouldn't it be played? But is it authentic performance if the African drum is being played by middle-aged white woman in New Mexico who I strongly suspect has never been to Africa and has no other connection to the drum's traditional culture? It was enough for the second woman and the man that the drum itself, the text, was authentic. Was this a moment of fetishistic consumption of the Other, on one hand, and appropriation, on the other, or was there something else going on here as well?

The more I have thought about this conversation, the less comfortable I have felt with my easy judgment, particularly my assumption of the central importance of authenticity—of the drum itself, the performer, and the context to which it was destined. Because I also heard mutterings of what a great idea a drum-coffee table was. The woman clearly valued her new drum; however, her valuation was not based on its connection to an authentic past rooted in the object's vernacular origins. It was not even based in the drum's genre as a musical instrument. She had changed its genre to home décor. Perhaps it was a memento of Santa Fe or a friend; perhaps the space she inhabited was important to her; perhaps her generic categories differed from mine, she liked round things or wooden things. Perhaps the man who made the drum felt like the Kyrgyz feltmakers and cared less about the authenticity than the income. The bus riders and I didn't even know if it was really authentic, we all just assumed so, because the maker, we assumed, had said so, and because of the context in which it was bought. Like the felt Christmas ornaments from Kyrgyzstan, it might have only been that the material was authentic. Just because I had trained as a folklorist, did I now have the right to exercise the privilege of insisting on my articles of faith as the most important? In doing so, did I have the right to deny the agency of another to value their world according to their own articles of faith?

I suggest here that, far from being a relic of folkloristics past, our articles of faith remain vital and often unquestioned parts of how we as folklorists define the objects and subjects of our study. Further, I believe that our faith in the importance of these valences has led us towards a specific hierarchy of "acceptable" subjects and methodologies, and I question what we may be marginalizing in our insistence on these categories of value. For folklorists, such faith may be likened to Mihaly Hoppel's concept of a "cultural belief language"—the idea that a community's language can limit what can be expressed or described, and that such language is based in and can help shape belief (cited in Ellis 2001: 95). It could be argued that folklorists had difficulty at first in dealing with the concept of folklore and the internet because we did not have the language to describe it. I would add to this formulation that it was not simply a failure of linguistics but of paradigm, those things, to paraphrase Hamlet, that cannot be dreamt of in our philosophy. Recategorizing authenticity, for example, from a keyword to an article of faith encapsulated my unease with how we talk about, fail to talk about, and value authenticity in the field of folklore studies. Bendix has claimed that part of the tension surrounding authenticity, and I would argue our other articles of faith, lies in the diversity of folklorists themselves: there are those who find the authentic or the vernacular "a major attraction" and those who see them as "an early disease long overcome by scholarly healing through the rigor in inquiry" (1997: 219). As with any faith, there are fundamentalists and atheists. The potential, for me, of looking at authenticity, the vernacular, genre, and our other articles of faith lies in being able to acknowledge both their slipperiness and their incredible influence. We cannot deny that these constructs have played a major role in the foundation of folklore studies and folkloristics and continue to exert tremendous pressure on how and who we study. That does not mean we cannot doubt.

NOTES

1. I use "we" and "our" throughout to refer to folklorists as a group. I am fully aware of the problems inherent in such pronoun usage.

2. Cf. Charles Briggs. "Disciplining Folkloristics." *Journal of Folklore Research*, Vol. 45, No. 1, Grand Theory (Jan.–Apr., 2008): 91–105.

3. The original special issue included seven articles. Some of these articles were heavily revised for the 2003 book, and Roger Abrahams' chapter "Identity" was added at that time.

4. Kyrgyzstan does have a vibrant pieced quilting tradition as well, which has led to a quilting and quiltmaker exchange.

5. For one definition of genre, see Bauman: "One order of speech style, a constellation of systemically related, co-occurrent formal features and structures that serves as a conventionalized orienting framework for the production and reception of discourse. More specifically, a genre is a speech style oriented to the production and reception of a particular kind of text" (2004, 3–4). It is possible to extend this definition to other, non-verbal areas such as foodways and material culture.

6. Many wits have enjoyed pointing out that technically speaking there is no such thing as a fish, since the animals contained within that classification go back to a diversity of evolutionary ancestors, unlike their land-dwelling cousins.

REFERENCES CITED

Baudrillard, Jean. 1994. *Simulacra and Simulations*. Translated by Sheila Faria Glaser. Ann Arbor: University of Michigan Press.

Bauman, Richard. 2004. *A World of Others' Words: Cross-Cultural Perspectives on Intertextuality*. Malden: Blackwell Publishing.

Bauman, Richard. 2008. "The Philology of the Vernacular." *Journal of Folklore Research* 45, no. 1: 29–36. http://www.jstor.org/stable/40206961.

Bauman, Richard and Charles Briggs. 2003. *Voices of Modernity: Language Ideologies and the Politics of Inequality.* Cambridge: Cambridge University Press.

Behar, Ruth. 1993. *Translated Woman: Crossing the Border with Esperanza's Story.* Boston: Beacon Press.

Ben-Amos, Dan, ed. 1976. *Folklore Genres. American Folklore Society Bibliographical and Special Series,* Vol. 26, Austin: University of Texas Press.

Bendix, Regina. 1997. *In Search of Authenticity: The Formation of Folklore Studies.* Madison: University of Wisconsin Press.

Benjamin, Walter. 1955. "The Work of Art in the Age of Mechanical Reproduction." In *Illuminations: Essays and Reflections,* edited by Hannah Arendt. New York: Harcourt Brace and World.

Bhabha, Homi K. 1985. "Signs Taken for Wonders: Questions of Ambivalence and Authority under a Tree Outside Delhi, May 1817." *Critical Inquiry* 12:1, 144–65.

Briggs, Charles. 1980. *The Wood Carvers of Córdova, New Mexico: Social Dimensions of an Artistic 'Revival.'* Knoxville: University of Tennessee Press.

Briggs, Charles. 2008. "Disciplining Folkloristics." *Journal of Folklore Research*, Vol. 45, No. 1, Grand Theory (Jan.–Apr.): 91–105.

Bronner, Simon. 1986. *American Folklore Studies: An Intellectual History.* Lawrence: University of Kansas.

Clifford, James, and George Marcus. 1986. *Writing Culture: The Poetics and Politics of Ethnography.* Berkeley: University of California Press.

Dundes, Alan, ed. 1965. *The Study of Folklore.* Englewood: Prentice-Hall.

Dundes, Alan, ed. 2005. Folkloristics in the Twenty-First Century (AFS Invited Presidential Plenary Address, 2004). *Journal of American Folklore* 118, no. 470: 385–408. http://www.jstor.org/stable/4137664.

Ellis, Bill. 2001. *Aliens, Ghosts, and Cults: Legends We Live By.* Oxford: University of Mississippi Press.

Fausto-Stirling, Anne. 2000. Sex*ing the Body: Gender Politics and the Construction of Sexuality.* New York: Basic Books.

Feintuch, Burt. 1995. "Introduction: Words in Common." *Journal of American Folklore* 108, no. 430: 391–94. http://www.jstor.org/stable/541652.

Feintuch, Burt. 2003. Eight Words for the Study of Expressive Culture. Urbana: University of Illinois Press.

Gencarella, Stephen Olbrys. 2009. "Constituting Folklore: A Case for Critical Folklore Studies." *Journal of American Folklore* 122, no. 484: 172–96. http://www.jstor.org/stable/20487676.

Gilman, Lisa. 2009. "Genre, Agency, and Meaning in the Analysis of Complex Performances: The Case of a Malawian Political Rally." *Journal of American Folklore* 122, no. 485 : 335–62. http://www.jstor.org/stable/40390071.

Glassie, Henry. 1995. "Tradition." *Journal of American Folklore* 108, no. 430: 395–412. doi:10.2307/541653.

Goldstein, Diane E., and Amy Shuman. 2012. "The Stigmatized Vernacular: Where Reflexivity Meets Untellability." *Journal of Folklore Research* 49, no. 2 : 113–26. doi:10.2979/jfolkrese.49.2.113.

Harris-Lopez, Trudier. 2003. "Genre." In *Eight Words for the Study of Expressive Culture,* edited by Burt Feintuch. Urbana: University of Illinois Press, 99–120.

Howard, Robert Glenn. 2008. "Electronic Hybridity: The Persistent Processes of the Vernacular Web." *Journal of American Folklore* 121, no. 480 : 192–218. http://www.jstor.org/stable/20487596.

Hughes, Langston. [1940] 1993. "Salvation." In *The Big Sea*. New York: Hill and Wang, 18–21.

Kapchan, Deborah A., and Pauline Turner Strong. 1999. "Theorizing the Hybrid." *Journal of American Folklore* 112, no. 445: 239–53. doi:10.2307/541360.

Kodish, Debora. 1993. "On Coming of Age in the Sixties." *Western Folklore* 52, no. 2/4 : 193–207. doi:10.2307/1500086.

Lawless, Elaine J. 1992. "'I Was Afraid Someone like You . . . an Outsider . . . Would Misunderstand': Negotiating Interpretive Differences between Ethnographers and Subjects." *Journal of American Folklore* 105, no. 417 : 302–14. doi:10.2307/541758.

Motz, Marilyn. 1998. "The Practice of Belief." *Journal of American Folklore* 111, no. 441: 339–55. doi:10.2307/541314.

Oring, Elliott. 1986. *Folk Groups and Folklore Genres*. Logan: Utah State University Press.

Pimple, Kenneth. 1990. "Folk Beliefs." In *The Emergence of Folklore in Everyday Life*, edited by George H. Schoemaker. Bloomington: Trickster, 51–59.

Pocius, Gerald. 2003. "Art." In *Eight Words for the Study of Expressive Culture*, edited by Burt Feintuch. Urbana: University of Illinois Press, 42–68.

Schacker, Jennifer. 2007. "Unruly Tales: Ideology, Anxiety, and the Regulation of Genre." *Journal of American Folklore* 120, no. 478 : 381–400. doi:10.2307/20487576.

Shuman, Amy. 2005. *Other People's Stories: Entitlement Claims and the Critique of Empathy*. Urbana: University of Illinois.

Sims, Martha, and Stephens, Martine. 2011. *Living Folklore: An Introduction to the Study of People and Their Traditions*. Logan: Utah State University Press.

Sokal, Alan. 2008. *Beyond the Hoax: Science, Philosophy, and Culture*. Oxford: Oxford University Press.

Stewart, Susan. 1991. "Notes on Distressed Genres." *Journal of American Folklore* 104, no. 411: 5–31. doi:10.2307/541131.

Email from Nebraska

Todd Richardson

In the final year of my PhD program, while I was scrambling to finish a dissertation of passable value, Roger Welsch contacted my advisor Elaine Lawless because he was looking to unload his copies of the *Journal of American Folklore*. He had decided the issues—every one since the early 1960s—were taking up too much shelf space, and he figured Elaine might know someone who could put them to use. Immediately, Elaine sent me an email informing me that I would be driving to Roger's home in Dannebrog, Nebraska, to pick up the journals so that I could add them to my own library. Never mind that every issue of *JAF* is accessible in virtually every library in North America or that I had enough trouble finding space for the print copies of *JAF* I had begun accumulating since joining the American Folklore Society a few years earlier. I would be taking Roger's library because, like him, I was a folklorist from Nebraska. Elaine figured it was destiny.

Like most Nebraskans I was familiar with the name Roger Welsch, as he's something of a regional celebrity. For a number of years in the late twentieth century he produced *Postcards from Nebraska*, short documentary pieces that aired on CBS News Sunday Morning. These vignettes showcased, as Welsch put it, "the extraordinary nature of ordinary people," focusing mostly on subjects and characters close to his home in Dannebrog. As an example, my favorite *Postcard* profiled Louie LaRose and his domesticated buffalo herd on the Winnebago Reservation in Northeast Nebraska. The last time I had heard Welsch's name had been a few years earlier when my then ninety-three-year-old grandmother asked me if I remembered "that old guy Roger Welsch." Because my grandma had died the year before Roger sent his email to Elaine,

I was, frankly, less shocked by the offer of his library than I was by him still being alive. *How ancient must this guy be*, I thought to myself, *if even Grandma Blanche considered him old?*

Dannebrog is in the center of Nebraska, a two-and-a-half-hour drive from Omaha, my hometown, so I decided to head home for spring break, during which I would make a day trip to pick up the library. Originally, my intention had been to continue shunning humanity by holing up in my house in Missouri over spring break to finish that confounded dissertation, but I convinced myself it might be best to ditch that plan as I no longer really even knew what my dissertation was about. People were always asking me that—"What's it about?"—but after having worked on it for two years, I had come to feel that even if there were some clever ideas in it, or at least some clever sentences, there were only a handful of academics who would find anything worthwhile in my highfalutin, posturing rhetoric and that it was, for the most part, about nothing at all. A break from that, I figured, couldn't be bad. Besides, it didn't matter much if I finished in a timely manner as I had a better shot at getting another year of financial aid than I did of getting a job.

I arrived in Dannebrog (population 360) early on a Wednesday afternoon. While Roger's place wasn't overly hard to find—he actually lives on Roger Welsch Boulevard—the place certainly looks like it wants to be hard to find. The first thing visitors see when turning into Roger's place, which appears to be nothing more than an innocuous grove of pines from the highway, is a large hand-painted sign warning "VISITORS NOT WELCOME." The sign's scowl was unsettling, and it had me wondering whether or not I should turn around. I convinced myself the sign's unique phrasing was likely a disclaimer rather than a boundary, a way of saying *you may visit, but you will not be welcome*. I kept going forward, driving around a thicket of trees and through what appeared to be a tractor graveyard before eventually pulling up to Roger's place.

Roger's house is a charming country home tucked alongside the Loup River, and it exhibits none of the curmudgeonliness of the road leading up to it. Most rural Nebraskan homes are severe-looking things, little wind-burnt boxes standing in defiance of the flatness around them, but Roger's house, nestled amongst so many trees, which are rarities on the plains, looked Shire-like. As I got out of my car, Roger stepped out of the house, and it was immediately clear to me that not only was he still alive, he was thriving. Strapping at well over six feet tall, he looked to me like a corn-fed Gandalf. Or maybe more like a corn-fed Andy Warhol. Either way, my grandmother, despite being twenty-five years his senior, could call him "That old guy" because, like Gandalf and Warhol before him, Roger stumbled on the secret to never aging: begin grey. He was wearing well-worn overalls, which I've learned is something of a uniform for him, with a hard-washed flannel shirt underneath. On any other folklorist, the outfit would have looked like a costume, but Roger, as they say, owned it, and I greatly envied that about him.

Following an appropriately understated Midwestern exchange of hellos, Roger led me to a stack of boxes just inside the garage, and we went to work loading his *JAF* library into my car. As we went back and forth from the garage to my car, Roger started talking to me in his sonorous baritone about his recent activities. He informed me that his house wasn't really his house, that he had returned the land on which he lived, the land on which I was presently standing, to its previous inhabitants, the Pawnee Nation. Following the sale of his property to the Pawnee for one dollar—government regulations, for some reason, discourage land gifts of such size, particularly when given to American Indians—he commenced renting his house back from the Pawnee for one dollar a year, an absolutely foolish arrangement by most American yardsticks. Roger had come to his decision after working closely with the Pawnee on the repatriation of ancestral remains that had been in storage at the Nebraska State Historical Society. Before that, he had worked closely with and was eventually adopted by the Omaha Tribe, experiences he was writing about in a new book he intended to self-publish. It became very clear to me that American Indians, the Pawnee in particular, had become the fulcrum of his identity and worldview.

I find his land gift to the Pawnee inspiring, the sort of act that improves my view of humanity. That being said, I didn't—and still don't—know what to make of Roger Welsch's identification with American Indians. At that moment when he first told me how strongly he affiliates with Indians, I was in the depths of graduate school cynicism, a station that rendered me all-too-ready to dismantle other people's meanings. In this case, that wasn't terribly difficult to do: Roger had "gone native," a traditional indiscretion within the folklife of folklorists. All manner of academic terms and concepts describe and deride the phenomenon—"anti-conquest," "appropriation," "objectification"—but, for me, it comes down to treating people as a means to an end rather than as an end in themselves: when you look to others to make your meaning for you, you're treating others poorly. I find the practice especially problematic when it's white people finding themselves through other, more conspicuously ethnic people, probably because I've been that guy before—I wore a red, black and green Malcolm X baseball cap throughout most of high school. Bottom line, when a colonizer tells you he likes your stuff, it's time to hide your stuff. And even if Roger isn't a colonizer, he is certainly closer to the center of a colonialist culture than the people whose culture he's claiming to celebrate.

Then again, it's not like Roger is Baby Huey, crushing other cultures with his clumsy attempts to make nice. He is cautious, thoughtful and humble in his approach to American Indians, and when he speaks of his interactions and relationships with them, he makes it clear he speaks mostly for himself: "I do occasionally speak up more when white people make themselves look particularly stupid," he writes in *Embracing Fry Bread*, "more to save my own race further humiliation than to explain or protect a culture and people who scarcely need yet another white guy speaking up for them" (2012: 9). His self-awareness, a quality all too rare in cross-cultural interactions, is admirable. Moreover, Roger isn't looking for some premodern, endangered authenticity in Indians. He sees himself, rather, as participating in a dynamic and postmodern culture, one that is far from endangered and certainly isn't in need of converts, thank you very much. For far too long, folklorists and folk enthusiasts have artifactualized and fetishized American Indians in order to distance themselves from normative American culture, and while I think there is a bit of this at work in Roger, it is tempered by that aforementioned self-awareness: "Over the years I have remained to some degree or another a mainstream, middle-class, educated white man." He writes, "While I haven't embraced all the ugly influences of white culture around me, I have at least consciously acknowledged them, speaking to what they are and what they do" (2012: 8–9).

As I said previously, I don't know what to think about Roger's approach to American Indian culture, but I do know what Roger has to say about me not knowing: "That's fine," he writes of those who object to his conduct, "But it really is irrelevant. How can someone change the experiences and impressions of another? . . . If your opinions, impressions or experiences differ from mine, don't try to change mine or argue with me about them. The thing for you to do is write your own book" (2012: 14–15). This sentiment is what I most love about Roger Welsch: he expresses and embraces a large-minded subjectivity, one that exhibits a faith in other people's ability to think and behave smartly.

Prior to his run on CBS News Sunday Mornings, Roger was a tenured professor at the University of Nebraska at Lincoln. Being recently tenured myself, I find it difficult to fathom the recklessness of giving up the security and control that comes with tenure in order to, as Roger put it, "live on my own good looks"; to do it from Nebraska no less, seems to me a form of mania. Nevertheless, Roger opted for the unknown because he felt there was a larger classroom out there with whom he might discuss the sophistication of everyday expressive culture. The best analogue for what Roger has done throughout his career, I think, is Will Rogers as he, like Roger, was a populist and popular entertainer closely associated with American Indian culture. More importantly, both Roger Welsch and Will Rogers used their gifts with words, bolstered by mass media, to share the invisible—or at least ignored—genius of everyday Americans *with* everyday Americans.

Roger entered my folkloristic life at the right time. I was running on intellectual fumes after years of reading scholarly writing on folklore, and discovering that there was someone out there who didn't write that way but wrote important stuff about folklore anyway completely changed my outlook on the field. I've learned a lot from Roger, whether he meant to teach me any of it or not. For instance, I've learned that people don't need to be told they're learning to learn something. Likewise, education doesn't need to always be entertaining, but it certainly helps, particularly when dealing with a subject like folklore that most people are both intimately and barely familiar with. And you don't need to have a thesis to have a point.

More than anything, I've learned that there's a much bigger audience outside academia. As much as I'd like to do what Roger did with *Postcards from Nebraska*, I'm too much of an introvert and I'm not as good-looking as him. Besides it wasn't the venue that makes Roger's work so important. It was, rather, the respect, humor and humanity he always showed both the people he was writing about and the people he was writing for, attributes that are abundant in his most recent works as well. Like Roger, I endeavor to show my audience respect by writing readably about difficult ideas.

I couldn't tell Roger all this at the time because I didn't know all this at the time. It was only after our unlikely encounter that I really started to look into the life and career of the guy whose *JAF* library now surrounds me. It's funny how if he had not sent that email from Nebraska, I likely would have gone about my career regardless, just a little differently and less hopefully. It is, however, these sorts of deeply personal, idiosyncratic, and improbable experiences that both make a worldview and make a worldview irreproducible. Roger's work is, in both its form and its content, a testament to this reality.

Years ago when Roger was still working in academia, he wrote a note for *JAF* about definitions. "But no logic, no research, no righteousness, no sincerity on the folklorist's part will permit him to legislate a definition for other conventions. Folklore for any social unit is what its members think it is, and this rationale is as valid as William Thoms's, The Kingston Trio's, or the American Folklore Society's, for that is the nature of meaning. Efforts can and may be made to alter the broader convention, but they cannot go forth under the banners of Truth and Logic" (1968: 264). He wrote this as a response to what has become the field of folklore's preferred definition, via Dan Ben-Amos, of folklore as "artistic communication in small groups." I used to cite Ben-Amos's definition frequently in my introductory courses. I did so not because I thought it was a particularly good definition, but because I knew it would shut down unwanted discussion, and I felt dirty every time I did it. After all, it didn't clear anything up for students; all it did was assert my institutional authority through a precisely phrased delineation of epistemological boundaries. After getting to know Roger and his work, I don't do that anymore. I'm now proud to take a fuzzy, understandable and, above all, humanistic approach to this stuff we call folklore.

After we packed the last box into the back of my car, Roger left me with some advice about coyote and how everything is unpredictable, but I didn't really get it. Or maybe I did, and that's what I'm talking about here. Whatever the case, I drove back through the trees and tractors and turned onto the highway leading back to Omaha, to the University of Missouri, to my dissertation, to my career in folklore, and I did so feeling a little more welcome in the field.

REFERENCES CITED

Welsch, Roger. 1968. "A Note on Definitions." *Journal of American Folklore* 81 (321): 262–64.
Welsch, Roger. 2012. *Embracing Fry Bread: Confessions of a Wannabe.* Lincoln: Bison Books.

On Fanfiction and the Amateur/ Professional Divide

Shelley Ingram

One inauspicious day in February, I posed a question on the (private) Facebook page of a group of folklorists: "If you were to write a fanfiction about folklorists, what would you write?" The very first response was, "Important Question: Can you ship them?" My answer: "Of course."

> Franz Boas x John Hunt high school!AU
> Margaret Mead and Ruth Benedict do fieldwork. Canonverse.[1]
> A mafia!AU between the early folklorists and anthropologists. With an enemies
> to lovers subplot maybe? Oh, wait—make it a breakup fic!
> Wilhelm Grimm's private diary. No shipping him with his brother, though.[2]
> Ghost of [redacted name of dead folklorist] seduces [redacted name of living
> folklorist] from beyond the grave. Coffeeshop!AU preferable.
> Malinowski/Conrad
> Stith Thompson—Star Wars crossover[3]

Within a matter of minutes, they had populated the entire disciplinary history of folkloristics with mayhem, grand romance, and everyday living, with narratives of secret lives and secret loves couched within the day-to-day mundanity of people known mostly from their texts. Here is what we learn from my Facebook query: fanfiction has its own rules and its own language, crafted over time by the members of fanwriting communities.

It reveals and creates meaning, bringing out dynamics that might have otherwise gone unnoticed. It deconstructs history and the text. It relies on in-group knowledge for its continued existence. In short, fanfiction writers are part of a folk group.

But it would serve us well to move beyond justifying fandom and its texts as part of folk culture, and even beyond an interpretation of the function and meaning of this digital folklore. The debates surrounding the proper place of fanfiction and other fan-produced work in the hierarchy of artistic production can also be an interesting corollary to discussions about fraudulent folklore, as one of the primary criticisms of fanfiction writers is that they often have the audacity to trespass on grounds best left preserved for the "professionals." Their very existence threatens the boundaries between expert and amateur, between trained artists and "usurpers." Even texts that are supportive of fandom and fan writers, like Rainbow Rowell's novel *Fangirl*, ultimately come down on the side of artistic authenticity, as the growth of Rowell's young protagonist is measured by her ability to put down her fanfiction to instead write *real* fiction, a move prompted and guided by her professionally sanctioned university writing professor. The debates about fandom and fanfiction, then, can give us a frame for delving into the complicated questions surrounding the nexus of academic and public discourse.

Let's start here: what, exactly, is a fandom?

I teach an upper-level undergraduate course on folklore and fiction, in which I often focus both on how folklore functions in literature *and* how literature has been taken up by folk culture. Fandom throws this process, the incorporation of literature into folk culture, into stark relief. If there are folklorists out there who still hold out hope for some kind of pure folk culture, you would be hard pressed to find a folk culture more pure than fandom. In class, I usually anchor this contention with two definitions. The first is Marilyn Motz's notion that folklore is "fugitive knowledge," an expression of culture that exists outside of institutionalized systems of belief. The second is the cultural theorist Henry Jenkin's definition of popular culture. He argues that "popular culture is what happens as mass culture gets pulled back into folk culture" (2006: 140). As Jenkins is the patron saint of fan studies, I bend to his will.

If you need more proof that fandom is a folk culture, think of it as a community "held together through mutual production and reciprocal exchange of knowledge" (Jenkins 2006: 27); it pulls from mass culture "narratives or genres and takes them into the culture of a self-selected fraction of the people" to be "reworked into an intensely pleasurable, intensely signifying popular culture" (Fiske 1992: 30). And it's not just that the community of fandom is a folk group. The "fantext" itself is an iteration of the group's folklore. Mafalda Stasi likens it to mythmaking, in the way that fanwriting "is a way of making and transmitting meaning through collective narrative creation" (2006: 124) Kristina Busse and Karen Hellekson locate *variation* as a key component of the fantext, the fantext being what is produced when "the community of fans creates a communal ... interpretation [of a source text] in which a large number of potential meanings, directions, and outcomes co-reside" (2006: 7). And Anne Jamison suggests that fanfiction "resembles all storytelling, ever. People like to swap stories, period, and the internet is like a big electronic campfire" (2013: 4).

Many folks have been critical of fandom and fanfiction writers. Camille Bacon-Smith's groundbreaking *Enterprising Women*, the first "official" ethnography of a fandom, decided to take the activity of fanwriting seriously, but even she could not quite get past the idea that these women, who sometimes wrote stories about an imagined romantic relationship between the two male *Star Trek* characters Kirk and Spock, were deviant. For those who may not know, stories in which two men have a romantic and/or sexual relationship is called "slash" fiction. Stories concerning two women are less prevalent, but they do exist and are often categorized as "femslash." However, slash and femslash are only part of a much larger corpus of fanfiction, and not all fanfiction is romantic or sexual in nature. It only seems that way because popular media tend to focus on these stories to the exclusion of all else, suggesting that we as a culture are still engaged by the lure of perceived "deviance" and that such deviance is still defined by its distance from or proximity to heteronormative conceptions of sex and sexuality.

Indeed, "deviance" had been the predominant criticism lobbed at fanfiction writers[4] (and still is, outside of academic circles). That is, until cultural theorists began to look more closely at what was really going—and as cultural attitudes concerning sexuality and sexual identity changed and access to these fan-produced works increased. What scholars discovered was a thriving folk community, though they may not all have used this term, and "a growing recognition of the communal dimensions of expression, as writing takes on more aspects of traditional folk practices" (Jenkins 2006: 188). These groups nurture artistic craft, provide a sense of belonging and identity, and facilitate an engagement with culture so deep that it might make the most ardent literature scholars blanche.

On an article about fanfiction posted on the pop culture website *Jezebel*, a commenter with the username JustTheTippiHedren wrote:

> It's so difficult to rec good fics without some fandom or subgenre as a guideline. Bad transcends. I don't have to know the work or the conceits of the subgenre to know something is terrible, but good stuff ... if you don't know the work how

can you appreciate beautiful canon compliant fiction that nestles elegantly into a gap in the original narrative? Or dialogue that is so spot on that it could be lifted but you know it isn't? AU fic that is perfectly reimagined, isn't an AU cliché, and serves to cleverly deconstruct the original text? And outside of simply great writing, how can I know how to recommend fetish fuel for you without a request or knowing your kinks? Even more than romance, fanfiction is a conversation that builds upon the relationships the writers have with the genre and the works that precede it.

An incredibly apt description of the communal, folk meaning-making at the heart of all fanfiction, this comment does more than simply define it as a "conversation." It makes clear the ways in which fandom has its own vocabulary, its own rules and conceits. It marks fanwork as an artistic *and* critical endeavor, and it likens it to any other discipline. In a 2015 issue of the *Journal of American Folklore* dedicated to "digital" folklore, Russell Frank says that he is not concerned with deciding whether or not "the expressive traditions of virtual communities" count as folklore, because that question "has largely been settled" (2015: 316). It is not hard to see why if you look at the comment above. And the range of papers presented at the American Folklore Society's recent annual meetings is clear evidence that folklorists *are* actively rejecting the notion that folk and digital culture exist in discrete realms. I, too, consider that question settled.

So what, exactly, is fanfiction, and what does it have to do with the fraudulent folklorist?

How many times have we as folklorists, when asked to define a type or genre of folklore, answered, "It's complicated?" This response is partly a simple recognition that definitions *are* complicated and that a resistance to the impulse for universalizing goes hand in hand with expert knowledge. But it also performs, I believe, a type of boundary work, another way to transcend the "triviality barrier" and to prove not just the complexity of our subject(s) of study but also the need for professionals to adequately parse them. The same is true in fan studies, as scholars resist an easy definition of "fanfiction." Perhaps the most succinct definition is "writing that continues, interrupts, reimagines, or just riffs on stories and characters other people have already written about" (Jamison 2016: 17). As Jamison rightly points out, this definition in practice envelops a lot of work that has, at various times, simply been called "writing," from Chrétien de Troyes and Shakespeare to Jean Rhys and P. D. James.

Yet fanfiction is *different* from fiction that simply tells stories using other people's characters. Take, for example, these two texts, "The Problem of Susan" and "We Need to Talk About Susan Pevensie." Both are about the character of

Susan Pevensie from C. S. Lewis's Narnia series, who was famously discarded in the last book, kept from Narnia because of her burgeoning interest in "nothing nowadays except nylons and lipstick and invitations." Both stories are a type of "fix-it," where the writer tries to work out a problem they have with the source text. Both stories have become well known in Narnia fandom, and both are written by C. S. Lewis fans. However, the first was written by Neil Gaiman, the second by a fanfiction writer named dirgewithoutmusic. That one was written by someone who *makes a living as a writer* and the other by someone who does not seems to be the only sure line of demarcation between a story that looks perfectly fine on a syllabus and one that could get me called to my department chair's office.

In *Camera Lucida*, Roland Barthes calls the amateur "an immature state of the artist: someone who cannot—or will not—achieve the master of a profession." And yet, as he also says, it is the amateur who stands closest to the very essence of art's being (1980: 99). We see this same dichotomy in popular perceptions of fandom: the fan is "deemed emotional (low class, uneducated)" while the "aficionado," like a scholar of Joyce or any other "elite, prestige-conferring" subject, is instead marked "rational (high class, educated)" (Jenson 1992: 21). The scholar, the professional, is educated, while the amateur has only their emotion, their passion, their closeness to the essence of the object's being, to draw from. Seen from this perspective, it makes sense that many scholars locate the beginnings of fandom as we know it by talking about Sherlock Holmes, whose fans have produced fantexts almost since the first publication of a Holmes story. He was, if you remember, an *amateur* detective.

And fans are not just writing literature. They are also doing the work of literary critics, like in the famous essays put out by the Sherlock Holmes fan group the Baker Street Irregulars and the "serious literary examination" of *Star Trek* episodes included in the book *"Star Trek" Lives!* (1975) (Coppa 2006: 47). Whether through an in-depth discussion of source texts, the formal analysis of scenes or single sentences, an eagle-eyed consideration of the creative act of world building, or the very act of writing fanfiction itself, fans act as critics who sometimes know the source text better than the creators do—as Deborah Kaplan says, fanwriting is always, first and foremost, an interpretive act (2006: 135). It could even be said that scholars of culture and its artifacts, like folklorists or literature professors, are simply fans who have found a way to legitimate their obsession within a culturally sanctioned space. Fan and scholar alike are at times adoring, at times critical, but always intellectually engaged with the object of their affection.

Jenson uses her binary formulation between fan and aficionado to discuss why fans are so often perceived as deviant—here, it is a matter of the Other, of creating a category of otherness by which the academic's own obsessions can seem, as she argues, "benign, even worthy." Even more than that, the popular view of the fandom is that it is "a bastion of the physically, socially, and literarily inept" (Jamison 2013: 90). This is partly why fantexts can really push the buttons of those whose work is being incorporated into fannish practices. The fan writer thinks she understands, in part because of the "collective intelligence" of fandom, the intricacies of the work of art in ways outside the purview of the people who actually make the thing. She thinks, in some cases, that she can "fix" the source text through her own artistic intervention (like Jacqueline Lichtenberg, one of the authors of *Star Trek Lives!* and a well-known science fiction writer, who said that her career as a writer began because she thought, "They're writing it all wrong!" (2013: 94). Fans should therefore keep their hands off of the product of the true artist. If they were *serious* about their work, they would be making their own art, not poaching from the professionals.

These same rhetorical moves were at the heart of the very creation of the so-called professional class, which began when the "gentleman scientist" sought to rise above "folk practitioners" as part of the Industrial Revolution's scientific turn (Fournier 2002: 123). The dichotomy between professional and amateur persists anywhere there is institutional support or monetary compensation for work, whether it be through universities or licensing boards or authorizing agencies. The "core defining criteria" for early professionalization included "formal education and entry requirements; a monopoly over an esoteric body of knowledge and associated skills," and "autonomy over the terms and conditions of practice" (Anleu 1992: 24). As Gerry Beegan and Paul Atkinson note, then, the very notion of professionalism "acts as a system of exclusion by setting up criteria that, intentionally or unintentionally, bar individuals and groups on the basis of money, class, ethnicity and gender," from its beginning constructing "social arenas that were largely middle class, white and male" (2008: 305). To be a professional, one had to have access to education and money. The creation of a professional class was an overt attempt to keep those at society's margins safely marginalized—or, to borrow Charles Briggs and Richard Bauman's language, to purify the construction of knowledge.

Professionalism therefore required the invention of the amateur, and words like "'amateur,' 'dilettanti,' or 'dabbler'" quickly came to stand in for "unprofessional" as a way to mark a person or thing as a "threat to professional status" (Taylor 1995: 504). Thus professionalism is not just the way we know ourselves to be *legitimate* and *not inept*. Its goals were and are more insidious. To be a scholar is to not be a quack, to be a professional is to not be an amateur—and both binaries are based on a desire to find new ways to enact old prejudices. These distinctions came about in part because of a desire to codify difference and to imbue the mostly white men who may have lacked access to excessive economic capital (i.e., the middle-class) with a hierarchical distinction, reinforcing their privileges of gender, caste, race, and education (Beegan and Atkinson 2008: 305). If we accept Jenson's formulation, then, the majority of the gatekeeping between "deviant" fan work and "worthy" artistic work is predicated on issues of class and education. The fan's low-class status is conferred in many ways: by a perceived lack of access to the means of production, by the accessible, mass-produced quality of their object and the cultural capital it thereby lacks, and by the fact that they do not get paid to do what they love. This last fact, that of the separation of fan work from capitalistic economy in the production of art, links the fan indelibly to the amateur.

Here is what I think we can take from this conversation. We should think about how we decry the mass production of the "folksy" and the commercialization of folk culture from one side of our mouth while we clamor against the amateur folklorist from the other. If there is one defining trait of boundary-work in folklore studies, it is the "zealous commitment to protect the discipline against usurpers" (Briggs 2008: 95). Usurpers, those *not-folklorists* threatening our field, come in various guises. There are the "gentleman scholars" who populated our early history and who continue to exist in one form or another, antiquarians who saw the study of newly named "folklore" as first and foremost a hobby (Zumwalt 1988: 1–2). There are the scholars of other disciplines who "enthusiastically proclaimed a fascination with things folkloric" and egregiously adopted the mantle of folklorist (Georges 1991: 5). There are the "amateurs who give our field a bad name," those who embrace, in one of Alan Dundes' primary examples, writers like Joseph Campbell (2005: 391).

Furthermore, we folklorists, even those of us with the "right" kind of training, are constantly pushing to get our subject of expertise taken seriously. We want people to view us as real scholars, and we want to be part of that learned world. Therefore, we had to create the role of the professional folklorist. The way we know ourselves to be "aficionados" rather than "fans" is the fact of our own existence. Thus class and race privilege always come into play with the public discourse of folklore, because underlying it all is an anxiety surrounding public uses of the word—when people engage the vocabulary of our discipline in their everyday lives in ways that are sure to set our teeth on edge. *Myth does not mean untrue.* But the word "folklore" is never neutral, whether employed in academic articles or in newspaper headlines. The history of its existence as a word denies its neutrality, and we should not ignore that ours is a term laden with an oppressive, hierarchical burden.

So we should remember that when we invoke the word "amateur" with disdain, or when we claim the status of "expert" as a way of setting our knowledge apart, we are making more than just a categorical move. We are participating in a system of belief that has roots in imperialist discourse. I am not suggesting that we abolish the distinctions between fact and fiction, or between the knowledge gleaned from careful, sustained study and the "gut instinct" that might arise after a cursory examination of the wrong evidence. I am instead reminding myself that there are many ways of knowing the world. Fanfiction is one of those ways. Its writers pay no heed to distinctions between amateur and professional; at least, not in a way that privileges one way of knowing over the other. Fanfiction writers choose their folk group, their fandom, because they want to interact more fully with the world of art and knowledge and culture that surrounds them. What else would an expert do?

NOTES

1. "Margaret Mead and Ruth Benedict Do Fieldwork." By Jessica Doble

Ruth held the camera, positioned the lens on Margaret who posed in her Tzantza mask. The camera hid the smile that played along Ruth's lips as she watched Margaret.

"You know the women of the tribe—"

"You promised no work tonight, Margaret."

"But every month," Margaret began. The shutter clicked and the lightbulb flashed, illuminating Margaret's pale skin, the smell of burnt flash powder.

"Oh, now I hope it's turned out. What do you think?" Margaret asked.

"It's lovely, just like the subject."

"You do flatter."

"Beg your pardon?"

"Flatterer!" Margaret exclaimed raising her voice.

"Who else takes a train and cab and walks 2 miles in those shoes?"

Margaret set the mask on the table next to Ruth as she finished with the camera. "I just had to catch you before returning to Columbia. You needed to stay at an inn so far away from the train station?"

"I like to explore the town and the people when I travel," Ruth lifted her chin in defiance. "It's the people in context that's important and I've taught you—"

"I know darling, 'the crucial differences which distinguish human societies and human beings are not biological. They are cultural.'"

"You tease me, but I am right."

Margaret wrapped her arms around her waist from behind. Right next to Ruth's ear, she said, "You are right, I do tease you, mercilessly."

Ruth leaned into her embrace. A knock sounded on the door and they parted.

"Dr. Benedict?"

"Hello?"

Margaret smiled. "Young Ruth is on the other side of the door."

"A moment, Ruth," Ruth called as she threw Margaret a withering look that only made her smile more.

2. "From Wilhelm Grimm's unpublished 'Strict Diary of Terms,' an autobiographical account of the making of the *Haus und kinder marchen*." By John Laudun.

12 August 1809.

Jakob has brought me more of these execrable stories from the many peasant women whose company he cultivates. I think perhaps he mistakes them for something other than they are, cow-faced creatures whose only worth is in the udders they proffer to their too many offspring. They seem to entrance him in direct proportion to how much they abhor me. Nevertheless, he insists upon remaining in their company, spending hours listening to their prattle and scribbling it down as if they were in any way comparable to such a poet as Heinrich Wilhelm von Gerstenberg, whose name will, I am sure, remain on the lips of those who cherish the art for centuries to come.

I will, as I have a thousand times before, thank him for the latest sheaf of papers, still wreaking of moldy bread and small beer, and then use them to stoke the fires of my study's hearth. As the flames leap up, cleansing me of the words of those women, I find myself free to spin stories of my own, stories that will, I am sure, torment children, filling them with dread for the terrible beasts that they will, I hope, discover lurking everywhere in their world. There will be, once I am done, no stories left to tell, and we will be rid of this dreadful notion that the common people themselves have anything more to offer than their backs. Having righted ourselves and made it possible for those blessed with the intellect and the will to pursue such courses, we will, at long last, have rid ourselves of the notion that stories can do anything more than blind us to that which reason illumines.

3. "Dr. Thompson." By Amber Slaven.

It was never really clear why Dr. Thompson spent such long evenings in his office during his later years. Although he still taught two graduate seminars a semester and served on dissertation committees, the four to five hour reclusion spells every Monday, Wednesday, and Friday seemed disproportionate to his work load. Most of his graduate students didn't think much of this and just assumed he was working long hours on the revised edition of The Motif-Index of Folk-Literature and didn't have extra time for mentoring. It had been several years since the last edition and we all knew how much the project occupied his mind. This fact was obvious from the stacks of note cards he still carried around in his coat pockets that displayed his neat and clear notation of individual motifs.

I started classes at Indiana University in the fall of 1970 in pursuit of my Doctorate in folklore. I was especially excited to work with Dr. Thompson, as I wanted to build on the tale research he had pioneered in the 50s. I worked for two years to develop a relationship with him so that he would agree to take on my dissertation project and help me navigate the waters of folk tale research. He was reluctant and often impartial to my attempts to develop a professional relationship. But I was persistent, and, at the end of my third year, he approached me and said he wanted to take me on as an advisee. He led me into his office and opened a drawer in his desk where a short, cylindrical shaped stick was stashed. He lifted it from the drawer and a beam of red light erupted from the end and revealed what appeared to be a light sword. Looking at me with yellow-tinged eyes, he said, "It's Sith, not Stith."

4. Jolie Jenson succinctly states that "the literature of fandom is haunted by images of deviance" (1992: 9).

REFERENCES CITED

Anleu, Sharyn L. Roach. 1992. "The Professionalisation of Social Work? A Case Study of Three Organisational Settings." *Sociology* 26(1): 23–43.

Bacon-Smith, Camille. 1992. *Enterprising Women: Television Fandom and the Creation of Popular Myth*. Philadelphia: University of Pennsylvania Press.

Barthes, Roland. 1981. *Camera Lucida: Reflections on Photography*. New York: Hill and Wang.

Beegan, G., & Atkinson, P. 2008. "Professionalism, Amateurism and the Boundaries of Design." *Journal of Design History* 21(4): 305–13.

Briggs, Charles. 2008. "Disciplining Folkloristics." *Journal of Folklore Research* 45(1): 95.

Bronner, Simon. 1998. *Following Tradition: Folklore in the Discourse of American Culture*. Logan: Utah State University Press.

Busse, Kristina, and Karen Hellekson. 2006. "Introduction: Work in Progress." In *Fan Fiction and Fan Communities in the Age of the Internet*, ed. Karen Hellekson and Kristina Busse, 5–32. Jefferson, NC: McFarland & Co.

Coppa, Francesca. 2006. "Writing Bodies in Space: Media Fan Fiction as Theatrical Performance." In *Fan Fiction and Fan Communities in the Age of the Internet*, edited by Karen Hellekson and Kristina Busse, 225–44. Jefferson, NC: McFarland & Co.

dirgewithoutmusic. 2014. "We Need to Talk about Susan Pevensie." https: //archiveofourown .org/works/1218274

Dundes, A. 2005. Folkloristics in the Twenty-First Century (AFS Invited Presidential Plenary Address, 2004). *Journal of American Folklore* 118(470): 385–408.

Fiske, John. 1992. "The Cultural Economy of Fandom." In *The Adoring Audience*, edited by Lisa A. Lewis, 30–49. London: Routledge.

Fournier, Valérie. 2002. "Amateurism, Quackery and Professional Conduct: The Constitution of 'Proper' Aromatherapy Practice." In *Managing Professional Identities: Knowledge, Performativity and the 'New' Professional*, edited by Mike Dent and Stephen Whitehead, 116–37. London and New York: Routledge.

Frank, Russell. 2015. "*Caveat Lector*: Fake News as Folklore." *Journal of American Folklore* 128(509): 315–32.

Gaiman, Neil. 2006. "The Problem of Susan." In *Fragile Things: Short Fictions and Wonders*, 172–81. New York: Harper.

Georges, R. 1991. "Earning, Appropriating, Concealing, and Denying the Identity of Folklorist." *Western Folklore* 50(1): 3–12.

Jamison, Anne. 2013. *Fic: Why Fanfiction is Taking Over the World*. Dallas: Smart Pop.

Jenkins, Henry. 2006. *Convergence Culture: Where Old and New Media Collide*. New York: New York University Press.

Jenson, Jolie. 1992. "Fandom as Pathology: The Consequences of Characterization." In *The Adoring Audience*, ed. Lisa A. Lewis, 9–29. London: Routledge.

JustTheTippiHedren, August 27, 2014 (6: 31 a.m.). Comment on Fan Fiction Tuesday: We have Questionable Taste, August 26, 2014, http: //backtalk.kinja.com/fan-fiction-tuesday -we-have-questionable-taste-1627246412/all.

Kaplan, Deborah. 2006. "Construction of Fan Fiction Character through Narrative." In *Fan Fiction and Fan Communities in the Age of the Internet*, edited by Karen Hellekson and Kristina Busse, 134–52. Jefferson, NC: McFarland & Co.

Lichtenberg, Jacqueline, Sondra Marshak, and Joan Winston. 1975. *"Star Trek" Lives!* New York: Bantam.

Motz, Marilyn. 1998. "The Practice of Belief." *Journal of American Folklore* 111(441): 339–55.

Stasi, Mafalda. 2006. "Toy Soldiers from Leeds: The Slash Palimpsest." In *Fan Fiction and Fan Communities in the Age of the Internet*, edited by Karen Hellekson and Kristina Busse, 115–33. Jefferson, NC: McFarland & Co.

Taylor, B. 1995. "Amateurs, Professionals and the Knowledge of Archaeology." *British Journal of Sociology* 46(3): 499–508.

Zeitlin, S. 2000. "I'm a Folklorist and You're Not: Expansive versus Delimited Strategies in the Practice of Folklore." *Journal of American Folklore* 113(447): 3–19.

TWO

Misanthropelore

Todd Richardson

Using outcasts, loners, lost souls, and misanthropes as his protagonists, Daniel Clowes's comics provide a sustained and blistering critique of the crudeness and commercialism of normative American culture. The society he presents is a society from which one would hope to be alienated. The most direct expression of Clowes's frustration with mainstream culture comes in "I Hate You Deeply" (1990), a short piece that appeared in the second issue of *Eightball*, an anthology series Clowes produced between 1989 and 2004 (fig. 1). In it, Lloyd Llewelyn, the title character of Clowes's first comic book series, who in this instance is functioning as a thinly veiled surrogate for Clowes's own feelings, lists things he detests, including but not limited to: *zillionaires, musclemen, military types, fashion plates, watered-down nostalgia hounds, occultists, new agers and anyone seeking simple, catch-all solutions to unanswerable questions, lowest common denominators, actors, models and/or anyone who places disproportionate importance on that kind of glorified service job, and people who hide behind cartoon characters to espouse their unpopular opinions.* As a whole, "I Hate You Deeply" offers an exhaustive and exhausting account of the worst in contemporary society, bringing to mind Sartre's maxim, "Hell is other people."

In the middle of Lloyd Llewelyn's hateful litany, an "instructional" panel appears, one that exemplifies a curiously folkloric, or at least folklore-adjacent, process discernible throughout Clowes's work, one that I am calling misanthropelore (fig. 2).[1] Framed as "How to Formulate Opinions," Lloyd Llewelyn

Figure 1: Clowes, Daniel. 1990. Title panel for "I Hate You Deeply." *The Complete Eightball: Volume One* (2015). Seattle: Fantagraphics: Issue 2, page 22.

explains that he generates his expressions and values oppositionally by figuring out what someone he dislikes thinks and then adopting the inverse as his opinion. It is identity through gainsaying or, more accurately, gainsaying *as* identity. In a 1999 interview with *Hermeneut*, Clowes said, "The only way you can define yourself is against types of people anyway. You sort of negate everybody else, and then . . . where are you?" (1999: 138). This philosophy, I suggest, animates the expressive strategies of Clowes's characters in that they assert their identities primarily through disaffiliating gestures. More than who they are, they strive to express who they are not.

Considering the hostile view Clowes and his characters possess of other people, he is an unlikely artist to consider folklorically. The field, after all, focuses on the meaning people make together, folklore being generated when two or more people develop a shared way of expressing themselves. In "I Hate You Deeply" and elsewhere, Clowes dismantles the value of sharing expressions, if not the idea of community itself. Nonetheless, Lloyd Llewelyn's formula for developing opinions is a sort of collaboration in that his expressions would not exist without assistance from other people. His ideas are shaped by the community, but they are not shared by the community, and if this is not artistic communication in small groups, it is at least artistic communication *through* small groups. I have introduced the term misanthropelore to describe the expressive strategies Clowes depicts, the ways his characters make meaning

Figure 2: Clowes, Daniel. 1990. Panel from "I Hate You Deeply." *The Complete Eightball: Volume One* (2015). Seattle: Fantagraphics: Issue 2, page 24.

through disaffiliation. It is misanthropic, but calling it misanthropy misses something essential. "I would hope that if you really read the work carefully," Clowes said in a 2010 interview, "misanthropy wouldn't be all you took away from [my comics]." He implies that, yes, misanthropy is there, but there is something more complex going on as well, and that is what I am trying to get at here, the ways such seeming negativity might be constructive.

While I am focusing on how Clowes represents this process in his work, these expressive strategies are present in real life as well. I believe, in fact, that the idea of misanthropelore can help people such as me better understand the function of folklore in our lives. Frankly, I have never gotten a meaningful view of my expressive customs in the field of folklore. I have taught undergraduate classes on folklore, and I have become rather adept at getting people to appreciate the often implicit expressive traditions they share with groups, yet the most resonant examples—hiccup cures always get a strong response—strike me as rather low-stakes in comparison with the traditions discussed in the "heavier" texts I assign. Simply put, the folklore many of my students acknowledge as their own—the folklore I acknowledge as my own—is rarely load-bearing. The expressive traditions I have been taught to appreciate as my own are largely incidental to my identity, unlike the folklore of other groups commonly addressed in folklore scholarship, groups for whom shared expressions are perceived to be foundational. Much of this has to do with my cultural middle-ness—I am a straight, white, middle-class, middle-aged, midwesterner—and I will discuss the significance of that shortly, but it is also because I myself am something of a misanthrope and prone to conspicuous disaffiliation.

DISAFFILIATION AND FOLKLORE STUDIES

Folklore as it is commonly conceived, both inside and outside academia, is ill-equipped to appreciate the expressive dimensions of disaffiliation. For the most part, people conceptualize folklore as an expression and/or sign of belonging. On the American Folklore Society's "What Is Folklore?" page, the second sentence reads, "Every group with a sense of its own identity shares, as a central part of that identity, folk traditions" (2018), an explicit emphasis on the shared aspects of folklore, which have long shaped the field and frame most discussion of the subject. A cursory scan of recent folklore scholarship reveals that a majority of it focuses on specific, discernible folk groups. Public folklore programs, as well, share an affinity for group expressions. When I was working with the Nebraska Folklife Network, it quickly became clear that programs always begin with an assumption of group cohesion, and program content was consistently framed as a showcase for the way a group, usually ethnic in nature, does things. Even when a genre of folk expression was used as the focus for an event, as was the case with the NFN's dance-themed program in 2015, the content was presented as a succession of group traditions (e.g. Irish, Omaha, Karen).

This focus on the group poses at least two problems when discussing what I call misanthropelore. For one, emphasizing the group makes it that much harder to appreciate an individual's way of doing things, and misanthropelore is definitely an expression of individual autonomy. Put another way, because misanthropelore is about differentiating an individual from a community, defining folklore through groups dismisses such expressions as aberrations or, more likely, belonging to a different expressive arena altogether. Moreover, conceptualizing folklore as a thing shared by a group gives preference to expressions of solidarity. Expressions that are critical of the group, even when they come from within the group, are less likely to be acknowledged within conventional folkloric frameworks as such expressions do not contribute, on the surface at least, to a cohesive, sustainable vision of the group. When folklore does not behave the way people believe it ought to—and consensus holds that folklore ought to unify a group—it does not register.

In "the Esoteric-Exoteric Factor in Folklore" (1959), William Hugh Jansen provides a vocabulary for discussing aspects of folklore that are simultaneously obvious and opaque, vocabulary that can help illuminate the fugitive nature of misanthropelore. In simplest terms, esoteric folklore consists of a group's representation and interpretation of itself. For instance, as a Nebraskan, I can tell you that within our regional group, we believe ourselves to be pragmatic, polite, and hard-working, and our shared expressive traditions generally emphasize those qualities. Exoteric folklore, on the other hand, consists of a group's representations and interpretations of other groups. Again speaking as a Nebraskan, I will confess that we generally believe coastal folk to be unscrupulous and narcissistic. "The esoteric applies to what one group thinks of itself and what it supposes others think of it." Jansen writes, "The exoteric is what one group thinks of another and what it thinks that other group thinks it thinks" (1959: 206–7). Both the esoteric and exoteric manifestations of folklore are crucial to identity, the former for obvious reasons and the latter because people's sense of themselves pivots on difference.

Jansen argues, "The esoteric part of this factor, it would seem, frequently stems from the group sense of belonging and serves to defend and strengthen that sense" (1959: 207). People generate a cohesive identity for the group, one that gives individuals both meaning and purpose in the process. Astutely, Jansen argues that the exoteric dimension also is "a product of the same sense of belonging, for it may result from fear of, mystification about, or resentment of the group to which one does not belong" (1959: 207). In a corresponding footnote, Jansen observes, "Much material rich in the esoteric-exoteric association springs from people who, forced by modernization or led by their own desires, have abandoned a group association or have tried to assume membership in another group than their own" (1959: 209n4). Those who have, in Jansen's terms, "abandoned a group association" are especially relevant to this discussion because they are exactly the type of people represented in Clowes's comics, people whose own desires lead them away from modernization (or at least people who desire to appear to be rejecting modernization).

Jansen suggests certain attributes encourage the development of exoteric folklore, chief among them a group's isolation. For example, occupational groups that work far from urban centers, such as miners or farmers, invariably have a great deal of exoteric folklore about them. As well, Jansen argues that groups that are isolated by other factors like language or education similarly attract exoteric folklore. In each case, it is a group's deviance from the mainstream, whatever the mainstream may be in that particular time and place, that makes such people magnets for exoteric interpretations. But when Jansen talks about isolation, he focuses on groups that are isolated. In this chapter, I am interested in characters who, whether by choice or circumstance, have isolated themselves and how they creatively express that isolation. They do not have exoteric folklore ascribed to them, or at least that is not what I am discussing here. Rather, they view groups they supposedly belong to exoterically as a way of disaffiliating.

People who distance themselves from a society still need to situate themselves culturally, and they can do so using exoteric folklore. It is a negative process, insofar as the individual is eliminating possibilities rather than creating them, but it is a folkloric process nonetheless as the individual is making meaning through groups (e.g. "I must be a good person because I am not one of the bad people."). There is, as well, an expressive dimension to the process as these disaffiliated individuals strive to make clear their position outside groups they are invited into or presumed to belong to. They generate an absence that conveys they belong elsewhere. Where that might be, specifically, may be unclear, yet they still convey their proper position as being on the outside. In general, belonging is understood inclusively, as in a person belongs when he or she is included, yet belonging can be interpreted differently, as in the case of the person who belongs on the outside. Alienation, in other words, is not inherently a bad thing as there are certain societies, such as the consumerist wasteland depicted in Clowes's comics, from which it is a good thing to be alienated (fig. 3). To belong elsewhere in such circumstances is a point of pride. Exclusion from a group may not situate a person as specifically as inclusion does, but it still situates a person.

In "Differential Identity and the Social Base of Folklore" (1971), Richard Bauman builds on Jansen's ideas. Bauman reconsiders the assumption discussed above that "folklore is a function of shared identity." He points out that when people think about folklore, they usually think of it as something expressed and exchanged between people within a cohesive, or at least identifiable, community. For better or worse, folklore is seen to express group character within group settings. Viewing folklore as performance, he contends, illuminates the complex social base of folklore by showing how folklore can be exchanged between people or groups with differential identities. In other words, performer and audience do not need to share a group affiliation in order for folklore to exist. Bauman credits Jansen for identifying this aspect of folklore in "The Esoteric-Exoteric Factor in Folklore," but he notes that Jansen still focuses primarily on the esoteric. Bauman cautions, "As long as folklore is conceptualized as a self-contained realm of cultural products abstractly connected with some homogenous body of people identified as a folk and participating in it collectively, the use of folklore in situations involving differential identity will be obscured from view" (1971: 38). Focusing only on in-group performances of folklore misses the point, as Bauman puts it, that "folklore may be as much an instrument of conflict as a mechanism contributing to social solidarity" (1971: 38).

Misanthropelore, which I have broadly defined as disaffiliating performances, is an instrument of conflict, or at least a way of placing contingencies on social solidarity. Because folklore as it is commonly construed has a blind spot for expressions that do not contribute to the cohesiveness of a group or

Figure 3: Clowes, Daniel. 1992. Title panel for "Grist for the Mill." *The Complete Eightball: Volume One* (2015). Seattle: Fantagraphics: Issue 8, page 21.

community, disaffiliating expressions might be acknowledged but they are likely to be dismissed as something else entirely. Misanthropelore, however, offers a vocabulary for discussing performances of disaffiliation as expressive traditions in their own right, not just as folkloristic anomalies or isolated speech acts. While misanthropelore is distinct from predominant conceptualizations of folklore, it, like conventional folklore, is defined through the same shared notions of a group. Much like a starving person and a gourmet are both defined by their relationship with food, misanthropelore and folklore represent an excess and shortage of the same thing, solidarity.

Some of the spirit of misanthropelore can be found in Leonard Primiano's concept of uniculture, which he outlines in "Vernacular Religion and the Search for Method in Religious Folklife" (1995). Primiano defines uniculture as "a processual system of conscious and unconscious knowledge, beliefs, behaviors, and customs particular to the individual to which he or she refers and which she or he employs as the basis of everyday living," and he presents the term as a way to highlight the idiosyncratic manner that people take in and reinterpret "official" religious beliefs and practices (1995: 49–50). More broadly, uniculture answers Primiano's call for the field of folklore to "enlarge its focus to emphasize the individual as the creator and possessor of a single folkloric world view, who constantly interprets and negotiates his or her own beliefs" (1995: 48). He continues, "This does not imply that an individual is not influenced by a number of physiological, cultural, social, and environmental forces, but that given the human capacity to interpret these influences, people develop their own folklore within as well as around themselves" (1995: 48). Misanthropelore, too, enlarges the focus of folklore studies by giving name to individuals' idiosyncratic interpretations of shared traditions, yet misanthropelore is distinct from uniculture due to its differential nature. While misanthropelore is, like uniculture, "a product of the personal creativeness of our daily lives," unlike uniculture, misanthropelore refuses the prevailing belief system in order to assert individuality. In short, uniculture internalizes social systems whereas misanthropelore externalizes them.

In "Solo Folklore" (2006), Jay Mechling offers his own analysis of idiosyncratic folklore, contending that "we can often perform traditional folk oral and customary texts with ourselves as the only audience" (438). Like Primiano, Mechling is concerned with the internalization of social systems, arguing that "solo folklore" is how people rehearse folk expressions in private, providing "a repertoire of events by which the brain develops plans for behavior and practices them offstage" (2006: 446). His argument, however, is ultimately more epistemological as he contends "solo folklore" demonstrates "that the observer's mind is the locus of reality of folklore" (2006: 444). Applying this to misanthropelore, the crucial audience and primary observer is the performer. While the performer may seek to make clear to others that he is she is not their "folk," the more important dimension is that the misanthropelore performance makes clear to the performer that others are not his or her "folk." More simply put, misanthropelore need not be evident to others to be effective, and might exist entirely in unspoken thoughts and feelings.

Dorothy Noyes's contribution to the "Keywords for the Study of Expressive Culture" special issue of the *Journal of American Folklore* provides a delineation of "group" that can further illuminate the irregular shape of misanthropelore. "Group," according to Noyes, designates the "productive tension" between network and community, the former comprising day-to-day interactions between individuals and the latter being the identity shared by a collectivity (1995: 33). Network, within this breakdown, is ontological and community is deontological. Adopting this conceptualization, misanthropelore can be thought of as a rejection of community that takes place in the network, which is not to say that misanthropelore is a strictly practical performance. Quite the contrary, actually, as misanthropelore depends on the deontological aspects of a group in that its meaning emerges through defiance of a group's felt reality: misanthropelore is the expression of personal identity through a rejection of shared identity. In her conclusion, Noyes discusses the difference between the village and the marketplace as analogues for folkloristic inquiry, arguing that the marketplace offers "liberty in relative abundance," while adding "equality and fraternity are goods in much shorter supply" (1995: 35). Borrowing her phraseology, misanthropelore denounces equality and fraternity in the name of personal liberty.

Likely the closest analogue to misanthropelore, both notionally and nominally, is Gary Saul Morson's concept of misanthropology, which he defines as "the study of the cussedness of human nature" (1996: 59). Discernible in works ranging from Dostoevsky's novels to the U.S. Constitution, misanthropology sees the threat of corruption in all human collectivities. Morson distinguishes misanthropology from misanthropy, which he argues is simply "reverse sentimentality," via their certitude. Whereas misanthropes are convinced of the accuracy of their worldview, misanthropologists adopt a more heuristic approach to human experience, eschewing theory in favor of the practical now. "Misanthropology," Morson writes, "looks not for timeless, absolute, and universal truths, but for something more clinical: it asks what to do now, in this locality with these people, in this unrepeatable situation—questions to be answered not by invoking timeless ethical laws but by meditating on accumulated experience" (1996: 61). Misanthropology is, in this manner, not so much a worldview as it is a strategy of social cautiousness.

Like misanthropology, misanthropelore is not monolithic nor is it necessarily negative. Rather than a catalogable body of customs and traditions, misanthropelore is an aesthetic strategy, one that individuals use to perform their deviance from a group or community without necessarily signifying membership in a different group or community.[2] Put another way, misanthropelore is more asocial than antisocial. The performances are as likely to appear as absences—a person might remain strategically silent during the recitation of an oath—as they are outright rejection of the prevailing order. The important thing to keep in mind is that an expression does not need to be hostile to be misanthropelore. As with misanthropology, it is socially cautious, but that does not mean it is necessarily antagonistic.

Arthur Schoepenhauer's porcupine parable may help illustrate the negotiation at work in both concepts. In *Parerga and Paralipomena*, Schopenhauer describes a prickle of porcupines huddling together to share their warmth in winter. As they draw close to one another, their quills begin to poke, so they decide to disperse, only to quickly grow cold again. A cycle of huddling and dispersing ensues until the porcupines eventually decide to remain distant from each other, *yet not so distant as to become unbearably cold*. Schopenhauer elaborates:

> In the same way the need of society drives the human porcupines together only to be mutually repelled by the many prickly and disagreeable qualities of their nature. The moderate distance which they at last discover to be the only tolerable condition of intercourse, is the code of politeness and fine manners; and those who transgress it are roughly told—in the English phrase—to keep their distance. By this arrangement the mutual need of warmth is only very moderately satisfied; but then people do not get pricked. A man who has some heat in himself prefers to remain outside, where he will neither prick other people not get pricked himself. ([1851] 2001: 651)

Misanthropelore expresses and maintains such a "moderate distance." It admits a certain need of social warmth while insisting on one's independence from others, even if that entails some discomfort. In Noyes's terminology, it might be thought of as the balancing of one's position in the network with one's place in the community. Such performances may appear to some, particularly those invested in the group, as an attack on shared values, but they are, more accurately, a tempering of one's affiliations, making such expressions more misanthropological than misanthropic.

To return to Jansen's notion of exoteric and esoteric folklore, misanthropelore allows individuals to approach their own groups, or at least groups within which they routinely operate, exoterically. I am, as already mentioned, Nebraskan, yet my affiliation with that social identity is tempered by strategic indifference to Nebraska football, which amounts to apostasy in my home state. I am, however, paradoxically proud of this indifference to Nebraska football. Not caring about the Huskers contributes to my social self. It differentiates me, and, being an American, my culture values personal independence. While there are many aspects of Nebraskan-ness that I do celebrate, I carefully calibrate my investment in *Nebraska as a shared identity* so as to avoid absorption in the whole. That indifference, which, for example, I express by deliberately not wearing red on game days, provides me with, in Shopenhauer's terms, a moderate distance from my ostensible group.

Sustaining such disaffiliations, or at least having them tolerated by others in the group, is much less challenging for those closer to the center of the network. I can say that *my* culture values expressions of personal independence because I am a straight, white, middle-class, Midwestern, middle-aged man. That I have the power to construct the terms of my own deviance is a paradoxical demonstration of my cultural normativity; as Noyes put it, "those who draw boundaries are those whose strength comes from their centrality" (1995: 24). Likewise, the protagonists in Clowes's comics are all white and mostly men, close to the center of the American mainstream, which means we (the characters and I) are unmarked and mostly free to define ourselves on our own terms, and while anyone can perform what I am calling misanthropelore and it can occur inside any group, it is incalculably easier for people in positions of power to make a spectacle of their personal deviance (e.g. When a rich man wears a stained shirt, he is eccentric, but when a poor man does it, he is dirty). The examples I provide throughout strongly skew toward white, middle-class experience and exhibit the privileges that come with such centrality, yet denouncing such expressions as selfish and insensitive acts does not diminish their reality, whether they occur on the page or in real life. I am not celebrating or condemning misanthropelore. I am simply trying to understand it.

All that being said, if the expressive mode I am identifying here is addressed, it is likely to be discussed as a pathology. No matter how much American culture appears to value personal independence, deliberately disrupting established customs, particularly those niceties that hew us closer to one another, is generally associated with antisocial personalities. However fraught misanthropelore might be, it is not de facto unhealthy. Learning to see misanthropelore not as the absence of belonging, or at least not exclusively so, but instead as the performance of a differential identity, albeit a non-specific one, can remove such expressions from the confining rhetoric of pathology, wherein they are dismissed as dysfunctions. Even when it manifests as absence, misanthropelore is a real and meaningful expression of a person's social identity, and that, in itself, makes it worthy of discussion in the field of folklore.

Within the field of folklore, Moira Smith comes closest to the mechanisms of misanthropelore in her article "Humor, Unlaughter and Boundary Maintenance" (2009). Building on Michael Billig's notion of unlaughter, which he defines as "a display of not laughing when laughter might otherwise be expected, hoped for or demanded" (2005: 192), Smith conducts readings of joke performances that elicit unlaughter, thus enforcing group boundaries. Her central example is a series of Mohammed cartoons published in a Dutch newspaper in 2006, which, she contends, were a deliberate attempt to elicit unlaughter, thus enacting the Western idea that one should "have a sense of humor." She writes, "Western folk ideas about the sense of humor label unlaughter as a sign of serious deficiencies in personality and a symptom of an inability to adjust to group norms" (2009: 166).

"Humor, Unlaughter, and Boundary Maintenance" is a crucial contribution to folklore studies for the way it makes absence available to analysis. It does not, however, seriously address absence in the form of unlaughter as, potentially, an identity-driven, differential expression by the one-who-does-not-laugh. Smith is right that unlaughter can be elicited in order to reveal and reinforce group boundaries; as she puts it, "The contemporary importance that is placed on the sense of humor . . . fuels strategic uses of humor performances to provoke humorless responses and, in so doing, to heighten social boundaries" (2009: 150). Yet unlaughter might also be a deliberate, constructive expression of an unlaugher's position in relation to others, a point Smith alludes to without elaborating on when she writes, "Unlaughter is not always just a regrettable accident but may be used deliberately by both joke instigators *and members of joke audiences* to highlight supposed differences between them and so heighten exclusionary social boundaries" (italics mine, 2009: 151). Rather than focusing on the one-who-does-not-laugh's inability to be on the inside, approaching the expression (or absence thereof) as misanthropelore focuses on how the unlaugher consciously creates a boundary by withholding an expected response. Put another way, not laughing is not a disqualifying reaction as much as it is a disaffiliating gesture. In Smith's analyses, unlaughter represents a lack of humor support, yet it can also be read as active support for different values. There may be a point where unlaughter becomes an expressive tradition in its own right, not just an idiosyncratic failure to conform to others' expressive customs.

One last example from my life may help clarify. Due to a secular upbringing, I do not identify with any specific religion. Nevertheless, I frequently encounter Judeo-Christian traditions, as they are common through Western culture, especially in the American Midwest, which is where I have lived my entire life. The majority of people I interact with maintain Judeo-Christian traditions in one way or another, and that means when I go to weddings, funerals, and other social gatherings, I am often invited to participate in some form of religious expression, most commonly the saying of grace. When a performance of grace is keyed and participants bow their heads, I keep my head raised. This is not meant to be an aggressive gesture or indictment of the group and its expressive customs. Rather, I keep my head up because, while I am familiar with the custom, the saying of grace does not express my identity. Not bowing my head is not, from my vantage, a failure to accept an invitation or meet group expectations: it is a positive expression of my differential identity. Indeed, just because I do not "belong" here, does not mean I do not belong anywhere. In fact, as often as not, a curious form of community emerges from my reaction as I will make eye contact with others who decline to participate in the ritual. Perhaps to the earnest participants, those of us not bowing our heads constitute an exoteric group—they may see us as heathens, gentiles, or seculars—yet to those of us on the "inside" of this emergent out-group, we have constructed our own community. We are not them, our only shared tradition being *not* sharing theirs.[3]

The illustrations thus far have focused on speech acts, but misanthropelore can be discerned in countless other disaffiliating expressions and gestures. Varying levels of dishevelment, for instance, express varying levels of investment in a group or community; an untucked shirt can be a mild rebuke to shared customs, whereas allowing oneself to have body odor can strongly differentiate a person within an American culture of compulsory odorlessness. Whenever and wherever a person opts not to comply with a tradition or custom they are familiar with, perhaps even fluent in, is a possible instance of misanthropelore. The important thing to keep in mind is that even if no other membership is implied, the expression might still be read as a positive identity claim, not simply a failure to comply. Conversely, a disaffiliating gesture should not be equated with total disaffiliation. Participation in a group's culture, even the participation of the most revered tradition bearer, is always incomplete and contingent, and misanthropelore is a conscious expression of an individual's incomplete and contingent participation. It is socially cautious but not inherently antisocial, and as shown through the porcupines in Schopenhauer's parable, keeping one's distance is not the same thing as complete abandonment.

A real, spatialized group can emerge through the shared act of not participating, as was the case with furtive eye contact made while not saying grace, yet misanthropelore does not always result in such a specific community. Misanthropelore may renounce all group affiliation as a way of asserting one's individual liberty, but even when this is the case, the group and, by extension, folklore are essential, as without them, there would be nothing against which the individual could define their individuality—there can be no nonconformity, after all, without conformity—and, for this reason, misanthropelore falls squarely within the field of folklore studies. Moreover, while the gestures might be inspired by allegiance to different groups with their own sets of values, they can also simply be misanthropelore, an expression of unwillingness to participate in any community. In other words, misanthropelore is an expression of difference as identity, not just a different identity, and, in this way, can be a constructive expression of one's social identity without requiring affiliation with any society specifically.[4]

GHOST WORLD

Instances of misanthropelore abound in Daniel Clowes's most famous work, *Ghost World*. Told episodically, *Ghost World* relates the experiences of Enid Coleslaw (an anagram of "Daniel Clowes") during the summer following her graduation from high school. A deeply cynical young woman unsure what she will do next, Enid meanders through an ethereal landscape—it is not quite suburban, not quite urban—with her closest friend Becky, encountering a menagerie of characters they, as often as not, treat as amusements, mocking and pranking them. Enid's cynicism and indecision, along with a shared attraction to a boy named Josh, strains her relationship with Becky, whom she was planning to move in with. Eventually, Enid decides she is going to go to college elsewhere, which critically damages her friendship with Becky, only to find out later she failed the entrance exam and will not be going anywhere. The individual episodes of *Ghost World*, which are shaded exclusively in a spectral blue, first appeared in issues eleven to eighteen of *Eightball* and would be published as a stand-alone book in 1997. In 2001, *Ghost World* was adapted into a film, and the screenplay, which was nominated for an Academy Award, was written by Clowes and Terry Zwigoff, the film's director.

The meaning of the title is appropriately vague. While "ghost world" appears as graffiti throughout, its significance is never addressed or explained, leaving it unclear why Clowes would name a book about a teenage hipster and the curious folk she encounters such an otherworldly title. In "The Ghost Worlds of Modern Adolescence," likely the most incisive scholarly analysis of the story to date, Pamela Thurschwell contends that the title refers to the developmental stage of the central characters, pointing out that "Ghosts, like adolescents, are defined by their liminality, caught between time frames. If ghosts exist uneasily between the world of the living and the dead, then adolescents exist uneasily between childhood and maturity" (2013: 147–48). Thurschwell goes on to argue that *Ghost World* exposes the empty promises Capitalism makes to young people and how it has become impossible to forge an authentic identity in a consumerist culture. Thurschwell is absolutely right about the importance of adolescence in the text, yet I think there's even more to Enid's ghostliness, that she is spectral not only in terms of her age, but also in the way she haunts her community rather than inhabiting it, a situation characterized by misanthropelore as I am describing it. With the possible exception of Becky, Enid treats people as objects, taunting and tormenting them, always begrudging the space she must share with others. She maintains an oppositional relationship with her ostensive communities, disaffiliating herself at every opportunity as a way of asserting her individuality through contradistinction.

Enid's oppositional stance is clear from *before* the first page. Below the Table of Contents of the book version of *Ghost World* is a picture of Enid giving the finger to someone or something slightly to the right (and definitely not the reader) (fig. 4). She and Becky are wearing graduation regalia, so, presumably, the subject of ire is her school, a fact confirmed in the film adaptation. While I suppose the case may be made, I am not suggesting that flipping the bird is misanthropelore. Rather, I mention this image because it succinctly frames the disaffiliation Enid asserts throughout the story, always separating herself from others as a way of defining herself through difference. A more representative

Figure 4: Clowes, Daniel. 1997. Image from *Ghost World*. *The Daniel Clowes Reader* (2013). Seattle: Fantagraphics: Page 45.

example of misanthropelore occurs in one of the comic's first panels when, after Enid denounces the readers of *Sassy* magazine of as a bunch of "trendy stuck-up prep school bitches," Becky suggests that Enid is "a stuck-up prep school bitch" (fig. 5). Enid strives to disaffiliate from groups she ostensibly belongs to in order to reassure herself that she is not what she appears to be to others. As Thurschwell suggests, there's something irreducibly adolescent about the exchange, and I suggest the same can be said about every instance of the expressive strategy I am describing. In adolescence, individuals assert their independence, which often entails denouncing identities thrust on them. I do not, however, want to suggest that misanthropelore is limited to a certain age range. When I suggest misanthropelore is irreducibly adolescent, I mean "adolescent" in a cultural sense, not as a stage of human development. For example, a frequent lament about contemporary American culture is that people live in a state of perpetual adolescence, never assuming the responsibilities of "true" adulthood.[5] Following this logic, misanthropelore, given its adolescent spirit, would be a strategy represented throughout American culture, not just among young people.

The most direct illustration of misanthropelore in *Ghost World* comes not from Enid herself but through Josh's assessment of her. When she asks him what he thinks her style is, he responds, "To defy definition" (fig. 6). It's a crystal-clear articulation of the expressive strategies Enid displays throughout *Ghost World*, the way she strives for inscrutability. In fact, Josh's assessment is hipsterism distilled. Defining hipsterism is a difficult thing to do, a fact articles on the subject are always quick to point out. Mark Greif, co-founder of the literary magazine *n+1*, wrote in the *New York Times*, "My colleagues

Figure 5: Clowes, Daniel. 1997. Panel from *Ghost World. The Daniel Clowes Reader* (2013). Seattle: Fantagraphics: Page 47.

and I started to investigate the contemporary hipster, what was the 'hipster,' and what did it mean to be one? It was a puzzle. No one, it seemed, thought of himself as a hipster, and when someone called you a hipster, the term was an insult" (2010). Overwhelmingly it seems, hipsterism is viewed disdainfully, even from 'within,' yet it, or at least the category that people extrapolate from a range of expressive behaviors, retains a strong allure, inspiring endless jokes, insults and blog post. Hipsterism, as far as I can tell, is an expressive strategy that materializes emptiness, which helps explain the difficulty of identifying it. For the most part, hipsterism does this through association with groups other than one's own, which is what Norman Mailer suggested in one of the first considerations of the idea, "The White Negro: Superficial Reflections on the Hipster" (1957). Hipsterism, in effect, transforms other people's customs into

Figure 6: Clowes, Daniel. 1997. Panel from *Ghost World. The Daniel Clowes Reader* (2013). Seattle: Fantagraphics: Page 106.

differential expressions, draining them of their "authentic" meaning. "Under the guise of 'irony,'" Christian Lorentzen wrote in an editorial for *Time Out New York*, "hipsterism fetishizes the authentic and regurgitates it with a winking inauthenticity" (2007).

A clear instance of such manipulation of authenticity occurs in *Ghost World* when Enid drags Becky and, eventually, Josh to Hubba Hubba: The Original 1950s Diner. While there, Josh wonders what is so special about the place, asking Enid, "Aren't there hundreds of places like this?" Enid replies, "Not hardly! This is the Mona Lisa of the bad fake diners" (1997: 81). On a previous trip to Hubba Hubba, Enid relentlessly mocked the inauthenticity of the place, its decidedly un-1950s menu—the specials were Pasta Vasilio and Spinach Tortelli—and the waiter's exuberant 1990s hairstyle. Nevertheless, Enid "loves" the place, referring to it as "God."[6] Enid generates meaning through ironic dislocation, cherishing a place for its awfulness. Irony, in fact, is a central trait of misanthropelore as it is a way of containing conflicting meanings, just as misanthropelore contains conflicting meanings in how it expresses, simultaneously, that a person both is and is not a participant in a community.

The sort of irony just described, as well as misanthropelore in general, can be insensitive and arrogant. Sharpening this aspect, the reason Enid, Becky and Josh travel to Hubba Hubba is because Enid was pranking someone, having responded to a "missed connections" personal ad, pretending she was interested in the man who placed it and wanted to meet him at the diner. The man, referred to in the book only as Bearded Windbreaker, shows up, only to leave after he quickly figures out he has been set up, stopping to glare at Enid, Becky and Josh as he walks away. It is a heartbreaking exchange, and even Enid feels guilt despite her perpetual disassociation, evident in the hangdog expression on her face as they drive home (fig. 7).

Such expressive appropriations should be called out for the privilege they exhibit, yet they are, nevertheless, meaningful. It would be worthwhile to read them as expressions of identity, not just as instances of cultural abuse and thievery. In his introduction to the *Treasury of American Folklore* (1944), B. A. Botkin distinguished between "folklore as we find it and folklore as we believe it ought to be." He elaborated, "Folklore as we find it perpetuates human ignorance, perversity, and depravity along with human wisdom and goodness. Historically we cannot deny or condone this baser side of folklore—and yet we may understand and condemn it as we condemn other manifestations of human error" (xxv–xxvi). So, too, can misanthropelore perpetuate "human ignorance, perversity, and depravity," but as discomforting as such expressions may be, they still express meaning and can reveal a great deal about a person's or group's values even if at first blush they seem deliberately inscrutable or abusive. In short, one does not have to approve of Enid's way of making meaning to acknowledge that there is meaning within it.

The last aspect of misanthropelore demonstrated in *Ghost World* that I want to discuss is nostalgia, which permeates the story. Enid consistently withdraws from contemporary concerns and relationships through nostalgia, using it as a way to further disaffiliate herself. In one of the book's most powerful scenes, Enid listens to her favorite record from childhood, "A Smile and A Ribbon," following a fight with Becky, and she breaks down (fig. 8). Earlier in the story, she refuses to sell a cherished toy from her childhood despite having put a price on it for her yard sale, insisting she does not want "some jerk with a trendy hair cut" possessing any of her "sacred artifacts" (1997: 53). Later, when she lets her yard sale be ransacked after she wanders off with Becky, she's grateful

Figure 7: Clowes, Daniel. 1997. Panel from *Ghost World. The Daniel Clowes Reader* (2013). Seattle: Fantagraphics: Page 84.

that "Goofie Gus," the toy she earlier refused to sell, is one of the only items left behind. There are, as well, less sentimental instances of nostalgia, such as when Enid dyes her hair green and dons a leather jacket, pointing out that she is not just another punk but a 1977 punk, as well as her expressed desire to put together an entire 1930s wardrobe, lamenting the fact that it would be so out of place: "The trouble with that is you look really stupid and pretentious if you go to a mall or a Taco Bell or something" (63). Throughout *Ghost World*, Enid uses anachronisms to differentiate herself from her milieu.

Recent psychological research has identified a social aspect to nostalgia as the memories people are most nostalgic for are memories of time spent with other people: "Holidays, family vacations, trips with friends, weddings,

Figure 8: Clowes, Daniel. 1997. Panel from *Ghost World. The Daniel Clowes Reader* (2013). Seattle: Fantagraphics: page 100.

religious ceremonies, and class reunions are the kinds of events people tend to be nostalgic about." Clay Routledge writes in *Nostalgia: A Psychological Resource* (2016), "The content of nostalgic memories suggests that nostalgia is about relationships and personally treasured objects or life experiences that remind us of or connect us to close ones" (2016: 16). In other words, when people are dissatisfied with or disconnected from their present society (or lack thereof), they conjure meaningful connections they have shared in the past in order to console themselves. Nostalgia, however, also erodes social ties as Stephanie Coontz, author of *The Way We Never Were*, points out. "Nostalgia can distort our understanding of the world in dangerous ways, making us needlessly negative about our current situation" (2013). Even if nostalgia does focus on social connections as Routledge and others aver, it places the most meaningful social connections in an inaccessible past, disaffiliating a person from more immediate social connections.

As important as nostalgia is in the comic book, it takes on even greater significance in the film adaptation through the character Seymour. An expanded version of "Bearded Windbreaker" from the comic (i.e. the man Enid pranked), Seymour becomes friends with Enid after she takes pity on him following her prank. Seymour is a single, middle-aged man with a record collection consisting of 1500 78s, having pared it down to "just the essentials." When Enid expresses envy for his record collection, along with all the other "cool stuff" he displays in his home, Seymour objects, "You think it's healthy to obsessively collect things? You can't connect with other people, so you fill your life with stuff. I'm just like all the rest of these pathetic collector losers," referring to his "friends" in the other room (2001). In effect, Seymour is a fetishist, by which I mean he is using objects to access traumatically inaccessible desires, and I think a strong argument can be made that collecting in general is a form of misanthropelore. Fetishism, in fact, may be the most misanthropic example of misanthropelore there is as it generally replaces human connections with objects. It substitutes messy, quixotic and difficult humans with predictable, controllable objects. Remembering a lost loved one through a picture or keepsake may be acceptable because it is really the only way to remain "in touch," but rejecting flesh-and-blood companions for a record or doll is something else entirely. It is the difference between accepting a loss and maintaining one.

I am, however, more interested in the anachronistic nature of the things Seymour collects, how he turns his back on modern society by collecting technology that is effectively obsolete.[7] And even more problematic is the vintage signage he collects for Cook's Chicken, a chain restaurant Seymour works for. Originally called Coon's Chicken, the restaurant used abhorrently racist imagery in its promotional materials, and Seymour has a large collection of its posters and menus. After looking through his collection of Coon's Chicken "memorabilia," Enid asks, "Are you saying that things were better back then, even though there was stuff like this?" Seymour responds, "I suppose things are better now, but, . . . I don't know, it's complicated." That Seymour thinks "it's complicated," especially in terms of normalized racism, demonstrates the problematic nature of nostalgia and misanthropelore. By eschewing contemporary connections, Seymour retreats into a world of his own making, one in which, due to his whiteness, he can dismiss the oppression of his neighbors. Modernity has its problematic aspects, but to hedge at all on the racist worldview expressed in Coon's Chicken signage exhibits a stunning insensitivity.

Nostalgia can be a misanthropic and dangerous indulgence as it devalues the present by placing the best meaning in the past. Yet as increasing research suggests, nostalgia can, on a personal level, be a beneficial thing as it helps people generate social meaning in isolation. Misanthropelore is similarly conflicted. While it may appear to be a negative concept as it devalues community, it also, on a personal level, can be quite useful and provide someone with a great deal of meaning. It is crucial, consequently, to discern how one's sentiments do or do not exploit other people. When nostalgia overlooks the experience of others in the past, it is selfish and dangerous. Likewise, when misanthropelore ignores the needs and contributions of others in the present, it is a selfish and dangerous form of social meaning making.

AWKWARDNESS

While I am relying on fictional instances of misanthropelore, as I suggested early in this chapter, I believe disaffiliating expressions are common throughout contemporary American culture, a culture that often praises independence over community. According to a study conducted by Miller McPherson, Lynn Smith-Lovin, and Matthew Brashears in 2004, the average American claims to have two confidants, a drop from three in 1985, and nearly one in four Americans claims to have no confidant at all (2006). In their book *The Lonely American: Drifting Apart in the Twenty-first Century*, Jacqueline Olds and Richard S. Schwartz contend that the day-to-day experience of Americans combined with the nation's individualist ideal has promoted a spread of social isolation:

> People in our society drift away from social connections because of both a push and a pull. The push is the frenetic, over scheduled, hypernetworked intensity of modern life. The pull is the American pantheon of self-reliant heroes who stand apart from the crowd. As a culture, we all romanticize standing apart and long to have destiny in our own hands. But as individuals, each of us hates feeling left out. In the interplay between these conflicting goals, our society has fallen into a trap, one that has been made even more inescapable by an abundance of technologies that ostensibly provide better tools for connection. (2009: 11)

In effect, the United States, both as a network and as a community, encourages people to separate themselves from one another, an aspect of American society that theorists have been commenting on at least since Toqueville, who, in 1835, observed that Americans "form the habit of thinking of themselves in isolation and imagine that their whole destiny is in their hands" (106–7).

There is, however, a peculiar potential for connection latent within Americans' shared isolation, a connection that is also a principal contributor to misanthropelore. In his book *Awkwardness*, Adam Kotsko identifies two modes of awkwardness, everyday awkwardness and radical awkwardness (2010). The former arises from "gracelessness" or an individual's inability to conform to the customs that guide social interactions. Radical awkwardness, on the other hand, arises from a society's inability to provide standards to which people are expected to conform. According to Kotsko, awkwardness became pervasive in Western culture following the cultural revolutions of the 1960s. Before then, a social hierarchy was in place that was oppressive, unfair and predictable, "But the events of the 1960s threw the normative model significantly off-kilter, making it impossible to embrace that model wholeheartedly" (2010: 19). No new social model replaced the flawed, old one; thus people were left without a guide in their social interactions and were forced to figure things out on their own. "By the 1970s, awkwardness, not the stability of Fordism," Kotsko argues, "had become the new 'default setting' of American culture" (2010: 19). He attributes a nihilism that became predominant in 70s culture to this absence of a guiding system for socialization, and, I would add, that this absence is a primary contributor to misanthropelore becoming a more prevalent form of expression in postmodernity. After all, following the events of the 1960s, affiliating one's self with mainstream culture meant allying oneself with an unjust and rightfully dying social order, and declaring independence from "normal folk" was laudable, even if it did not come with a corresponding affiliation elsewhere.

Kotsko sees in both forms of awkwardness the potential for greater connection: "The experience of awkwardness, then, is an intrinsically social one. And this means that, paradoxically, certain violations of the norms we rely on to navigate our way through social encounters—either violating specific rules, as in everyday awkwardness, or more broadly violating our expectation that there will be rules applying to every situation, as in radical awkwardness—actually create a weird kind of social bond" (2010: 9). Awkwardness, in other words, is defined by a failure to meet social norms, which makes it, despite being an absence, a fundamentally social phenomenon. In a similar vein, even though misanthropelore defies certain expressive traditions, there can be a "weird kind of social bond" forged through its performance if only people acknowledge, perhaps even embrace, such absences as expressive customs in their own right. Folklore as we find it is different from folklore as we wish it to be, and a weird and contingent social bond is better than no social bond at all.

As awkward as many of Enid's encounters are, her awkwardness is paltry compared to that of Wilson, protagonist of Daniel Clowes's book of the same name. *Wilson* is composed of seventy single-page, six-to-eight panel cartoons, all of which focus on the book's protagonist's struggle with other people. Presented, presumably, in chronological order, they follow the paunchy, balding and be-spectacled Wilson as he struggles connecting with people throughout his middle years. "Fellowship," the first comic in the book, opens with a cheery Wilson walking his dog (fig. 9). He declares himself a "people person." After lamenting a diminished sense of community within the human family, he encounters another dog walker and inquires into her well-being. She proceeds to tell him of her troubles, specifically about her computer that just crashed, and as she continues to tell Wilson about her attempts to fix the problem, he interrupts her: "For the love of Christ, don't you ever shut up?" Most of the comics in *Wilson* follow a similar trajectory, always ending with Wilson at odds with other people. The drawing styles range from funny-pages basic to realistic, and the content ranges from sentimental to absurd. Often, style and content are paired counterintuitively, such as in "The Old Neighborhood," when a crudely drawn Wilson, having just left his father's deathbed, falls down on the field where he used to play ball and cries out, "Oh Daddy Daddy Daddy." Conversely, "Post Office" is presented in a realistic, sepia-toned style, yet the comic ends with Wilson asking an elderly woman to hold onto a package and guess how much it will cost to send before telling her it is filled with dog excrement.

Throughout the book, Wilson attempts to connect with people, often strangers but also people from his past, only to have the efforts fail. He calls his father for the first time in years only to learn that his father is dying. Wilson later gets in touch with Pippi, his ex-wife, and learns that he has a daughter she gave up for adoption. Together, they figure out where their daughter is and gradually build a relationship with her that culminates in a family road trip that, technically, qualifies as kidnapping. Following an argument, Pippi turns Wilson in to the authorities and he spends the next six years in prison, during which time his beloved dog Pepper dies. Following his release, a mellowed Wilson approaches his relationships more sincerely, yet his attempts to connect with others are almost always rebuffed. He does end up in a stable-but-loveless marriage, and his daughter allows him to Skype with his grandson, yet the boy shows zero interest in building a relationship with his biological grandfather.

To call Wilson awkward is insufficient. He is a prophet of awkwardness, sharing the gospel with everyone he encounters. By conventional metrics, this would be a bad thing, yet viewing his expressions from Adam Kotsko's generous perspective on awkwardness shows that no matter how clumsy and negating he may be, Wilson is incredibly social, simply in an unsettling way. Kotsko suggests, "It's difficult to deny that there are people for whom awkwardness is a kind of perverse skill, who bring it with them wherever they go. We are only able to identify someone as awkward, however, because the person does

FELLOWSHIP

Figure 9: Clowes, Daniel. 2010. "Fellowship." *Wilson*. Montreal: Drawn and Quarterly.

something that is inappropriate for a given context. Most often, these violations do not involve an official written law—instead, the grace that's in question is the skillful navigation of the mostly unspoken norms of a community" (6). Whether he realizes or not, Kotkso is talking about awkwardness's relationship with folklore, how the expressive customs people share might be made visible through their violation. I would further suggest that what he outlines is misanthropelore and that such disaffiliating performances render intelligible the implicit affiliation people share with one another. Misanthropelore is, in this sense, folklore's shadow, an absence that signifies the presence of something else.

I do not, however, want to suggest that the value of misanthropelore as I have been describing it comes primarily from it being folklore's other. For one, no matter how much his awkward performances of misanthropelore may offend others, Wilson still connects with people. In his own way, he has his folk and it includes people like Daniel Clowes. When asked why he would write an entire book about such a despicable misanthrope, Clowes replied, "Likeable characters are for weak-minded narcissists. I much prefer the Rupert Pupkins and Larry Davids and Scotty Fergusons as my leading men. And I actually kind of like Wilson. He'd be fun to hang out with in short and finite increments" (2010). Misanthropes, outcasts and losers, it seems, can form their own community, figures brought together not in spite of their differences but because of them. In "Nostalgia and Its Discontents," Svetlana Boym introduces the idea of "diasporic intimacy," which she writes "is not opposed to uprootedness and defamiliarization but is constituted by it. So much has been made of the happy homecoming that it is time to do justice to the stories of non-return and the reluctant praise of exile." She concludes, "Diasporic intimacy does not promise an unmediated emotional fusion, but only a precarious affection—no less deep, yet aware of its transience" (2007: 16). As Boym sees it, people exiled from their communities, whether involuntarily or voluntarily, connect with one another through the shared experience of exile, generating meaning through a familiar absence. It is, in effect, displacement as community, and I suggest that shared disaffiliation might offer a similar sort of intimacy, perhaps even a solution to the Marxist paradox of never joining a club that would have one as a member.

In issue three of *Eightball*, Lloyd Llewelyn returns to apologize: "I was accused of being a one-sided cynic and a whining impossible-to-please pessimistic mope! Please! It was certainly not my intention to offend! And especially not YOU of all people, dear reader! Please accept the following few pages as an apology of sorts, a testament to my positive intentions and an expression of goodwill toward All Human Beings and especially you, my cherished reader." The comic is titled "I Love You Tenderly" (fig. 10), and among the things he

Figure 10: Clowes, Daniel. 1990. Title panel from "I Love You Tenderly." *The Complete Eightball: Volume One* (2015). Seattle: Fantagraphics: Issue 4, page 11.

expresses affection for are "Polite, pleasant, unthreatening, innocuous, silent sexless wallflower types; Rejects, Losers, has-beens and never-weres; and wimps, dweebs and fuck-ups" (figs. 11 and 12). Llewelyn, predictably, loses focus and begins listing more things he hates deeply, yet it is significant that even when he names the things he loves, they are distinguished by their position outside the norm. While the formula may be negative, much like his earlier panel "How to formulate an opinion," the result is positive as he manages to generate affinity with others, even if it comes from their shared isolation.

This, more than anything, is what I hope misanthropelore contributes to folklore studies: a way of identifying and analyzing the types of cultural expressions that occur in communities that enable and encourage social isolation on a grand scale. A consensus has emerged that communal ties have weakened despite the increased connectedness of a culture rife with digital technologies. Mediatized relationships, the thinking goes, are not "real" relationships, and they come at the expense of more meaningful connections. Moreover, industrialized society supports social isolation on an unprecedented scale, and as many as one in four American households are now single person households. All of which is to say, we do not rely on one another for our social needs in the same ways we used to, and our shared expressive customs are necessarily changing. Folklorists can play an integral role in bringing greater awareness to social dislocation, whether deliberate of forced, and misanthropelore can facilitate that process by providing a way of talking about the expressive dimensions of cultural isolation.

Figure 11: Clowes, Daniel. 1990. Panel from "I Love You Tenderly." *The Complete Eightball: Volume One* (2015). Seattle: Fantagraphics: Issue 4, page 11.

Figure 12: Clowes, Daniel. 1990. Panel from "I Love You Tenderly." *The Complete Eightball: Volume One* (2015). Seattle: Fantagraphics: Issue 4, page 11

NOTES

1. Do we need another lore? Probably not, but I'm going with it because it helps me understand myself as both folklorist and folk. Besides, even if we don't need another lore, if we begin to question the utility or need of scholarly conceits, our entire academic universe might unravel—I'm not the first and I certainly won't be the last to wedge my ideas into an already overcrowded scholarly marketplace.

2. A collection of misanthropelore, even if not a catalogable body of customs and traditions, would be a fascinating exhibit.

3. Misanthropelore is, in some sense, tricksterism, in that both are deliberate attempts to unsettle shared standards of right and wrong. When, in *Trickster Makes This World*, Lewis Hyde suggests, "Trickster creates a boundary, or brings to the surface a distinction previously hidden from sight," he could just as easily be talking about misanthropelore (7). Misanthropelore, however, is not a narrative conceit and it certainly isn't mythological, and I feel that to equate it with trickster or tricksterism would be falsely ennobling, akin to saying that because trickster once quilted, quilting is tricksterism.

4. Learning to identify and understand misanthropelore requires rethinking the ontology of sociality, and, fortuitously, such a rethinking is occurring on an epic scale because of the omnipresence of social media and digital technologies. In this chapter, I avoid examples of misanthropelore that rely on digital culture and social media as I do not want to portray performances of disaffiliation as I theorize them as a "new" thing—disaffiliating gestures as an expressive strategy likely have been present throughout human history—but it should not be hard to see that digital technology and misanthropelore are ideally suited to one another.

5. U.S. Senator Ben Sasse of Nebraska wrote a book, *The Vanishing American Adult*, built on this idea, arguing that "ours in now an odd nation of both delayed grown-ups and adult children." Of course this adolescent national spirit has, from a certain perspective, been with the United States since the beginning. The Declaration of Independence is a visionary statement, but, as a student once commented in a class I was teaching, the list of grievances within it reads, at points, like a teenager proclaiming his right to run away from home. The United States has long had an adolescent spirit, caught between where it comes from and what it wants to become. It seems fitting, then, that the country's expressive traditions would have some adolescence to them.

6. On a few occasions throughout the story, Enid refers to ironic pleasures as "God"—she called Joey McCobb, a painfully unfunny comedian, "our God"—echoing, however unintentionally, George Lukas's suggestion that irony is the voice of God in a world abandoned by God.

7. I know you can still get record players and new vinyl is being produced as a high rate, but we are talking about 78s!

REFERENCES CITED

American Folklore Society. 2017. "What is Folklore." http://www.afsnet.org/?page=whatisfolklore.

Bauman, Richard. 1971. "Differential Identity and the Social Base of Folklore." *Journal of American Folklore* 84(331): 31–41.

Billig, Michael. 2005. *Laughter and Ridicule: Towards a Social Critique of Humor.* London: Sage.

Botkin, B. A. [1944] 1993. *A Treasury of American Folklore.* New York: Bonanza.

Boym, Svetlana. 2007. "Nostalgia and Its Discontents." *The Hedgehog Review* (Summer): 7–18.

Cacioppo, John T., and William Patrick. 2008. *Loneliness: Human Nature and the Need for Social Connection*. New York: Norton.

Clowes, Daniel. 1997. *Ghost World*. In *The Daniel Clowes Reader* (2013). Seattle: Fantagraphics: 39–118.

Clowes, Daniel. 1999. "*Ghost World*: An Interview with Daniel Clowes by Joshua Glenn." *The Daniel Clowes Reader* (2013). Seattle: Fantagraphics: 135–44.

Clowes, Daniel. 2001. *Ghost World*. Written by Daniel Clowes and Terry Zwigoff. United Artists.

Clowes, Daniel. 2010. "Interview with Hillary Chute." *Time Out New York*, April 26, 2010.

Greif, Mark. 2010. "The Hipster in the Mirror." *New York Times*, November 14: BR27.

Hyde, Lewis. 2010. *Trickster Makes This World*. New York: Farrar, Strauss and Giroux.

Jansen, William Hugh. 1959. "The Esoteric-Exoteric Factor in Folklore." *Fabula* 2(2): 205–11.

Kotsko, Adam. 2010. *Awkwardness*. Washington: Zero Books.

Lorentzen, Christian. 2007. "Why the Hipster Must Die." *Time Out New York*, May 30. https://www.timeout.com/newyork/things-to-do/why-the-hipster-must-die

Mailer, Norman. [1957] 2007. "The White Negro." *Dissent*, June 20. https://www.dissent-magazine.org/online_articles/the-white-negro-fall-1957.

McPherson, Miller, Lynn Smith-Lovin, and Matthew E. Brashers. 2006. "Social Isolation in America: Changes in Core Discussion Networks over Two Decades." *American Sociological Review* 71: 353–75.

Mechling, Jay. 2006. "Solo Folklore." *Western Folklore* 65 (4): 435–53.

Morson, Gary Saul. 1996. "Misanthropology." *New Literary History* 27(1): 57–72.

Noyes, Dorothy. 1995. "Group." *Journal of American Folklore* 108(430): 449–78.

Olds, Jacqueline, and Robert S. Schwartz. 2009. *The Lonely American: Drifting Apart in the Twenty-First Century*. Boston: Beacon Press.

Primiano, Leonard. "Vernacular Religion and the Search for Method in Religious Folklife." *Western Folklore* 54 (1995): 37–56.

Routledge, Clay. 2016. *Nostalgia: A Psychological Resource*. New York: Routledge.

Schopenhauer, Arthur. [1851] 2001. *Parerga and Paralipomena*. Oxford: Oxford University Press.

Smith, Moira. 2009. "Humor, Unlaughter, and Boundary Maintenance." *Journal of American Folklore* 122(484): 148–71.

Toqueville, Alexis de. [1835] 1945. *Democracy in America*, ed. Phillips Bradley. New York: Knopf.

Revelry: Shirley Jackson and Stanley Edgar Hyman

Shelley Ingram

> Being impossible, an abstract belief can only be trusted through its manifestation, the actual shape of the god perceived, however dimly, against the solidity he displaces.
> —Shirley Jackson, *The Sundial* (1958)

Shirley Jackson was a witch. A witch who, according to her college-professor husband Stanley Edgar Hyman, specialized in "small-scale black magic and fortune telling with a tarot deck." Stories of her witchcraft were used in publicity material for her first novel, *The Road Through the Wall* (1948). Indeed, the blurb of the novel, written by Hyman, called her "the only contemporary writer who is a practicing amateur witch." Perhaps the most famous of the witchcraft stories Jackson told is this: she made a voodoo doll representing Alfred Knopf and used it to force a fall that broke his leg. Interviewers got a lot of mileage out of this story, obviously. But many critics, both contemporary and current, dismiss such claims of witchery as merely clever marketing. She can't actually *believe* in witchcraft, they say, because she's a phenomenal writer. Phenomenal writers don't believe.

But Judy Oppenheimer, Jackson's first biographer, claims that Jackson had "the ability to see beyond reality, to pierce the veil into other realms. Shirley was, in fact, psychic" (1988: 18). Darryl Hattenhauer, in one of only two published full-length critical monographs on Jackson's work, takes particular issue with this representation. Such assertions, Hattenhauer argues, "are not just laughably illogical. They are reactionary. They enable the sentimentalizing [and] erasure of Jackson as the complex political writer who compares with the best of her generation" (2003: 9). I, too, get frustrated with the tendency to ascribe so-called irrationality to women in service of their erasure, as if women are not capable of irony or literary play. But Hattenhauer's claim betrays a fundamental privileging of a particular ideology rooted in the superiority of reason and intellect. You can't be "the best of a generation," he says, and also believe in ghosts. He feels perfectly comfortable declaring with unquestioning authority that "Jackson did not experience the supernatural" (Hattenhauer 2003: 10).

Here is a place where folklore and literature intersect on a literary, disciplinary, and personal level rarely seen. The critical consensus seems to be that it was all a big joke, and that Hyman manipulated this vision of Jackson as witch both because it made them money and because he occasionally enjoyed painting her as a bit silly. Three of Jackson's children, however, *did* believe that their mother was psychic. Hattenhauer dismisses the children, suggesting instead the more palatable alternative that perhaps "they regard their mother as not literally psychic but virtually so by dint of her extraordinary mind." He goes on to say that "at any rate, the views of her children recalling the perceptions of childhood seem less reliable than the views of Jackson's adult contemporaries," many of whom believed that Jackson was merely "playing" witch (2003: 198n17). But Jackson's children explicitly claim that it was to *them* that she let the truth of her belief slip out—their mother loved them best, they said, when they were young, because that was when their minds were open to the fantastic. Perhaps, then, the fraud she perpetrated was actually on her circle of adult contemporaries, a circle dominated by her academic husband. After all, as David Hufford points out, the "neutral" academic stance is always one of non-belief (1995). The witch playing the not-witch playing the witch

But it is not by her witchcraft that we know her. We know her instead by what happened on June 26, 1948, the day that the *New Yorker* published her story "The Lottery." "The Lottery" is a tale of a ritual human sacrifice that sustains the way of life of a small, modern farming community. "Lottery in June, corn be heavy soon" says Old Man Warner, fully connecting the stoning ritual to sacrificial fertility. Why not my daughter, asks Mrs. Hutchinson, the woman being stoned by her own son, irrevocably connecting the ritual to the horrors of motherhood. "The Lottery" is undoubtedly Jackson's most famous piece of fiction, and it resonates still throughout contemporary culture (see the *Simpsons* episode "Dog of Death"). Many an hour in the classroom has been whiled away by literature students debating the symbolism and structure and purpose of both the story and the ritual itself, the discussion dominated by the question "but what does it *mean?*" As Ruth Franklin notes, the letters that poured into the *New Yorker* after the story's publication fell into two general camps: those that asked this same question, what "it" meant, and those who asked where they could go to see the ritual play out (2013). The story seemed to tap into a deep desire for ritual participation, even if that participation resulted in the death of a woman at the hands of her family and her community. It spoke, it seems, to something dark inside of us.

Jackson wrote to H. W. Herrington, one of her former professors, to say that the story had all started in his folklore class (Oppenheimer 1988: 131).

• • •

> The experience of ritual communion ... is a true collective act, a temporary merger of individual identity in a collective whole that is larger than the sum of its parts, and at its conclusion releases its individual units purged and fulfilled, as though they had been cast up from the belly of the whale.... The only culture trait we [Americans] possess which might fairly be called a full ritual communion—collective, purgative, and overwhelming—is the lynch mob.
> —Stanley Edgar Hyman, "The Symbols of Folk Culture"

Stanley Edgar Hyman was a folklorist. Though he is most often remembered as a literary critic or "Shirley Jackson's husband," he nonetheless considered himself a folklorist. And he was not one of those "amateurs purporting to represent our field" whom Dundes critiques, "blissfully ignorant of earlier studies of their subject matter" (2005: 401). No, Hyman was at the very center of the era's debates about the origins and meanings of myth. He was perhaps best known for his fanatical adherence to George Frazer's (and Lord Raglan's and Jane Harrison's) theories of myth and ritual. Hyman believed that all folklore was a product of the devolution of myth, and that all myth was generated through ritual, the narrative, à la the Cambridge school, created to accompany and sanction ancient rites. The issue of the *Journal of American Folklore* that published Claude Levi-Strauss's essay "The Structural Study of Myth" also included Hyman's article "The Ritual View of Myth and the Mythic," and he published additional articles and myriad book reviews in *JAF*. Hyman identified himself as a "literary folklorist" and claimed folklore as his "own field" (1953).

Inside the pages of his wife's first novel is the deceptively simple dedication "To Stanley, a critic." This was, in fact, his primary vocation. His talents, said his second wife, were "mainly of a destructive order with a highly developed instinct for the jugular" (Pettingell 1978: xi). Hyman was particularly critical of anthropology—or more precisely, anthropologists—saying that "it is hard to see" how their academic output "could have any use at all for the serious folklorist." He calls Boas's students (and their theories) "absurd" and flat out states that folklore as a field will never progress until it frees itself "from the omnipresent anthropologists" (1950: 728). He says that the ideas of William Bascom, particularly those concerning myth, "are the pricked bubbles of obsolete theory," whose "irrelevant defenses of primitive potentiality" seems "a relic of the old days when anthropology was as much a form of social exhortation as an heuristic science." There are "many factors," Hyman says, that keep anthropologists like Bascom "from being adequate folklorists" (1958: 154). Here is what he says about the *Journal of American Folklore*'s decision to publish essays by anthropologists:

> It would be difficult to imagine *The American Anthropologist* giving its space to an article on anthropology by a literary folklorist like myself unless the article displayed at least a respectable acquaintance with the field and had something original or useful to say. That [such a] superficial rehash of what we all know much better should have been delivered at a meeting of the AFS and published in the *JAF* suggests that our standards are far too low, our respect for professional ethnologists far too high, or both. (1953: 238)

Hyman did not limit his scorn to anthropologists who dared to write about myth without genuflecting at the altar of George Frazer and Lord Raglan (for that was, in reality, the crux of his objections). He was also anti-racist and pro-proletariat, a holdover from his Marxist college days. He excoriated John Lomax, for example, in a review of Lomax's *Adventures of a Ballad Hunter*, saying that Lomax's book "shows us . . . an absolute want of taste or discrimination, an enormous gullibility, a vast ignorance, a substantial musical illiteracy, and a total human failure in regard to the Negro singers he did so much to discover." He called Lomax's condescension to "little men" (i.e., the proletariat) "disgusting," and added, "Lomax becomes a kind of unconscious advocate of the Southern penitentiary system, because only under its segregation and barbarities is the purity of Negro folk song preserved" (1948: 485–93). These remarks, as harsh as they may seem, were in fact trenchant criticisms of Lomax and his ilk. For example, Hyman pointed out Lomax's "Jim-Crowed" acknowledgments, where "white sources are credited in one section, Negro 'boys' in another" (1948: 485). He was less vitriolic in his condemnation of Stith Thompson's *The Folktale*—calling it an invaluable though bland example of the "pointlessness" of the Finnish school—but still he quickly points out the "chauvinism [of its] assumption that any interesting or complex tale must be of European, probably northern, origin" (1948: 485). While his *ad hominem* attacks were unseemly, sometimes he got things right.

If you push aside his pomposity and bluster, Hyman was putting forth a definition of folklore that is familiar, if dated in its mythic insistence. While he maintained until the very end that all folklore derived from myth, he also believed that new folklore arose out of the scraps of myth as technologies and social needs arose. He said that if he *were* to define "folk culture, it might include some such categories as these: the hero, ritual communion, the cycle of the year as a pattern of life related to the earth, the symbols of worship, and the dignity of occupation" (1964: 308). Hyman gives the following example: Franz Shubert's belief that breaking a mirror brings bad luck is folklore; his original compositions are not. If Shubert's compositions entered into folk culture, Hyman would call this art "folk transmitted" (1948: 492). Perhaps most compellingly, he thought that folklorists ought to think more about *process*, about the modes of transmission and the transformations of folklore such transmissions bring about (1949a: 471).

Richard Dorson seems to have been something akin to a fan. He called Hyman's work on ballads "ingenious," particularly Hyman's claim that it was the "American ethos" that turned majestic ballads into bad poetry. He mentions favorably Hyman's rants against the "cult of the folksy," and several times cited Hyman's assessment of the field of folk study as "monstrous."[1] One can also imagine that Dorson was gleeful at Hyman's utter contempt for the "eccentrics" who were destroying folk studies, whose "frauds and popular amusements are an affront and an abomination" to folklore scholarship (Hyman 1950: 726). Hyman abhorred the attempt to pass off either popular *or* elite culture as folklore, and felt disgusted by the attempts to cash in the desire to be "folksy" (1949b). He was speaking, in many regards, Dorson's language.

Hyman enjoyed taking on the leaders of the field, never questioning his own position relative to the likes of Boas, Bascom, and Lomax. In addition to pointing out folklore's monstrosity, he suggested that there was a "critical sickness" afflicting folk study in America that included bias, provincialism, and ignorance (1950: 722). And yet, Hyman never gave up his belief in the value of the field. He was a fierce advocate for recognizing the importance of folklore, arguing that "sponsors of folk study should fight for a central, even a required, place in the curriculum" (quoted in Dorson 1950: 346). There is joy in his vitriol and much to be said in favor of the iconoclast. He was an often mean and petty writer, and he refused to let politeness stand in the way of what he saw as the raison d'être of academic study: to argue and to advocate and to rile. So confident was he in his own infallible rightness that he accepted no other view of reality. He was never afraid to take on even the most esteemed of his colleagues, and no one and nothing was sacred.

Except, of course, for Frazer. This is his irony. His iconoclasm was pointed in the wrong direction. Hyman was part of a vanishing breed of myth scholars, out of sync with most of his contemporaries, someone who could only watch in vain as post-structuralism and modern ethnography made him and his criticisms increasingly irrelevant—ultimately rendering him not a radical but simply a man out of time. After all, who reads Hyman anymore?

• • •

> Mr. Arnold Waite—husband, parent, man of his word—invariably leaned back in his chair after his second cup of breakfast coffee and looked with some disbelief at his wife and two children. His chair was situated so that when he put his head back the sunlight, winter or summer, touched his unfaded hair with an air at once angelic and indifferent—indifferent because, like himself, it found belief not an essential fact of its continued existence.
> —Shirley Jackson, *Hangsaman*

It is rumored that Kenneth Burke, Hyman's friend and mentor, once said to him, "You write about myth, your wife creates it." This perhaps best encapsulates the dynamic between these two writers, wife and husband, rivals and lovers. According to all biographical accounts, their relationship was deeply dependent, unhealthy, and loving; in short, it was complicated. Oppenheimer writes:

> Stanley scooped [Jackson] up, dazzled, amazed, and overwhelmed her; he tucked her in his pocket and brought her home to show off to his friend. In the years to come he would variously terrify her, amuse her, teach her, encourage her; protect, dominate, enrich, and enrage her; he drove her nuts, he kept her sane. (1988: 62)

Hattenhauer believes, and most Jackson scholars would agree, that "the greatest influence on Jackson was Hyman," and that he "did not just influence her. He controlled her . . . he was the master and she the apprentice" (2003: 15). And yet, she made most of their money; she received most of the acclaim. Picture this: Stanley in his study, surrounded by books, writing furiously. Shirley is everywhere else, tending their four children while bringing in the groceries from the car, since she is the only one in the family who drives. She hands him a check, proceeds from her latest publication in *Good Housekeeping*, then heads into the kitchen. He continues writing, both oblivious to the wife who performs all of the domestic duties and begrudging of her power as moneymaker. But at least it frees him up to do *real* work: folkloristic literary criticism.

But there is another, equally probable, scene from the Jackson/Hyman household: the dining room is filled with friends, intellectual luminaries (like Burke or Ralph Ellison, or, if they're lucky, Dylan Thomas), and local academics. There is drink and food and cigarettes and card games, and the party runs deep into the night. Stanley may have invited his current mistress; if so, Shirley is probably fuming. Arguments happen and stories are written and alliances formed or broken. Shirley practices her witchcraft, Stanley attempts to craft her narrative. Stanley's friend tries to unnerve Shirley by telling her that in his knapsack is "a dead baby, which I shall eat tonight in the woods, roasted over a campfire," but she just nods her head and says "It's always nice to have a little snack along in case you get hungry." It is chaos and it is revelry (Oppenheimer 1988: 67).

This kind of unabashed enthusiasm for play and irreverence made its way into both of their work. As their youngest son said, "They were rebellious little shits" (Oppenheimer 1988: 134). Their lifestyle was finally destructive, as Jackson's early death and Hyman's relative lack of academic legacy attests. But it is also a bit beguiling. I wish at times that I had more freedom to be a witch, to call out racism where it exists, to cast spells on a recalcitrant editor or to feel little need for censorship (or good sense) in my critiques. Ultimately, history has shown Hyman's ornery flamboyance to be far from unique, most of his insights generally not particularly insightful. Jackson, though—her work is a marvel. She wrote sentences like this: "The trees around and overhead were so thick that it was always dry inside and on Sunday morning I lay with Jonas, listening to his stories. All cat stories start with the statement: 'My mother, who was the first cat, told me this,' and I lay with my head close to Jonas and listened" ([1962] 2006: 53).

There is a character in Jackson's novel *Hangsaman* named Arnold Waite. Arnold is the father of the protagonist, Natalie, and theirs is a relationship fraught with tension: academic, domestic, sexual. Arnold is a scholar, and he calls Natalie into his study each morning in order to read and critique Natalie's writing. In this room are books on demonology and "an abridged copy of *The Golden Bough*." Arnold writes Natalie a letter after she goes away to college, claiming to be the knight "caroling lustily under her window," seeking to save his Natalie from the dragon that is surely keeping her away from home. He speaks to her in the language of myth and fairy tale, while Natalie grows increasingly distant. Ultimately, as I have argued elsewhere, Natalie is subsumed into Frazer's vaunted myth of the dying king, led to a copse of trees by a woman named Tony, a woman who may or may not be real. But the sacred grove here is a closed-up amusement park, with stale popcorn and remnants of bathing suits strewn through the streets, an ugly revision of Diana's bucolic forest. Natalie "slays" Tony through the rejection of her touch. She re-writes and is re-written by Frazer's primordial myth, and Natalie ends the novel in a state of liminality, unsteady and ambivalent but remade.

Hyman's presence is manifest throughout all of Jackson's work. In *Hangsaman*, the character of Tony is clearly a stand-in for Arnold, and there is no better representation of Hyman than Arnold in all of Jackson's oeuvre. She turns her husband into the father into an imagined woman whom she slays, reconfiguring Hyman's entire academic worldview and replacing it with one that is both pre- and post-modern. In "The Lottery," the action hinges on the proverb "Lottery in June, corn be heavy soon." It is fruitless to say what this story is "about," except it has something to do with a scapegoat and with an ugliness underpinning all communities. But the proverb traditionalizes and ritualizes the annual murder by connecting it to fertility rites. This is a proverb made up by Hyman, spoken one morning over the breakfast table. Understanding Hyman's role in the ritual debates of the time helps us to better read *Hangsaman* and "The Lottery"—and everything else Jackson wrote—and understanding her as deeply conversant in her era's academic discourse of folklore offers new ways into her texts. Knowing Hyman's role as myth critic and rabble-rouser, philanderer and autocrat, is invaluable.

Literature and language and culture all live and thrive in a world with people who have folklore, and that folklore invariably worms its way into our texts. As Hyman once wrote, "Our world is a multiverse and complex one, and our literature accurately reflects it" (1978: 20). He was arguing in favor of the critic who "knows everything," who knows and understands anthropology, folklore, psychology, and history. Reading Jackson and Hyman both and together gives us new understandings of her fictions, and new insights into those mythy modernists are revealed—such concurrent reading might not allow us to know everything, but it certainly helps us to know more. Jackson creates myth, yes, but she also writes *about* myth, and in particular her husband's mythic brand of folklore studies. She simultaneously undercuts it and rewrites it and pledges allegiance to it. And remember, it all started in a folklore class.

NOTES

1. See Dorson 1951a, 1951b, 1959, and 1963.

REFERENCES CITED

Dorson, Richard. 1950. "The Growth of Folklore Courses." *Journal of American Folklore* 63(249): 345–59.

Dorson, Richard. 1951a. "Five Directions in American Folklore." *Midwest Folklore*. 1(3): 149–65.

Dorson, Richard. 1951b. "Folklore Studies in the United States Today." *Folklore* 61(3): 353–66.

Dorson, Richard. 1959. "A Theory for American Folklore." *Journal of American Folklore* 72(285): 197–215.

Dorson, Richard. 1963. "The American Folklore Scene." *Folklore* 74(3): 433–49.

Dundes, Alan. 2005. "Folkloristics in the Twenty-First Century." *Journal of American Folklore* 118(470): 385–408.

Franklin, Ruth. 2016. *Shirley Jackson: A Rather Haunted Life*. New York: W. W. Norton & Co.

Franklin, Ruth. 2013. "'The Lottery' Letters." *Newyorker.com*. June 25. ttp: //www.newyorker .com/books/page-turner/the-lottery-letters.

Haring, Lee. 1998. "Stanley Edgar Hyman." In *The Encyclopedia of Folklore and Literature*, edited by Mary Ellen Brown and Bruce A. Rosenberg, 320–21. Santa Barbara: ABC-CLIO.

Hattenhauer, Darryl. 2003. *Shirley Jackson's American Gothic*. Albany: State University of New York Press.

Hufford, David. 1995. "The Scholarly Voice and the Personal Voice: Reflexivity in Belief Studies." *Western Folklore* 54(1): 57–76.

Hyman, Stanley Edgar. 1948. "Some Bankrupt Treasuries." *Kenyon Review* 10(3): 484–500.

Hyman, Stanley Edgar. 1949a. "The American Folksy." *Theatre Arts* 33(3): 42–5.

Hyman, Stanley Edgar. 1949b. "Myth, Ritual, and Nonsense." *Kenyon Review* 11(3): 455–75.

Hyman, Stanley Edgar. 1950. "Discent on a Dictionary. Review of *Funk and Wagnalls Standard Dictionary of Folklore, Mythology and Legend. Vol. I: A-I*, by Maria Leach." *Kenyon Review* 12(4): 721–30.

Hyman, Stanley Edgar. 1953. "The Anthropological Approach." *Journal of American Folklore* 66(261): 237–38.

Hyman, Stanley Edgar. 1955. "The Ritual View of Myth and the Mythic." *Journal of American Folklore* 68(270): 462–72.

Hyman, Stanley Edgar. 1958. "Reply to Bascom." *Journal of American Folklore* 71(280): 152–55.

Hyman, Stanley Edgar. 1964. "The Symbols of Folk Culture." In *Symbols and Values: An Initial Study*, edited by Lyman Bryson, 307–12. New York: Cooper Square.

Hyman, Stanley Edgar. 1978. *The Critics Credentials*. New York: Atheneum.

Ingram, Shelley. 2016. "Speaking of Magic: Folk Narrative in *Hangsaman* and *We Have Always Lived in the Castle*." In *Shirley Jackson: Influences and Confluences*, edited by Melanie R. Anderson and Lisa Kröger, 54–75. London and New York: Routledge.

Jackson, Shirley. [1948] 2013. *The Road Through the Wall*. New York: Penguin.

Jackson, Shirley. [1951] 2013. *Hangsaman*. New York: Penguin.

Jackson, Shirley. [1958] 2014. *The Sundial*. New York: Penguin.
Jackson, Shirley. [1962] 2006. *We Have Always Lived in the Castle*. New York: Penguin.
Oppenheimer, Judy. 1988. *Private Demons: The Life of Shirley Jackson*. New York: Putnam.
Pettingell, Phoebe. 1978. Introduction to *The Critics Credentials*, by Stanley Edgar Hyman, vii–xviii. New York: Atheneum.

THREE

The Footprints of Ghosts: Fictional Folklorists in the Work of Gloria Naylor, Lee Smith, Randall Kenan, and Colson Whitehead

Shelley Ingram

[Al] asked Guy what kind of business he had in town. "I'm looking into the legend of John Henry," he responded, thinking in a moment of self-importance that this might impress the man. Al looked at him with a queer expression. He muttered, "Funny line of work."
—Colson Whitehead, *John Henry Days* (2001)

There is a whole cottage industry of books that chronicle the often absurd and petty world of academia. As members of a field usually shuttled to the margins of English and anthropology departments, academic folklorists are generally absent from most of these literary depictions of the university. That does not, however, mean that we are not fictionalized—we are. But it is a marker of our professional marginality and the field's historically problematic relationship with the public that we tend to show up in novels where there is a question of representation, or of authenticity; where there is a question of a community's meaning making, or of its ghosts. Such fictional representations of academic folklorists reveal a gap between how we perceive ourselves and a public understanding of our work. To echo a call made by Barbara Kirshenblatt-Gimblett (1998), it is important to take popular representations of the folklorist's work seriously, even if we believe such representations misrepresent who we are and what we do.

To that end, this chapter looks at four works of fiction that insert an academic folklorist as a character: Gloria Naylor's *Mama Day*, Lee Smith's *Oral History*, Randall Kenan's "Let the Dead Bury Their Dead," and Colson Whitehead's *John Henry Days*. The purpose of this chapter is not to point out all the ways in which these writers get folklore, not so much the "object" but the profession, wrong. While that exercise might be enjoyably cathartic, I am more interested in reading these texts for what they are—literary fictions, works of art that, for better and worse, are not obligated to have their content vetted for academic integrity. Kirshenblatt-Gimblett has argued that the "common usage today" of the vocabulary of folklore "preserves specialized understandings from the past" (1998: 296). These fictions by Naylor, Smith, Kenan, and Whitehead provide a way for us to better understand such "common usages" and to directly engage with the problematic legacies of folklore studies that persist, even as we continually work to disrupt them.

There is a constellation of qualities uniting these four texts, with the folklorist situated right at its center: a textual self-consciousness, an exploration of epistemology and its violences, a questioning of authenticity and a subsequent resistance to touristic reading, and a rendering of ghosts. Each of these works are a bit self-conscious, as they are in many ways about the construction of narrative, drawing attention to themselves as textual artifacts. They play with the representation of reality and fiction in order to expose the constructedness of both, calling into question not just the nature of authenticity, but the possibility of representing anything at all, serving as a challenge to the act of touristic reading. These texts anticipate and even resist the critical impulse to classify them primarily as arbiters of authenticity, implicating at various points the reader, the writer, the critic, and the narrative itself. Furthermore, the stories use their self-consciousness in order to make claims about epistemology: about the politics of Western institutions of knowledge, representation, and ethnography, and the ownership of culture and narrative. In doing so, they render the act of folklore—that is, the products of our intellectual endeavors—ghostly.

The ghostly is not an arbitrary signifier here. These stories all involve actual hauntings, suggesting that there is a deep connection between the way that the authors construct the work of the fictional folklorists and the absences that the ghostly figure. The folklorist is situated as a structural device through which absences in the narrative are revealed; only, it is not the folklorist or, perhaps more pointedly, not the folklorist's *text*, that ameliorates the absence.

The folklorist does not even realize the absence exists. Instead, it is the narrative itself that fills the space the folklorist has unwittingly created. These fictional folklorists are all searching for answers, for history, for ghosts, for some kind of truth—but they can never reach it. Their failure can only instigate the narrative, as it is the text itself that steps self-consciously into the void to do the work of the folklorist.

INDELIBLE AUTHENTICITY AND THE FAILED FOLKLORIST: *MAMA DAY* AND *ORAL HISTORY*

Gloria Naylor's 1988 *Mama Day* is a novel about belief, community, and, perhaps most importantly, listening. Set primarily on the Sea Island community of Willow Springs, a stateless locale populated by descendants of former slaves, the novel is an account of the courtship and marriage of Cocoa, a daughter of the Island, and George, an orphan from New York with an engineering degree and a love of Shakespeare. The novel follows the events of the summer that George and Cocoa decide to visit Willow Springs. While there, Cocoa falls victim to a dark, ambiguous, and, the novel implies, not entirely natural illness. She survives, but George does not, and he is buried on the island. The novel is made up of alternating first-person accounts in which George and Cocoa speak to each other, interspersed with chapters from a third-person narrator that follow Cocoa's great-aunt Miranda, an island healer called Mama Day. The reader only discovers at the end of the novel that the conversations between Cocoa and George, which seem so immediate, so present, happen as Cocoa sits by George's grave.

The back cover of the novel promises a "timeless yet indelibly authentic" look at a place still governed by the power of folk belief and the ancestors. I believe that this is a misreading of the novel, one that critics have tended to replicate over the years. Such misreadings occur in part because critics tend to accept the presence of an easily identifiable folk culture as permission to approach a work of fiction as if it were a mimetic representation of cultural authenticity. Rosemary Hathaway argues that, in literature, "Ethnographic material may serve only to reify preexisting cultural expectations, regardless of how it is presented," as if "folklore offers some sort of unmediated grounding in cultural authenticity" (2004: 171). Thus, "When readers encounter folk material in 'literary' fiction," the expectation is that it will "evoke the essential authenticity of the folk culture from which it is drawn" (2004: 172). Folklore has been constructed, in part because of the history of the discipline, as an authenticating agent.

In critical readings of *Mama Day*, the folklore serves to authenticate the culture of Willow Springs as that of a pre-modern Other, one able to return the characters, and by extension the readers and critics, back to their "authentic" selves. However, if one is not blinded by the desire to find in the novel a particular sort of cultural authenticity, even a cursory reading of the novel reveals a different perspective. Cocoa and George—or Willow Springs and New York, or the rooted and the rootless—do not offer dichotomous or competing versions of a way of life. Instead, the novel "undercuts the notion that Cocoa's cultural authenticity is superior to [George's] rootlessness" (Lamothe 2005: 163). Perhaps this dynamic is most explicit in Miranda's discussion of Candle Walk, the winter tradition in which the residents of Willow Springs "take to the road—strolling, laughing, and talking—holding some kind of light in their hands." During this ritual people exchange gifts, as an unspoken function of Candle Walk is to be "a way of getting help without feeling obliged" (110). However, "There's a disagreement every winter about whether these young people spell the death of Candle Walk. You can't keep 'em from going beyond the bridge, and like them candles out on the main road, time does march on" (111). Candle Walk was different when Miranda was a child, and it was "different still" during her father's childhood, and his father's before him. There was "nothing to worry about," she says, because when future generations forget about Candle Walk entirely, it will only be because the world will have changed—Candle Walk's disappearance will signal that there is no longer a need for it (111).

Naylor has thus written resistance into the text, a warning to readers who may look to *Mama Day* out of a nostalgia for an unadulterated and unchanging past. As Cocoa tells George, when he is enthralled by the mysticism he finds in Willow Springs, "Sure, it's nice in the summer. But the other nine months of the year, there is absolutely nothing going on," and that making a living on Willow Springs would "take back-breaking work" (220). Hathaway has cautioned folklorists and literary scholars alike against engaging in George's kind of nostalgia, which may manifest in literary criticism as "touristic reading." Touristic reading is what happens when we approach a work of fiction as if it is a tour guide to some authentic, exotic, Other culture. An interesting result of this touristic impulse is that almost every scholarly treatment of *Mama Day* mentions Reema's boy, a character who only appears in the short prologue and who is constructed entirely through dialogue. Why does such a minor character attract such critical attention? Because he is the folklorist, the ethnographer who returns home to Willow Springs to collect the story of the island.

Reema's boy stands as a comic figure, an object of ridicule to those who live in Willow Springs and a symbol of the corrupting world beyond the bridge that connects the island to the mainland. This ethnographer, "Reema's boy—the one with the pear shaped head," had gone away to college and come back "dragging his notebooks and tape recorder and a funny way of curling up his lip and clicking his teeth, all excited and determined to put Willow Springs on the map" (7). He appears in the prologue, an eight-page section placed between images of a family tree, an 1819 deed of sale for a woman named Sapphira, and, in fact, a map of Willow Springs. The prologue is thus an intermediary text, negotiating between the iconographic and artistic renderings at the beginning of the novel and the narrative of George and Cocoa, a narrative that recreates the events of that summer fourteen years before. This position allows the prologue an authority rooted in historical, empiricist, and anthropological discourse. It is the only part of the novel told in first person plural and is meant to represent the collective, though not communal, voice of the island. The first mention of Reema's boy is embedded in the middle of this section in the middle of a paragraph, his introduction eliciting no fanfare. The "we" of Willow Springs is thus claiming the power of ethnographic representation by displacing Reema's boy as the shaper of the text and by showing themselves capable of putting Willow Springs on the map—the map that they include at the beginning of the novel.

This is how they see him, Reema's boy: a product of a fancy college who "rattled on about ethnography, unique speech patterns, cultural preservation, and whatever else he seemed to be getting so much pleasure out of" (7). He wanted to know what "18 & 23" meant, and they told him, and he did not believe them, and he wrote a book about it, but he got it all wrong because he said *they* got it all wrong, deciding that the folks of Willow Springs were "'inverting their hostile social and political parameters,' cause see, being we was brought here as slaves, we had no choice but to look at everything upside down . . . everybody else in the country went on learning good English and calling things what they really was—in the dictionary and all that—while we kept on calling things ass-backwards" (8). Furthermore, they connect Reema's boy, the ethnographer, the academic, to the property developers who have "upped the price and changed the plans, changed the plans and upped the price," exploiting the land and the people, teaching the people of Willow Springs that "anything coming from beyond the bridge gotta be viewed real, real careful," because "Look at what happened to Reema's boy" (7). Academic folkloristic research here is a product of the same capitalist system that seeks to take advantage of the relatively self-sustaining community of Willow Springs. "If the boy wanted to know what 18 & 23 meant," they say, "why didn't he just ask?" (8).

So far, this is a rather typical, even stereotypical, character: the hometown child who goes away to college and returns only to show that he has not learned anything at all, a "stock figure of Eurocentrism, assimilationism, and cultural imperialism" (Blyn 2002: 243).[1] His character is a not very subtle attack on the politics of representation, on the academic impulse to not just "study" the Other, but to speak in their place without asking or listening, and on the connection between ethnography, capitalism, and exploitation. Moreover, Reema's boy is *more*, because he is *of* the Island. He is the so-called "hybrid" ethnographer that Alan Taylor warns us about when he talks of the problematic romanticization of the "bicultural man and woman" (1996: 434). He may be of Willow Springs, but the novel's narrator nonetheless aligns him firmly with Western institutions. He furthermore stands in contrast to the novel's focal characters, Cocoa and George, who *also* had education and experience beyond the bridge, who *also* bring to Willow Springs incomplete knowledge, but who finally learn to listen. Reema's boy is the framing character, the one who creates the empty space in which the autoethnographic narrator puts the story.

He "fails miserably" at being an adequate folklorist because he, as one critic argues, is not "authenticating shared ways of knowing [and] telling" (Donlon 1995: 27). Another critic says he is a "failure" because he could not learn to listen, yet another that he "symbolizes one (failed) model for modern African Americans" (Tucker 1994: 173; Lamothe 2005: 162). His failure seems to be a critical necessity. Yet he made a career, he published a book—if that is what it takes to get tenure, Reema's boy does not fail. There may even be something to his analysis, whether the people of Willow Springs accept it or not. Nonetheless, Reema's boy's success as a folklorist is inversely proportional to his failure as child of the island. It would seem that he cannot succeed in both worlds.

But then things get interesting. The collective narrator says, "Think about it: ain't nobody really talking to you. We're sitting here in Willow Springs, and you're God-knows-where. It's August 1999—Listen. Really listen this time: the only voice is your own" (10). The book was first published in 1988, so the date 1999 unsettles the narration. It calls attention to the construction of the text, and it places the reader in the same future-world as the fictional ethnographer. Self-conscious fiction, or fiction like *Mama Day* that gestures toward self-consciousness, often plays with the relationship between the implied author, the narrator, the characters, and the audience. Doing so disrupts traditional reading patterns and violates, in some way, the unwritten contract between reader and book. We see this betrayal played again in the ethnographic "we" of Willow Springs. Rather than presenting the "objective" point of view many critics seem to long for, this voice cannot be authoritative; in fact, it *refuses* claims to empiricism and absolute truth. Sapphira Wade, for example, is a legendary figure "satin black, biscuit cream, red as Georgia clay: depending upon which of us takes a mind to her" (3). There is no objective truth, and those who look for one, whether it be Reema's boy or the critics who read Reema's boy as only a foil to the true ethnographer, miss the point.

The metafictive elements of the novel implicate the reader—they tell us that the Willow Springs of the narrator is just as constructed as, and in fact *is*, the text we are about to read. Furthermore, the story can only be told through an engagement with our ghosts. Readers seeking the "indelible authenticity" of *Mama Day* might rightly rejoice in the dismantling of the colonizing rhetoric of the ethnographic project through the figure of Reema's boy, but until they learn to attend to Miranda's musings on Candle Walk or the beautifully drawn portrait of George's New York or the importance, finally, of the bridge between Willow Springs and the mainland, they too have failed to listen to what the ghosts have to say. The figure of the folklorist, creating as he does the absences representative of Western institutions of knowledge, serves as a warning to readers: don't be Reema's boy.

Lee Smith's *Oral History* has a similar frame. It also involves the return of a child, now grown into a college-educated adult, to her ancestral lands. And like Reema's boy, Jennifer is also acting as a folklorist, someone who seeks to turn the stories of her family and their ghosts into a tangible text—in this case, an essay for her folklore class and, perhaps more important, a valentine to Dr. Ripman, her folklore professor. When she tells Dr. Ripman about her family, whom she has never met, and their haunted house, which she has never seen, his "eyes lit up like big Miami stars" (17). So she drives her baby blue Toyota to Hoot Owl Holler, Virginia, chasing the perfect class project: the capturing of a ghost. She hikes up to the old family home and leaves her tape recorder running, looking to find something where there seems to be nothing. Jennifer's story is told in the un-numbered first and last sections of the novel, which are set in the present day and which, at the very end, tell us the future. The story captured between this frame is that of the Cantrell family, told in a mixture of first and third person accounts that begin in the 19th century. Some of these accounts are given by Jennifer's ancestors and relatives, while others are from townspeople who lived in and around Hoot Owl Holler. Taken as a whole, the novel presents a messy portrait of a century of marriages, deaths, births, and changes. But as with Reema's boy, Jennifer does not hear that story. All she hears is the emptiness of the tape recorder and the absence of a ghost.

Smith clearly constructs Jennifer as an incompetent scholar. Jennifer writes in florid undergraduate prose, filling her notebooks with observations she feels Dr. Ripman will appreciate (and he does, since she gets both an A and, eventually, a marriage proposal). Jennifer writes sentences like, "I feel nothing so much as an outpouring of consciousness with every pore newly alive. I shall descend now, to be with them as they go about their evening chores" (20). She labels Lil Luther Wade, the man she believes to be her grandfather, "a real treasure," and she works hard to block out the details that would sully her romanticized notions of Appalachian living, notions that only really bloomed during her college folklore course. "Salt of the earth," she says of this family, as the sirens from an episode of *Magnum, P.I.* wail in the background (16). Jennifer thought she was entering the world of *Songcatcher*, when in reality she was entering the house of Uncle Al, a man who makes his fortune selling Amway.

Jennifer eventually finds a way to explain the markers of a modernity that she has tried to ignore. When Al sexually assaults her by forcing a kiss, she says, "Some things may seem modern, like the van, but they're not, not really. They are really very primitive people, resembling nothing so much as some sort of early tribe. Crude jokes and animal instincts—it's the other side of the pastoral coin" (284). We could read the rest of the novel as an attempt to balance these sides of the "pastoral coin." For Jennifer, the Cantrells are either living bucolically in an edenic place outside of time and history, or they are savages. She is not capable of imagining a non-binary portrait of the family living in Hoot Owl Holler. In fact, she knows nothing about them. She believes that the old couple living with Al and Ora Mae, and Little Luther are her grandparents. But they are not, and no one ever tells her so—and she never thinks to ask.

This first section of the novel ends with Al running down from the ancestral home where Jennifer had left her tape recorder, scared of what he heard and saw. "Did you hear something?" Jennifer asks, but he does not answer. It is then that a storm comes down the mountain. The storm "has voices in it," says the narrator, "and Jennifer on the steps and Ora Mae in the yard inclined their heads in the wind like they're listening" (24). In the top right corner of the next page, which is mostly blank, there is a single, handwritten line: "Almarine Cantrell ~1876." As the book progresses, each new section is prefaced by such a page, with the list of names and dates growing longer until they finally take up all available space. This family tree is an iconographic representation that seems to fill the emptiness Jennifer captures on her recording.

Paula Gallant Eckard thus argues that in the narrative proper of *Oral History*, "Each character has a different perspective . . . that, when assimilated, tell the complete story of the Cantrells and Hoot Owl Holler" (1995: 122). This approach sees *Oral History* as a novel that exposes the limits of academic folkloristics, the facile nature of oral history projects, and a distrust of an "American academy which has traditionally refused to authenticate the value of oral storytelling" (Donlon 1995: 30). The complicated nature of storytelling is indeed set in contrast to the romanticizing superficiality of the folklorist. Furthermore, Jennifer is read, like Reema's boy, as a failure. She "fails to comprehend the history, spirit, and realities undergirding her family," says Eckard (1995: 127). Jennifer simply "fails as a folklorist," says Suzanne Jones (1987: 104). The ridiculousness of Jennifer's approach primes the reader to see the novel as Eckard does, as the real story, the "complete" story, of Hoot Owl Hollow. Jennifer's failure creates the space for the story, and it is the emptiness on the tape recorder, her feeble attempt to capture the ghosts of her past, that precipitates the storm that carries with it the voices of the hollow.

But as in *Mama Day*, things in *Oral History* are not quite so simple, and the book itself seeks to complicate readings like Eckard's. Jennifer does not really stand in for the ineffectual folklorist. She is instead the touristic reader, representative of those who pick up *Oral History* expecting a story of the strong but simple folk who populate Appalachia, those who look to the past as an exemplar of better times gone by. One reviewer who posted on Goodreads, a book review website, said the novel was a "window into a different culture," while another praised Smith's ability "to capture the lives of a culture that is disappearing." These popular reviews echo language already in the book, anticipated by Smith and incorporated through another textual artifact, the journals of Richard Burlage.

Burlage's journals make up a substantial portion of the middle of the *Oral History*. He is an outsider who comes from the city—Richmond—to Hoot Owl Holler to teach in fall of 1923. As he arrives in the Hollow by train, he decides that "such beauty cannot but proceed . . . from the divine" (105). He believes that this region is populated by people who are "simple, unassuming" with "a kind of peasant dignity, a naturalness inherent in [their] every move" (102). He, like Jennifer, is disoriented when he realizes that life here is not as he imagined. That is, until he falls in love at first sight with Dory Cantrell. After reading of the love affair feverishly recounted in Richard's diary, we discover that Dory and Richard are Jennifer's actual grandparents, with Dory giving birth to twins after Richard leaves to return to Richmond. Richard never learns about his children.

Thus the family tree, the one that progressively takes up more space in the novel, does not reflect Jennifer's true heritage, as Richard's name never appears. The tree is as incomplete as the oral history Jennifer turns in for class. This is only one of the ways the novel resists telling "the complete" story of the Cantrells. Smith has said that she is "endlessly fascinated by the idea that it is always the teller's tale, that no matter who's telling the story . . . and you never *finally* know exactly the way it was" (Arnold 1984: 246). We see such negotiations of truth throughout the novel, forcing the reader (more and less successfully, as reviews attest) to acknowledge truth as subjective, as speakers in the novel are all the time emphasizing that the story they tell is true: "I'll swear it. To this day" (29) and "you know I'd die before I'd tell a lie" (173). The repudiation of doubt can only introduce doubt, as it calls attention to the constructed nature of the first person accounts, a process with which we as folklorists are well acquainted.

Smith explicitly deconstructs the nature of legend, and what legend says about truth and subjectivity, with the story of the haunted Cantrell family home.

We learn that the story of the "curse" and the haunting that followed was the creation of a woman named Rose Hibbit, who was angry about her rejection by Almarine. But the story stuck. Hotel proprietor Justine confesses a belief in the curse, looking back at prior events and changing them to justify her belief. But Justine's conclusions are challenged by her friend Aldous. "He kilt her," Justine says of Almarine, and Aldous replies, "We don't know that." Her response is "well, we just as well as know it" (182). Finally, Aldous says "you could make up something about anybody up in any of those hollers [...] and once it starts, it just goes on by itself, it takes on a life of its own no matter who may be hurt in the process" (183). In fact, we do not know for sure whether or not Almarine killed anyone. That story is only referenced obliquely, though rumor and conjecture.

Even more than the negotiation of truth, then, absence is a constitutive element of the narrative. Dory, for example, is the centrifugal force of the novel. The stories that come before her seem to be leading to her birth, and the stories that follow all seem to take her as their center. Yet she never speaks for herself, and her motivations and interiority can only be supposed. As daughter Sally says of Dory, "A place inside her was empty that we couldn't fill," including, it would seem, her story (244). The multitude of speakers in the text often reference other such absences, gesturing toward stories never to be told. Granny Younger, the novel's first first-person narrator, says of Almarine, "He was gone almost five years. And whatever happened to him in between, that's his story. He never did tell a word" (31). Important events, like Almarine's own murder and even Dory's pregnancy, are only ever talked around and are never directly addressed. There are people named in the family tree, like Nun and Isadore, whose stories are not included and who are mentioned so rarely in the text that they only exist as filled-in genealogical blanks, situated beyond the scope of the narrative and outside of readerly knowledge. What we see is that the telling of each story only creates new gaps.

This tension, between presence and the absence such presence necessarily creates, is perhaps most overtly addressed when Richard returns to Hoot Owl Holler ten years after his first visit, bringing his camera along to "capture a bit of the past" (217). Like his granddaughter Jennifer, Richard is the outsider whose voice is heard only through the written word, his journals. And like Jennifer, he is in the dark about his family in the Hollow, the reader knowing what Richard does not. As he notices the logging and the mining going on all around him, he realizes that it was not a new enterprise. It was happening before, but he was not able to see it. He says it "makes me wonder what else I might have missed" (224). Richard and Jennifer thus represent absences in institutionalized knowledge, as they come from the city into the country searching for something they can never find. They have grandiose ideas about their roles in the history of the Hollow; one a teacher, the other a student, they cannot see that they are not welcome, and it is no accident that they both write where others speak. They are structurally important to the novel, as Jennifer's portion frames the narrative while Richard's props up the middle. They think they are going to fill in the gaps of Hoot Owl Holler, either through education or through oral history, and they both, in the end, fail.

It is this failure that interests me. In *Mama Day* and *Oral History*, the character of the folklorist is accused of "failing" in some essential way. The overwhelming critical consensus is that their failure is, at its core, about perception. Reema's boy did not listen to what his people told him, while Jennifer failed to record the voices of the holler. Both Naylor and Smith intend these characters to be foils to the knowledge of the community, suggesting that knowledge does not need to be gathered and analyzed and interpreted by any representative of an institution—because such representatives will only get it wrong, as Jennifer and Reema's boy privilege their own personal truths over the truths of the people around them. Furthermore, they both gain materially from their work; instead of signifying failure, their scholarly output leads to a measure of professional and personal success, as they effectively trade their folk culture for caste status. This success, though, has no correlative positive impact on the community. Neither writer is subtle in her satire.

Critics have been only too happy to follow this lead, especially since the presence of a consciously constructed folk culture pushes the reader to expect the authenticity of the oral over the written, or the folk over the academic. Critics thus use Reema's boy and Jennifer as the failures who can authenticate the text. However, both *Mama Day* and *Oral History* complicate the very paradigm they construct by playing with questions of truth and authenticity through a metafictive self-consciousness, by refusing any possibility of a "complete" story, and by likening the process of oral history to a conversation with ghosts, full of gaps and silences. This suggests to me that Naylor and Smith were *also* anticipating that critics would misread—mishear—the stories they were trying to tell. The folklorist is not a character separate from the reader. The folklorist *is* the reader, the critic, as the novels' metafictional aspects ask us to consider our own complicity in the failures of the folklorists.

THE TRUTH, NEAR BOUT: "LET THE DEAD BURY THEIR DEAD" AND *JOHN HENRY DAYS*

Randall Kenan's "Let the Dead Bury Their Dead" and Colson Whitehead's *John Henry Days* are different in their representation of the folklorist. These folklorists are not bumbling and clumsy nor are they foils for the superior knowledge of the folk, as Kenan and Whitehead take a more thoughtful, less obviously parodic approach to the project of folkloristics. Yet their folklorists too construct and reveal absence, they too are representations of the incomplete knowledge of institutions, each serving to question the type of knowledge that academics endeavor to produce. Kenan's long short story "Let the Dead Bury Their Dead" is the last in the 1992 collection by the same name that centers around the fictional town of Tims Creek, North Carolina. It begins with an intertextual appeal to academic tradition that makes reference to Kenan's other major work of fiction, *A Visitation of Spirits*, blurring the line between fiction and reality from the outset. "Let the Dead" is furthermore constructed as an edited version of a found text. James Malachi Greene, the oral historian of Tims Creek, loved the town, and the evidence could be found in his book *Let the Dead Bury Their Dead*, a manuscript discovered among his papers after his death. The story is being presented to the reader as an essay edited by one Reginald Kain (whose initial "RK" appear throughout the story), a professor in the Department of Anthropology and Folklore at Sarah Lawrence College. The story has two title pages: one for the "abridged and edited" version by Kain, complete with acknowledgements and a dedication page, and one for the "original" found text (though there are really *three* title pages, if you count the title page of the collection, with Kenan listed as author).

The editor Reginald Kain writes a scholarly introduction for the text, which is where the reader discovers that Greene died in a car accident in 1998. As Kenan's collection was first published in 1992, he, like Naylor does in *Mama Day*, displaces the reader by situating the telling of this origin story of Tims Creek in the future. We are consistently telling non-folklorists that folklore does not mean *old*, that it can be emergent and new. The reason we have to preface all of our first-day-of-class lectures with such claims is that the willingness to locate folklore primarily in the past—the older the better—is probably the most persistent legacy of folklore's scholarly history. The stories Naylor, Smith, and Kenan tell may be about the past, but they each consciously decide to move the narrative frames, the ones that include folklorists, into the future. Perhaps this is a way to destabilize the notion that folk communities exist as representatives of some kind of primordial era, living in a land that time forgot. The people do move forward.

Or, perhaps this is simply one more facet of the metafictive impulse, to show that time and text are always only constructions, as the scholarly preface does more than destabilize time. The paratext of "Let the Dead" quotes from Hobbes and Bakhtin and Hurston, offering Hurston's famous warning that we are now "going to hear lies above suspicion." The inclusion of these epigraphs frames the story as academic historiography at the same time it warns us against such assumptions. Kain then explains that he has excised "three minor passages" and blames Rev. Greene for the "oddly positioned" intrusions of letters, diaries, and scientific treatises into what is otherwise a transcript of a conversation. The story proper is full of footnotes that reference real books and books not yet written, an incursion of academic discourse into an oral and then literary space. It is a disorienting reading experience. We do not know what is fact and what is fiction or why we are reading such an amalgamation of voices and forms.

The story is too complex to fully relate here, but it is about the founding of Tims Creek, traced to a man called Pharaoh. Pharaoh escaped enslavement and started a colony out beyond the boundaries of the plantation, and his ghost is said to haunt the land. The story of Pharaoh, which ends with a showdown between Pharaoh's spirit and the devil, is told through the oral history given by Rev. Greene's great uncle and aunt, Ezekiel and Ruth Cross. But the story is also about Rebecca Cross, white wife of the plantation owner, her story told through diaries, and her son Phineas, his told through letters. These Crosses had the power of text and writing, but they are texts that could not be part of any institutionalized epistemology. All of these characters have narratives that have been repressed or excised from official history, both written *and* oral: Pharaoh's genealogy and history as a formerly enslaved African, Ezekiel and Ruth's as African Americans who were born during reconstruction and lived through Jim Crow, Rebecca's as a woman in the pre-Civil War south, Phineas as a gay man disowned by his plantation-owning father.

Kenan thus manages to touch on a variety of themes that we have come to expect in self-conscious fiction. The most obvious, perhaps, is the instability of history and its writers. If it had been up to Kain, the letters and diary entries of the Cross family might not have been included. Kain seems to prefer the oral to the written—at least, he prefers the *folk* to be oral. But Kenan chooses to return the inherent polyvocality of historical and ethnographic discourse that was initially absent from the ethnographic project. He reveals silenced voices, and he stresses that silencing is still occurring, as the transcript of the conversation between Ezekiel and Ruth is full of enforced patriarchal silences. Ruth is consistently shushed by Ezekiel and is limited to making short, though subversive, statements. This is a reversal from Kenan's earlier novel *A Visitation of Spirits*, in which Ruth's voice dominates. The reversal emphasizes the masculine nature of public storytelling and highlights the sort of absences that could be found in the work of folklorists. If all we had to go on was the transcript, we would not have the power of Ruth's voice or the knowledge gleaned from the diaries and letters. It is through the intertextual nature of postmodern fiction that the absence created (or, at least, unacknowledged) by the folklorist is revealed.

There are footnotes, though—many, many footnotes. These are inserted by the academic folklorist and the oral historian both, and they disrupt the oral history, often pushing the printed transcript off the page and relegating what we assume to be the primary story to the margins, threatening to displace it. But at the same time, the footnotes insert another crucial narrative, one concerned with a discourse of slavery, colonialism, and diaspora, situating the intimate localized origin story of Tims Creek within a global discourse of migrations both willing and forced. Kenan further places himself in the text by giving the folklorist/editor the initials "RK." By aligning himself with the academic through biography and language, and by linking to his previous novel through Greene and the Crosses, Kenan collapses the distinction between officially sanctioned conduits of knowledge, hidden texts, and folk history. So even though it is true that "by presenting an oral narrative that weaves a variety of forms and genres into its text, Kenan reclaims lost cultures and their contributions" (Wester 2012: 217), instead of that conjunction between oral and written speaking to a more substantial authority of representation, it is used to force the reader to acknowledge the writer's own complicity. That is, the character of the folklorist is one that can be exploited to reference the writer's own concurrent position of authority and fallibility.

At the end of the transcribed oral history, Ezekiel begins to speak about the generation that followed the last appearance of Pharaoh, a man who fought off the devil to finally bring "fire rain[ing] down from the sky just like the Lord sent to the cities of Sodom and Gomorrah." This cleansing, according to Ezekiel, left only two people alive. These two "hung together and started over again over here where we is today," with Elihu, the younger survivor, presumably an ancestor to many in the town (332). Ezekiel stops himself, though, because "that's another story." In *Oral History*, that space may have been left empty, a testament to the inherently incomplete nature of storytelling. But here, the absence is filled—twice. First it is filled by Greene, the oral historian, and Kain, the editor/author. Greene cites Kain's book *Tims Creek Chronicles* in a footnote so that the reader will have the "real" story of Elihu. To further underscore the instability of textual artifacts, the reader should by now understand that *Tims Creek Chronicles* could be the title of Kenan's *Let the Dead Bury the Dead*, as the stories included are either set in or make direct reference to Tims Creek.[2]

The second telling comes from Ruth. In her longest section of dialogue, she finally says "Good Lord, man, ain't you told this boy enough foolishness." She goes on to clarify that Elihu was just a man with a family who moved to town, and she proceeds to offer non-supernatural explanations for all of the strange events and unusual topography in Tims Creek that Ezekiel attributes to various hauntings: from Indian burial grounds to "geo-ology" to shooting stars. "But is sure as the devil wont the Lord destroying devils and dead folk," she says. "And you know it yourself, you old fool" (334). She undercuts not only Ezekiel's story, but the project undertaken by Greene and, subsequently, Kain. Ezekiel can only offer in response, "All I know is what my granddaddy told me, and boy, that was like I told you, word for word, near bout. Near bout" (334). "Near bout" is the last sentence of the story and of the collection, a negotiation of the contract between speaker, writer, folklorist, and reader; between the silent and the spoken, truth and fiction.

That the most metafictional of the stories in Kenan's collection is also the one that includes a folklorist is telling. Kenan, like Naylor and Smith before him, seems to seize on the possibilities for questioning truth and inscription that metafiction provides, recognizing the instability inherent in the collecting of folklore and the difficulty of "representing" anything, including a self or an Other. He challenges a notion embedded within the scholarly discourse of folklore and literature that sometimes inscribes a colonial passivity to writers of color in a way that suggests that writers are simply vessels for the presenta-tion of folk culture, the kind of passivity that can deny the ways in which the oppressed interact with their oppressors, the way that writers *write*. Kenan struggles with the relationship between inscription and the power inherent in inscribing, using the metafictive folklorist as the figure at the center of these negotiations. But where Naylor and Smith seem to implicate the reader, Kenan makes it clear that it is also the writer—whether of fiction or of scholarly texts—who has a stake in the construction of authenticity and the ghosts it creates. Kenan lays bare the ways in which the folkloristic project is, in the end, about the presentation of a text. His story actively resists a touristic reading by confounding expectations of authenticity and by meticulously cataloging the various ways and means of textuality.

Where Naylor and Smith align the folklorist with a particular type of reader, and Kenan with a particular kind of writer, Colson Whitehead makes folklor-ists of us all. And while in *Mama Day*, *Oral History*, and "Let the Dead Bury Their Dead" we get the feeling that there is a complete story somewhere that we simply do not have the means to access, in *John Henry Days* Whitehead seems to suggest that is no such thing, that all stories are absences. And yet, John Henry *as a story* is incredibly present, so much a part of traditional and popular culture that it has becomes a site of meaning-making across time, region, race, gender, and class. *John Henry Days* is simple in its premise but complex in its execution. In the narrative present, we follow J. Sutter, a journal-ist seeking the record for most publicity junkets attended in a single year. He lives off the free food and lodgings such junkets provide as payment for writing short fluff pieces about whatever it is the people in charge want to sell. The novel finds J. in Talcott, West Virginia, in 1996, attending a festival celebrating the unveiling of the John Henry commemorative stamp.

J.'s is the story Whitehead keeps returning to, but his is by no means the only story being told. The novel is made up of short chapters that jump through time and space, dropping in on many people—both historical and fictional—who engage, in one way or another, with the legend of John Henry. There is the young girl sneaking the sheet music of the ballad into her piano lessons against the wishes of her mother, for example, and the old bluesman who records the song but cannot seem to recreate on vinyl the power of his live performance. Paul Robeson makes an appearance, reflecting on his failed attempt to play a racist caricature of John Henry on Broadway. We even get a series of powerful, and realistic, chapters from the point of view of a man named John Henry, who works for the railroads and whose labor is used in horrific ways. To complicate matters further, we learn at the beginning of the novel that a man has opened fire during the festival and that two people are dead. We never learn the identity of the dead men, only that J., at the end of his marathon quest to beat the machine—for him, a seemingly endless parade of publicity junkets—may or may not be one of them.

At first glance, this novel seems decidedly different from *Mama Day, Oral History*, and "Let the Dead Bury Their Dead." And in many ways, it is. In those texts, the folklorist exists only as part of the frame—even in "Let the Dead," which includes an interview transcript, there is no sign of the folklorist outside of the metafictional paratexts of the story. The frame of *John Henry Days* is the man himself. Or rather, the legend of the man himself. The prologue consists entirely of fourteen short descriptions of John Henry, from "he was Jamaican, yellow-complected" to "he was a white man they say;" locating him as a "native of Holly Springs, Mississippi," or "a native of Alabama;" testifying to "the last time I saw John Henry" or proclaiming that "I think this John Henry stuff is just a tale someone started." These descriptions are uncredited and completely decontextualized. Critics have discovered that twelve of the fourteen accounts are taken directly from the work of folklorists Guy Johnson, Louis Chappell, and John H. Cox, but the reader has no way of differentiating between the "real" and the "fictional" descriptions of the man (Collins 2013: 289). The accounts are contradictory, even incoherent, once again revealing the absence that is at the heart of narrative and legend. So instead of the frame being woven around the absence created by the folklorist, here it is predicated on the absence at the core of the *product* of the folklorist: the collection, the text. Whitehead thus "exploits huge discrepancies in folk sources" in order to probe the simulacra that is culture (Ramsay 2007: 780). What we have are infinite iterations of the legend, but no clear pathway by which to access the "real" John Henry. "I can study the legend," says one collector, "but I cannot conceive of the man" (162).

At the same time, Whitehead makes clear that these variants, these distorted copies, are just as real, just as present, as any authenticated truth. The people throughout the novel who engage the legend, whether through singing or writing or marketing, do so with full faith that their John Henry is real or, more importantly, meaningful. Even the festival, with its "bad food, tacky souvenirs, and cheap carnival atmosphere" has its own "powerful meanings" (de Caro 2006: 15). Pamela, the daughter of the man who owned the world's largest trove of John Henry memorabilia, said that her father once told her, "If you can't remember the right words you make up your own to fill in the gaps . . . what you put in those gaps was you." It is by this process that "you've assembled your own John Henry" (373). *John Henry Days* is thus an exploration "not of the actual John Henry, but of the dissemination of the folktale of John Henry," using "the tale of John Henry as a site for the exploration of history as process, rather than as content" (Collins 2013: 290, 289). But more than that, the novel captures the actual work of folklore while implicitly critiquing the nature of folkloristics.

It does so through its fictional folklorist. This character is not pivotal to the novel's plot, nor is he is particularly emotionally compelling. And yet, this folklorist is so present in the text that the ten pages devoted to him (out of the novel's four hundred) are, once again, addressed in most of literary criticism. The folklorist is Guy B. Johnson, historical author of the 1929 book *John Henry: Tracking Down a Negro Legend*. In *John Henry Days*, Johnson has come to Talcott to explore the dissemination of the John Henry ballad, and though he continually reminds himself that "the veracity of the man's existence has no bearing on his mission here," he yearns for "the affirmative, irrefutable proof" that John Henry lived (163, 161). But all he finds are faulty memories, the absence of belief. "John Henry," one informant says, "who's that?" Johnson has a number of motivations for his work, each of which speaks in a fundamental way to the foundations of folkloristics. First, he wants to publish his book, even if it only contributes "one little thing" to the existing scholarship. His desire to publish is driven partly by professional jealousy. He laments Louis Chappell's "better credentials" and thinks with "a bit of envy" of John Harrington Cox, whose subject John Hardy was "without a doubt, a real, breathing person." All Johnson has to go on is "what people can wring from the years, hard-fought drips and drabs" (160). This book will be a way to prove his might as a scholar.

But there is more to his project than a desire for academic recognition. Whitehead's Guy Johnson is black, and he knows that "a Negro in the world of academics must be twice the scholar, and twice the tactician, of his white colleague." He has at times been protected by the "whiteface of scholarly research," but in Talcott in 1920s America, he feels the "grip of Jim Crow, ever clenched around his people" (157). What follows is a record of the troubles he runs into in his search for the elusive John Henry. Doors are slammed in his face, people recant their previous testimonies, and his movement around town is restricted.[3] As he leaves yet another failed interview, he asks, "What's another spade of dirt thrown up on a mountain?" At one point, Johnson says that "some have heard the ballad so many times that they manufacture their own spectatorship" (155). What is clear in this section is that Whitehead's Johnson has not manufactured his own spectatorship of John Henry's battle with the steam engine. He *is* John Henry: the academy is his mountain, his white colleagues the steam engine. He is thus bound, like our other fictional folklorists, to fail.

There are many such John Henrys in the novel. One of Whitehead's primary goals is to expose the exploitation of black male labor in the service of industrial society by returning to the John Henry legend the subversive power that had been stripped from it, in no small part because of the action of folklorists—including the historical Johnson. Johnson was in reality white,[4] and he and Louis Chappell consistently privileged in their scholarship the versions of the ballad they collected from white informants. Their interpretations furthermore revealed a "refusal to acknowledge the aspects of racial protest" that had persisted in the ballad (Fitzwilson 1995: 35). The refashioning of John Henry from a powerful resistance to white supremacy into a "national property, shared by singers and composers, writers artists, listeners and readers" (Dorson 1965: 163) has no better exemplar, Whitehead seems to suggest, than a festival in 1996 in West Virginia filled with funnel cakes and carnival games.[5] Whitehead's Johnson is the vehicle by which the author examines this academic treatment of John Henry, going back to the moment in history when institutions of knowledge were codifying an official version and interpretation of the ballad. He asks, "Who else is there to preserve the body of Negro folklore against the march of time? White folks?" (160).

Thus the fictional Johnson is also motivated by the problems inherent in how other academics were presenting and preserving the ballad. He says of Milton Reed, "Reed takes that tale of John Henry to be the God's truth—it coincides with his romanticization of the Negro, his ascription to the colored people qualities Reed cannot find in his own" (160). Reed "resembled a carnival barker gleefully describing the nether parts of the Hottentot Venus, with his frothy thin lips and wild eyes" (161). And perhaps most importantly, Whitehead's Johnson wants to make known the simple fact that John Henry did not belong to white people. *John Henry Days* exposes the attempts made by those who studied folklore "to mainstream John Henry's legend rather than focusing on the legend's subversive potential as a story of a heroic black man" (Tettenborn 2013: 276). A pointed attack against the ways in which intellectuals, academics, and, yes, folklorists were fetishizing and re-appropriating African

American culture at the turn of the century and beyond, this chapter on Guy Johnson reveals the complicit nature of folkloristics in perpetuating systems of structural inequality.

Yet *John Henry Days* also makes clear what we all believe to be true: folklore itself finds a way. It survives where it is needed, despite the efforts of folklorists to redirect its meaning. Whitehead, incorporating (but not citing) the historical Johnson's own words, reiterates that "the legend itself is in reality a living functioning thing in the folk life of the Negro" (Johnson 1929: 54; Whitehead 161). This is perhaps the central paradox at the heart of *John Henry Days*. As Peter Collins argues, "History is epistemologically uncertain, multiple, and hence a subjective construct open to interpretation," while at the same time it "has an existence outside of interpretive frameworks, a reality that continues to hold sway over people and that is dangerous to ignore." Folklore is what Whitehead uses to mediate this contradiction (Collins 2013: 289). And it happens in spite of, rather than because of, the folklorist, who is but one of the myriad agents of epistemological violence to appear throughout the novel. Through J., we see the end result of this violence, a man who has been interpolated into a system that refuses the lived experiences of people in favor of the hyperreality of signs: junkets and souvenirs. It is only at the end that J. realizes that the reason Big Bend Tunnel, the place in West Virginia where John Henry met his end, has not been walled up is because "they need something from it. Need their ghosts" (321). He realizes that he, too, is John Henry.

CONCLUSION: THE FOOTPRINTS OF GHOSTS

Ghosts are everywhere in *John Henry Days*—the ghosts of lives lived, of lives *not* lived, of history, of labor. It is a haunted text, as the mountain will forever be "alive with the ghosts of men" (107). But there is also an *actual* ghost. John Henry haunts the Talcott Motor Lodge, and only Josie, the proprietor's wife, can sense him. On this particular weekend, John Henry's ghost is haunting the rooms of both J. and Alphonse Miggs, the man with the gun. This literal ghost, though, is only one of the spirits inhabiting the novel. At the beginning of his stay in Talcott, the folklorist Johnson looks around his cluttered room and overflowing desk, noting that "this is the method of gathering folklore, accumulating, sifting, tracking with ineffectual magnifying glass the footprints of ghosts" (155).[6] If ours is a profession doomed by faulty tools and ephemeral tracks, if this is what they believe we do—track the footprints of ghosts—no wonder all of our fictional folklorists fail. There is no path to victory, because ghosts do not sit still for interviews; the harder we search for them, the less likely they are to be found.

What is it about fictional folklorists, then, and ghosts? *Mama Day* is revealed to be a discussion between Cocoa and her dead husband, George. *Oral History* ends with the second Almarine opening a theme park called Ghostland, appropriating for his own economic gain the haunted voices that come down the mountain. "Let the Dead Bury Their Dead" is animated by the specter of Pharaoh and the return of the town's dead. *John Henry Days* is fully populated by the ghosts not just of its eponymous hero, but of all the people that lost their lives racing to beat the machine. And like in most of the literature of haunting, these literal ghosts function as literary mechanisms for moving about a haunted world, for dealing with the trauma of historical existence, for expressing anxieties about modernity, for reckoning, as sociologist Avery Gordon argues, with the repression of the past in the present (2008: 183). There is a nexus here, between folklorists and absences, between authenticities, ghosts, and textualities. But what meanings arise from their convergence?

It would seem natural to find folklorists in books about ghosts. After all, we are the ones who, in the public imagination, search for quaint, bygone ways of believing. Despite our best efforts, folklore is still perceived as regional, rural, and old. We are the ones who, in a past we can reject but never escape, sought out superstitions that belonged not to "sophisticates" like ourselves, but to "the backward races, as the natives of Australia and our Indian tribes; the European peasant, Southern negroes and farmers, and others out of touch with towns and schools and railroads" (Vance quoted in Bronner 1998: 74). The Enlightenment-driven colonial rhetoric underpinning the early history of folklore studies continues to have a firm grip on the public imagination. And since the golden age of folklore as a discipline has passed, there are simply not enough of us to mitigate the damage done. Even if we *were* more numerous, it would hardly matter. The word "folklore" has a forceful and dynamic currency outside the academy, as it is a word that gets used conversationally every day. Though it began as a disciplinary term, there is no putting that horse back in the barn. The fact that folklorists for many decades were less than enthusiastic about the study of ghost narratives has not kept non-folklorists from assuming they are our professional bread and butter.

I believe there is more to it than that, though. Barbara Walker has argued that belief in the supernatural persists because, in a world of hypervisibility, "The supernatural acts as a balance," allowing a space in which "it becomes comfortable and acceptable to not 'know it all'" (1995: 6). In fiction, the folklorist acts both as an affirmation of the failure of Western institutions of knowledge to ever really "know it all" *and* as a destabilizing element in cultural representation. The ghosts in these novels represent, in part, the continued existence of the unknowable and a challenge to institutional representatives who think that they can understand the complex shapes of a community's narrative or the complex interactions of past and present. Folklorists may think of ourselves as somehow set apart from such institutions of knowledge because we often take as our object of study that which people do in defiance of official structures. But we are not, and these four writers seem to believe that we cannot find the ghosts we seek. Instead, the folklorists unwittingly create the absences into which the ghosts can put their own stories, can speak for themselves. Thus fiction dooms the folklorists to fail, because they keep trying to capture that which is ephemeral, that which moves between past, present, and future in defiance of the physical laws of our corporeal world.

Ultimately, these four writers are questioning the academic provenance of the ways that people know and live. That the folklorist is the character through which they choose to explore this particular type of epistemology, and through which they caution the reader and writer against literary tourism, is something to which we should continually attend. Perhaps one day I will write an essay about the ways in which these writers get our profession wrong: many of us do indeed consistently strive for reflexivity and actively repudiate colonialist ideology, taking seriously the power differentials inherent in any academic research focused on real, living cultures. Many of our essays and books attempt to do what these writers ask us to. And while they rightly demand that we resist a touristic reading of folk culture, it is not always clear that they fully know the academic field of folklore studies.

But maybe that is okay—our frustration about being misrepresented is not as important as the very real problems these fictions address, problems that are often at the root of structural inequalities and oppressions. Because ultimately these are fictions about the writing of fiction, about the constructs that shape how it is we "know" anything at all. They are not about real people, they are not about *us*. Instead, they are about the epistemologies at work in contemporary American society. Thus the folklorist—because of the phantoms of romantic nationalism that haunt our history and continue to drive the public discourse of folklore—is a metonymic signifier of the absence always present in the representation of cultures, able to be manipulated to stand in for the reader, the writer, and the textual artifact. It is a funny line of work indeed, tracking the footprints of ghosts.

NOTES

1. Blyn, in a refreshing change of critical pace, takes to task literary critics, and to some extent Naylor herself, for failing to adequately parse the complicated relationships between cultural relativism, ethnography, and colonialism (2002).

2. Except, of course, for the fact that there are references to one "Randall Kenan" in the footnotes.

3. These incidents in *John Henry Days* are most likely pulled from Johnson's *John Henry*. Here, the historical Johnson recalls, with barely concealed frustration, instances in which informants who had previously discussed John Henry refused to speak with him. For example:

> "John Henry, John Henry," Uncle Beverly said, as if he were speaking to himself. After a moment: "Which John Henry do you want to know about? I've known so many John Henry's [*sic*]."
>
> "I want to know about the one who was a steel driver at Big Bend Tunnel." I explained.
>
> "Big Bend Tunnel—John Henry—Yes, seems like I remember." He paused, and a faint smile cam over his face, as if he were at the point of recalling mothing. But the something wouldn't cross the threshold of his memory. He frowned and added. "No I guess I didn't know anything about that John Henry." (1929: 33).

Johnson, who was white, never overtly entertains the possibility that Beverly Standard, an "old colored gentleman . . . every bit of ninety," and the others who refused to speak to him were doing so because they wanted to keep their version of John Henry away from the white academic in a Jim Crow south. Whitehead, perhaps unintentionally, flips the script.

4. John C. Inscoe suggests that Whitehead replicated an error made by the anthropologist Brett Williams, who also claimed that Guy Johnson was black (2004: 89).

5. See Fitzwilson for a thorough examination of the ways in which folklorists revised the John Henry ballad and legend.

6. This is perhaps a reference by Whitehead to the best-known literary folklorist, Zora Neale Hurston, who famously claimed the "spyglass of anthropology" in order to see herself "like somebody else" ([1935] 2008: 1).

REFERENCES CITED

Arnold, Edwin T. 1984. "An Interview with Lee Smith." *Appalachian Journal* 11(3): 240–54.

Blyn, Robin. 2002. "The Ethnographer's Story: *Mama Day* and the Specter of Relativism." *Twentieth Century Literature* 48(3): 239–63.

Bronner, Simon. 1998. *Following Tradition: Folklore in the Discourse of American Culture.* Logan: Utah State University Press.

Collins, Peter. 2013. "The Ghosts of Economics Past: *John Henry Days* and the Production of History." *African American Review* 46(2/3): 285–300.

DeCaro, Frank. 2006. "'Authentic Local Culture': *John Henry Days* and the Open Textuality of a Folk Tradition." *Folklore Historian* 23: 3–18.

Donlon, Jocelyn Hazelwood. 1995. "Hearing Is Believing: Southern Racial Communities and Strategies of Story-Listening in Gloria Naylor and Lee Smith." *Twentieth Century Literature* 41(1): 16–35.

Dorson, Richard M. 1965. "The Career of 'John Henry.'" *Western Folklore* 24(3): 155–63.

Dundes, A. 2005. Folkloristics in the Twenty-First Century (AFS Invited Presidential Plenary Address, 2004). *Journal of American Folklore* 118(470): 385–408.

Eckard, *Paula* Gallant. 1995. "The Prismatic Past in *Oral History* and *Mama Day*." *MELUS* 20(3): 121–35.

Fitzwilson, Mary Ann. 1995. "With Hammers of Their Own Design: Scholarly Treatment of the John Henry Tradition." *Missouri Folklore Society Journal* 17: 33–54.

Gordon, Avery. 2008. *Ghostly Matters: Haunting and the Sociological Imagination*. Minneapolis: University of Minnesota Press.

Hathaway, Rosemary. 2004. "The Unbearable Weight of Authenticity: Zora Neale Hurston's *Their Eyes Were Watching God* and a Theory of 'Touristic Reading.'" *Journal of American Folklore* 117(464): 168–90.

Hurston, Zora Neale. [1935] 2008. *Mules and Men*. New York: Harper Collins.

Inscoe, John C. 2004. "Race and Remembrance in West Virginia: John Henry for a Post-Modern Age." *Journal of Appalachian Studies* 10(1/2): 85–94.

Jones, Suzanne W. 1987. "City Folks in Hoot Owl Holler: Narrative Strategy in Lee Smith's *Oral History*." *Southern Literary Journal* 20(1): 101–12.

Kenan, Randall. 1992. *Let the Dead Bury Their Dead*. San Diego: Harcourt Brace & Company.

Lamothe, Daphne. 2005. "Gloria Naylor's *Mama Day*: Bridging Roots and Routes." *African American Review* 39(1/2): 155–69.

Naylor, Gloria. [1988] 1993. *Mama Day*. New York: Vintage Contemporaries.

Ramsey, William. 2007. "An End of Southern History: The Down-Home Quests of Toni Morrison and Colson Whitehead." *African American Review* 41(4): 769–85.

Smith, Lee. 1983. *Oral History*. New York: Ballantine.

Tucker, Lindsey. 1994. "Recovering the Conjure Woman: Texts and Contexts in Gloria Naylor's *Mama Day*." *African American Review* 28(2): 173–88.

Taylor, Alan. 1996. "Captain Hendrick Aupaumut: The Dilemmas of an Intercultural Broker." *Ethnohistory* 43(3): 431–57.

Tettenborn, Éva. 2013. "'A Mountain Full of Ghosts': Mourning African American Masculinities in Colson Whitehead's *John Henry Days*." *African American Review* 46(2/3): 271–84.

Wester, Maisha L. 2012. *African American Gothic: Screams from Shadowed Places*. New York: Palgrave Macmillan.

Walker, Barbara. 1995. Introduction. In *Out of the Ordinary: Folklore and the Supernatural*. Logan, UT: Utah State University Press. 1–7.

Whitehead, Colson. 2001. *John Henry Days*. New York: Anchor Books.

The Folklore of Small Things

Willow G. Mullins

Vignettes, John Dorst has argued, "typically appear in marginal spaces" (1989: 120). Some have claimed the same of folklore. The field has often perceived itself as a study of the marginalized, the non-elite, the vernacular. One might think, then, it was also a study of the vignette, of those moments where something illustrative occurs. If the vignette "could be said to mediate between the page itself and the printed text inscribed upon it" (Dorst 1989: 120), we might further say that folklore mediates between the group and the creative expressions of that group.

But Dorst suggests that a vignette offers more than this mediation. It also performs an inversion, where it becomes unclear whether it is the paintings on the wall or the gallery itself, the text or the page, that should be the center of our attention. Similarly, modern folkloristics have taken the elements we study together, such that neither text nor context nor performance leaps to the fore. In this view, from what Dorst calls "the middle distance," folklore and vignettes share much in common. However, while folklorists have tried to show the extraordinariness of the commonplace by highlighting the moment of folkloric immanence, vignettes have tended towards the opposite, the shockingly mundane, the small things. One might wonder what has been missed in the search for those moments of performative excellence. What of the folklore of small things, the folklore that appears in unrecorded moments, just before or after the recorder is on or in spaces where we did not think to record in the first place because we were off the folklorist clock?

It is not that folklorists are unaware of the small things, but despite an attention to the details of everyday life, folklorists have remained relatively slow to study them. Our textbooks reference encoded forms of greetings, claims of knowledge and disclaimers of the same, the moments of community formed in the brief interludes of school pickups and post office lines, the creativity that may lighten the labors of daily life. We have recognized that these mundane genres are important and that they exist, but as a field we have continued to shy away from documenting them.

The difficulty might be one of our own participation within the very social fabric and constructs that we seek to study, what Dorst calls "the inseparability of the objects, instruments, and processes of production from the concrete social relations through which they are enacted and deployed" (1989: 131). If one of the initial problems that folklorists have had with the internet lies in the constructedness of its communities and folk forms, then those groups and art forms that are too close might also fall outside the spectrum of visible scholarship. Perhaps there are times we cannot escape the weight of our own cultural histories and social order enough to see the processes of production, or perhaps there are times we choose not to.

Simultaneously, the difficulty with analyzing such small things might be one of gender. Much of the folklore of the mundane that has been written has been subsumed under the rubric of women's folklore. Claire Farrar in 1975, Margaret Yocom in 1985, and Patricia Sawin in 2002 noted that folklorists have tended to focus more on public spaces, where men are more likely to perform and genres are more likely to be competitive. Turning to specifically women's genres brought the folklorist into the private sphere and in doing so revealed different genres, different concerns, and different narrative strategies. Women's folklore appeared to be more cyclical, more collaborative, and more supportive (Kalcik 1975; Jordan and Kalcik 1985; Yocom 1985). Yet in 2004, Alan Dundes could simultaneously acknowledge the systematic omission and suppression of women's voices and question the validity of feminist theory (2005: 6). It is possible that the lack of a folklore of small things is due to the gendering of such things as feminine.

Yet women's folklore has been documented and studied, even if not given its full due, particularly since the 1970s, and gender would seem only to explain part of the lack. We all have mundane aspects of our lives, and the tactics of adaptation and resistance that get us through them form a common thread, whether our daily lives find us in an office, a playground, or at home. It is important to note the ways such tactics are gendered—men at the suburban playground have different conversations than women—but it is helpful to know what both groups are saying about themselves and each other, and how each is performing their group identities, including gender, through those conversations.

Again, part of the reason for the omission of such small folklore from folklore study might also be definitional, laying in the move from folk text to performance. If we require that folklore be separate from general conversation, something noticeable by its special codes and appeals to tradition, then perhaps we miss those other codes and traditions that are so much a part of how we move through the day as to be unremarkable. It is difficult to put parameters on a text, to even find the text, when the folklore is happening in an amalgam of noncontiguous instants. There are, however, distinct moments of folklore that could be pointed out. If we assume folklore is always happening, how do we know what to look at? It is hard to be prepared for the folklore of small things.

Or perhaps these small things are simply too boring? The difficulty with studying small things may rest in the very mundanity of such folklore that makes it hard to recognize up close. Many can recognize the appearance of such small folklore in retrospect, but it is harder in the moment. James Deetz touches on this problem with his title *In Small Things Forgotten*, claiming that it is the very recovery of the meanings of such small things that is at the heart of historical archaeology (1996: 4). What of those things now? I cannot count the number of stitched samplers I have been shown, each owner proud of the family memento of a bygone era and convinced that their sampler bears value on the open market as a relic of history. The original stitchers most likely made them as a form of homework, however, not a treasure to be handed down. They may have been souvenirs of school days or simply show a distaste for throwing things away. Yet showing off a sampler is little different from showing off a child's phonics worksheet, saved for a century until phonics worksheets appear anachronistic. The bulk of the perceived value of a sampler lies in the object's longevity. The very smallness of the sampler, however, also has value. It shows us that we have replaced instruction in stitching alphabets with instruction in phonics. It shows us how our culture genders education and how that education in turn genders our children. It reveals an individual creative mind at work in the shapes of the letters, the pictures drawn in the margins. The trick, of course, is to see the value in the small things now.

•   •   •

Come in. I'm just making tea [you know that I was not, that I had put the kettle on because I knew you were coming, but upholding the fiction is important, it's Manners, and we'll both play]. Would you like some? The mugs are just up there.

I just got back. The most interesting thing happened at the airport.

[Let me begin by disclaiming my performance.] I'm not much of a knitter, as you know. I only make very small things, but make them I do, all the same.

I brought my knitting to the airport, found a seat among the early morning travelers, and having checked the time to see if I could work instead [look at me, preferring to work I say, marking myself as a certain kind of feminist and a certain class of American], opted to knit.

An older woman wearing a large necklace, who had smiled at me in the way of airport strangers who know that you are about to sit facing them while pretending they aren't really there, commented, "You knit like I do. You throw the yarn. Or did. When I knit." [She was clearly using special codes, referencing knitting styles, appealing to tradition.] Someone snickered. Four women traveled together. They all had children and grandchildren; they were not interested in talking about them. They were headed away for a cruise. They were scattered around me. I had joined their folk group by choosing an empty seat. I smiled back and disclaimed my performance, "I'm not much of a knitter. My mother-in-law knits amazing things." [Let me invoke my community.]

"What are you making? A sweater?"

"A sweater for my daughter."

"How old is she?"

"One and a half."

They let out a collective "aw." I felt well and truly patted on the head. These are formal stylistic devices, I thought, formulae we invoke from one hand-worker to another, one parent to another. Here I am, I thought, a picture of American womanhood in a modern age, knitting a sweater for my daughter from a pattern I found online, my laptop in my bag, invoking the sisterhood and genealogies of the distaff, even though I travel alone—mothering most traditionally from afar. I taught myself to knit from a book, because my grandmother, being left handed, refused to teach me. And here are these women, not knitting, finding me adorable.

"I always liked crochet better. It goes faster," said the one with the large necklace. She looked down the row at her friend, "Did you knit?"

"Lord no! I had a sewing machine," replied the one with dyed black hair and makeup that reminded me of my other grandmother, the non-knitter. As though that were all that needed to be said: you knit or you had a sewing machine. Did a sewing machine preclude knitting? Had the modernity of the machine taken over from the knitting needles? Should folklorists, Cecil Sharp style, hurry to document knitting while it still lasted? The chat groups of Ravelry, the knitting website, suggest the craft is hardly in danger. She continued, "I don't have it anymore." And so began their conversation of sewing machines gone by. Sewing machines they had owned or bought or been given. Singers and Brothers and Whites. Sewing machines their mothers had had and sewn on and tried to cover up the gold paint on because they thought it looked tacky. Sewing machines they universally could not be bothered to care about, but said something all the same, about them or their families or the people who thought they knew them. The women could have been a classical folklorist's dream, talking about their roles as mothers and grandmothers and the things they sewed with their beloved machines.

But they were not. They refused. Their sewing machines were gone. They were not knitting. Their families were not there. They were going on vacation.

The one next to the large necklace, with a cane and a too-big blue bag, commented, "My parents gave me a machine when I graduated from college. I still don't know why. Tools would have been more useful."

"I gave mine to my daughter. Not that she uses it either."

"I sold mine for $20, but the lady didn't want the cabinet. It was a good cabinet with drawers on both sides."

"Mine had a special bobbin. They were hard to get and it skipped a stitch every few inches. I hated that machine."

"You'd think she'd take the cabinet. Use it for an end table if nothing else. The cabinet was more use than the machine."

"Who needs another end table?" I wondered how long it would be before my own needles sat unused for years. Or my own sewing machine. So much for being "folksy," I thought.

•   •   •

Here was a group, certainly, engaging a non-defined genre, a kind of material memorate or maybe a bit of oral history. There was every indication of performances here, by me and by them. Traditions were being called up, evaluated in the harsh halogen lights, and laid down again. We enacted our identities, as mothers and daughters and makers and non-makers in the age of late capitalism and cruises. But there my folklore training began to break down. I had no way to describe and define this conversation as verbal art, but I was certain that it was folklore. I prefer to knit small things—they can be finished in the pieces of time in between. Between getting home and making dinner, while a child brushes their teeth before being tucked in, between waking up and heading to work. They can be made of small bits of yarn, no worry about dye lots or matching or buying enough. This exchange was a folk performance of small things, between here and there, in a momentary community, about the small things of daily life.

As Deetz, speaking historically, and Arundhati Roy (1997), speaking literarily, have said, the folklore of small things is a folklore of resistance and adaptation on a micro scale that is also imbued with larger polities. It is the small things that tip balances, formed by and forming larger social and political constructs. In the folklore of small things, resistance has been well documented, particularly under the rubric of feminist folklore (cf. Radner and Lanser 1993). For Michel de Certeau, drawing his language from military parlance, tactics form resistances—they allow people to survive their daily interactions with power structures (1988: xix). We have documented the stories and works of graffiti artists and women who burn dinners. Resistance disrupts and through its disruption, it becomes visible. The woman at the airport who sold her sewing machine earlier than the others resisted the gendered role of "sewer," and in doing so she created a visible absence in her home. An absence noted by family and friends and able to be filled in other ways, by items more closely attuned to her sense of her own identity (cf. Musello).

Such small things, however, are not always about resistance. They also embody tactics of adaptation. The folklore of adaptation appears in our narratives of making do, in the questions asked of colleagues and neighbors when we move to a new home or a new city. As a group, military and diplomatic spouses are masters of such tactical adaptations. In playgrounds and grocery store lines, "when we lived in . . ." or "do you know . . ." introduces and invites folklore of adaptation. Recently, I followed in awe as the wife of an Air Force pilot about to be relocated to my area tapped into a local school's Facebook group. She used the group's online network to find housing, make friends, figure out which grocery store chains were considered to have the best produce. Her tactics of adaptation extended to finding nearby after school activities and determining which set of clothes, from all of their previous postings, would best suit the climate. Internet communities may have made such folk learning easier and accessible from afar, but it is neither new nor necessarily homely. Letters spanning centuries attest to the persistent need to find good doctors and good meat, housing and schools, jobs and community. Adaptations appear in how we respond to a lack of a refrigerator in the office or knowing what to do when our car breaks down. At the airport, there was adaptation in the repurposing of the sewing machine table, and adaptation was at work as one woman's mother asserted her taste over the gaudiness of the sewing machine. Resistance and adaptation may be woven into the same cloth, as we accommodate to local conditions on the ground, choosing moment by moment what we will adopt, adapt, and reject. And writ through them all are ideas about how and where we work, class, social relations, gender, political movements, and also race and colonialism.

We have folk ways of setting up and keeping our lives that extend not only to the ways in which we move through our days but also in how we structure and enact the tactics of daily life. It is exactly in those small things that much of what makes each of us folk takes place. Without a folklore of small things, I had no way to categorize and describe this profoundly folkloric performance I found myself engaged in while knitting at the airport. Without a folklore of small things, we may lose the unremarkable by which we measure the remarkable; we may lose the remarkable in our everyday lives.

REFERENCES CITED

deCerteau, Michel. 1988. *The Practice of Everyday Life*. Translated by Steven Rendall. Berkeley: University of California Press.

Deetz, James. 1996. *In Small Things Forgotten: An Archaeology of Early American Life*. New York: Anchor Books.

Dorst, John. 1989. *The Written Suburb*. Philadelphia: University of Pennsylvania Press.

Dundes, Alan. 2005. Folkloristics in the Twenty-First Century (AFS Invited Presidential Plenary Address, 2004). *Journal of American Folklore*, 118, no. 470 (Autumn), 385–40.

Farrar, Claire, ed. 1977. *Women and Folklore*. Austin: University of Texas Press.

Jordan, Rosan, and Susan Kalcik, eds. 1985. *Women's Folklore, Women's Culture*. Philadelphia: University of Pennsylvania Press.

Kalčik, Susan. 1975. "'. . . Like Ann's Gynecologist or the Time I Was Almost Raped': Personal Narratives in Women's Rap Groups." *Journal of American Folklore* 88, no. 347: 3–11. doi:10.2307/539181.

Radner, Jo, and Susan Lanser. 1993. *Feminist Messages: Coding in Women's Folk Culture*. Urbana: University of Illinois.

Roy, Arundhati. 1998. *The God of Small Things*. New York: Random House.

Sawin, Patricia E. 2002. "Performance at the Nexus of Gender, Power, and Desire: Reconsidering Bauman's Verbal Art from the Perspective of Gendered Subjectivity as Performance." *Journal of American Folklore* 115, no. 455 : 28–61. doi:10.2307/542078.

Yocom, Margaret, 1985. "Woman to Woman: Fieldwork in the Private Sphere." In Rosan Jordan and Susan Kalcik, eds. *Women's Folklore, Women's Culture*. Philadelphia: University of Pennsylvania Press, 45–53.

The #Landmass between New Orleans and Mobile: Neglect, Race, and the Cost of Invisibility

Shelley Ingram

Right here children, between New Orleans and Mobile . . .
Nothing ever happened to anyone.

On August 27, 2017, the *Seattle Times*, in a now deleted tweet, published a map of the potential path of Hurricane Harvey, a massive storm threatening the Gulf Coast that would eventually bring devastating winds, surge, and rain to the Texas coastline. But one state did not have to worry about Harvey, because according to the map it no longer existed. Mississippi was mislabeled "Alabama," starting a short-lived but potent round of twitter gotcha. The hashtag #PrayForMississippi accompanied re-tweets of the map, humorously suggesting a stealth disaster: while we were all waiting for Harvey, Mississippi had been wiped from the map. #PrayForMississippi provided a moment of levity in what was otherwise a tense and painful week for residents of the United States Gulf Coast. Yet it also served to remind the people of Mississippi, on the twelfth anniversary of Hurricane Katrina's approach and landfall, of their invisibility. After the *Seattle Times* offered a quick apology and a new map, Twitter users responded in kind, with wry comments like "Thank you, Portland!" One user simply said "No worries. . . . apology accepted #Landmass."

The hashtag #Landmass refers to another meme that had made its way through social media almost exactly five years before. On August 26th 2012, while tracking the path of a hurricane named Isaac, a forecaster on the

Weather Channel is reported to have said that Isaac was a threat to "the landmass between New Orleans and Mobile." No video of the event exists, but the founder of a "Landmass" Facebook group writes that "from what I have read, it was a headline in a newspaper that was referring to a comment from TWC [*The Weather Channel*]." Within hours of the alleged gaffe, social media was flooded with mocking, disbelieving, and sometimes angry comments, directed first at the *Weather Channel* and then at larger media outlets and the nation as a whole. The landmass between New Orleans and Mobile actually has a name, you see. It is known to locals as "Mississippi."

Two iterations of the "landmass" meme followed, both built on the core assumption that the Mississippi Gulf Coast was, to the rest of the nation, invisible. The first involved simply replacing the word "Mississippi" with the word "Landmass." For example, there was a picture of a Mississippi beauty pageant winner wearing a sash stitched with the word "Landmass." "Ole Miss" became "Ole Mass." Welcome signs and license plates substituted the new name for the old. An aspiring country singer reworked the words of a popular song to include lyrics like, "No one talks about Mississippi / Ignoring is all they want to do" and "In the Land Mass / Escaping waves and hurricanes fast on the move / Somewhere in between Mobile and New Orleans is / The place that I grew up in / Ain't no one noticing." And my personal favorite, a picture of William Faulkner with a version of the words so often attributed to him (itself a piece of literary folklore): "To understand the world, you must first understand a place like Land Mass."

The second iteration of the meme played with Mississippi's reputation as backwards and uncivilized, revealing the continued impact of H. L. Mencken's assertion that the south was "almost as sterile, artistically, intellectually, culturally, as the Sahara Desert" (1917: 157). A mock-up of the cover of a magazine called "Landmassippi" ran headlines such as "Who Needs Teeth? Poll Results on Page 23," "Shame on Him: Resident Marries Outside His Family," and "Don't Buy This Magazine . . . You Can't Read!" An editorial cartoon showed members of the national media landing on the shores of the landmass in colonial-era boats, exclaiming, "Why there's civilization here after all." And a woman lamented "that awkward moment when The Weather Channel realizes that television and internet do exist in Mississippi." The nerve that "landmass" touched was exposed: in our cultural imagination, Mississippi was a place so full of ignorance and poverty that the rest of the country couldn't be bothered to call it by its name. However, the folklore of the landmass meme cycle, which could easily be neglected or dismissed as an inconsequential bit of fun, is also part of a larger pattern of expressive culture that, when examined, reveals the disturbing systems of oppression—racial, economic, cultural—still at work in the region and, consequently, the nation.

• • •

Finally a story about Mississippi (that land mass between Alabama and Louisiana).
—Kspiers, Amazon.com review of John Patterson Smith's *Hurricane Katrina: The Mississippi Story.*

August 27, 2017. August 26, 2012. August 29, 2005. The reaction of Mississippians to the *Seattle Times* picture in 2017 was really in remembrance of the #Landmass incident of 2012. And the reaction of Mississippians to #Landmass in 2012 was really in remembrance of Hurricane Katrina, a way to retroactively articulate feelings of loss and neglect. By any metric, the landfall of Katrina in 2005 ranks as one of the worst natural disasters in United States history. With a final death toll hovering around 1800 and over a hundred billion dollars' worth of damage done, the images that emerged during this national horror helped define the new century. For those in Mississippi affected by the storm, however, the images—of bodies floating in a clay-colored urban swamp, of a woman (her name is Ethel Freeman) dead in her wheelchair on a city sidewalk, of the unhomely spray-painted Xs marking houses as receptacles for the dead—also served to highlight the absence of representation of their own suffering.

On December 14, 2005, the Mississippi newspaper the *Sun Herald* ran an op-ed piece with the title "Mississippi's Invisible Coast." In it, the author says simply, "In the shadows of the New Orleans story, the Mississippi Coast has become invisible and forgotten" (2005). Four years later, the same writer pointed out that this invisibility had solidified into a "universal" part of the Katrina story, as the people of the Mississippi Gulf Coast "receded into the hazy status of non-people whose story is untold" (2009). Gulf Coast native Natasha Trethewey writes, "I ask [audiences] what they remember when they hear the words *Hurricane Katrina*. Almost all of them say 'New Orleans'. . . . Almost never does anyone answer 'the Mississippi Gulf Coast'"(2010: 2). The #Landmass and #PrayForMississippi meme cycles makes present the invisibility of the region, and their power comes in part from the lingering damage inflicted by the absence of Mississippi from the national narrative of Katrina.

In 2012, I was teaching at Mississippi Gulf Coast Community College. I asked the students in a literature class to come together as a group to produce a creation story for their small corner of the world. This is what they wrote.

When the Earth was young, the first brothers fought so much that they had to be separated. One was given dominion over the land, the other over the sea. The King of the Sea at first was delighted that his kingdom was so much larger than his brother's. He soon realized, though, that his brother, the King of the Land, got to live in the company of people, and he grew increasingly jealous. He wanted the same companionship. This is why every ten years the King of the Sea sends his water onto the shore, commanding the sea to bring him his brother's people so that he will have company too.

People in Mississippi haven't forgotten.

• • •

I was living in Missouri when Katrina made its final landfall. I could only watch in horror as the storm "wobbled" at the last minute, shifting a little eastward and putting my hometown firmly on the "dirty side" of the storm. The distinction, between the good side and the "dirty" side, is important to Mississippi's narrative of itself. Those who have dealt with the threat of hurricanes their whole lives understand that a storm packs its strongest, deadliest punch in its upper-right quadrant. To be to the right of the eye is to be in danger, to be to the left is almost like being in the clear. For the residents of the Mississippi Gulf Coast, without power for days and weeks after landfall, all they knew was that New Orleans was on the "good" side, the clean side, the easy side. With only sporadic access to the stream of media reporting the unfolding catastrophe in New Orleans, residents of the Mississippi Gulf Coast had little framework through which to interpret the national attention on the city. They didn't, couldn't, see what was happening there. They couldn't understand what all the fuss was about.

But would it have mattered if they had been able to see the devastation brought about by the levee and governmental failures in New Orleans? Would it have made their own losses any more bearable? I was able to fly into Gulfport, Mississippi, in November 2005 to visit family for the holidays. The flightpath took us out over the Gulf, where we turned around to approach the city from the south. Following the path of Katrina, then, we were able to see the miles and miles of destruction spread out below us. I do not have words to describe the quality of silence on the plane that day, as we looked out of our windows at a coastline we no longer recognized. Familiar landmarks were gone as the coast was reduced to forty-six million cubic yards of debris (Smith 2012: 36). Cities and homes destroyed, barges deposited on top of hotels, bridges collapsed, tens of thousands of trees either gone or stripped of their bark. And yet, not long after, a friend of a friend in Missouri asked, "Why are they doing fundraising for Katrina in Mississippi? It didn't hit them, do they think we're stupid and will just give them money?"

"That's okay," I could imagine many of the people who live along the Gulf Coast saying, "We don't need your money. We can take care of ourselves."

• • •

James Patterson Smith's *Hurricane Katrina: The Mississippi Story* collects oral histories of Gulf Coast residents. "Here amidst the chaos," he writes, "people often crafted life-saving responses on their own," with "individual ingenuity and local initiative in times of crisis" (2012: 59). It was "individual commitment" and a "willingness to accept personal responsibility" that "powered the businesses and local governments that somehow got back on their feet" (62, 66). While Smith maintains that the citizens, in the end, weren't "small-government ideologues," the rhetoric of self-reliance still dominated everyday conversation, and "we take care of ourselves" was a familiar refrain that I encountered over and over again (192). This response was in part protective, trying to pretend that everything was okay so that everything would, perhaps, *be* okay, even without outside help. They were taking care of themselves and each other, they said, and the evidence was in the apparent lack of violent crime and looting—they said, "That's why we didn't turn into New Orleans."

Indeed, Smith writes, "The common plight of loss and suffering drew people together across religious, socioeconomic, and racial lines" (65). For example, Douglas Brinkley points to five white men, "A couple of them great-great-grandchildren of Confederate soldiers," who risked their lives "for a black family unknown to them" as evidence of racial harmony in the aftermath of the storm (2006: 155). But just as saying that "we don't need the federal government's help" did not stop people from (rightfully) cashing their FEMA checks, saying that the community came together in ways that transcended barriers of race and class does not necessarily make it so. Trethewey, a former Poet Laureate of the United States, tells of her friend Aesha, a black woman evicted from her apartment the week after the storm, made to feel by her landlord's daughter "as if this apartment to which she still had a month's claim was something she was stealing" (2010: 19). Author Jesmyn Ward, winner of two National Book awards and also a Gulf Coast native, tells of how she was forced to ride out the storm in a pick-up truck with five other members of her family—including two elderly relatives and her visibly pregnant sister—because their family home was inundated with water. They tried to take shelter with their white neighbor, but the neighbor refused to let them in (BBC). She incorporates this episode into her novel *Salvage the Bones*, where the family of her young African American protagonist is forced to cling to tree limbs and rafters during Katrina in a fight for their lives.

So which story are we to believe? The one that chronicles a post-racial catastrophic coming together that flies in the face of conventional wisdom about Mississippi? Or the story that recognizes dog-whistle "bootstrap" rhetoric for what it is, the one that cannot so easily divest itself of the "racism and inequality and poverty" that Ward notes still defines the region? The one that cannot ignore the "ongoing experiences of so many poor people whose lives have yet to be rebuilt" (Trethewey 2010: 90)? The one that reminds us instead that "everybody knows about Mississippi goddam" (Simone 1964)?

In the weeks and years after Katrina, I saw the tension between these conflicting, but not mutually exclusive, narratives play out in the anger directed at New Orleans and at the media's fixation on the city. "We're not getting any attention because we're not running around killing each other," I remember one man saying to me, "New Orleans didn't even get hit, not really." His anger was fed in part by the area's invisibility. That invisibility had a real, tangible impact on the region in terms of federal aid and rebuilding commitments. It also helped compound trauma, as a lack of recognition of the suffering of the people of the coast made it more difficult for them to fully come to terms with their loss.

But lurking beneath this understandable resentment was a more insidious belief that *southern white people in pain* were invisible. As simply as I can state it, there was a belief that New Orleans was receiving all of the attention because the victims primarily were black, that it was 'political correctness' run amok. Not that there weren't people of color in pain in Mississippi, not at all, but it is part of the ever-present racism of the region that the experiences of people of color are often erased from dominant southern narratives.[1] My conclusion here is drawn from many conversations—with white acquaintances, with white people in line at the grocery story, with white people taking smoke breaks outside of dentists' offices. That "we came together and took care of ourselves and each other" was so often attached to phrases like "not like what happened in New Orleans," or to words like "handouts" and "violence" and "looting" and "thugs," is a rhetorical move that suggests a thread of white resentment running through the discourse, fueled by a resistance to the narrative of the backwards (white) southerner and an embrace of pervasive anti-black, white supremacist stereotypes about the inherent laziness and criminality of blackness.

I interpreted many of the words said to me, a white woman from the Mississippi Gulf Coast, as part of a "larger institutionalized nostalgic whiteness that celebrates individual achievement and personal responsibility" in contrast to the outspoken words of resistance, interpreted as "complaining," of those who are explicitly working to dismantle systems of oppression (Ryden 2012: 87). This is a rhetoric of individuality and self-reliance that allows "white rage," as Carol Anderson calls it, "to maintain not only the upper hand but also, apparently, the moral high ground" (2016: 4). The residents of the Mississippi Gulf Coast might not have been able to see the horror in New Orleans in the weeks after the storm, but they did hear about Kanye West saying "George Bush doesn't care about black people," they did hear the conversations, uncritically perceived by many of them as "complaining," about the ways in which systemic racism and poverty were at the heart of the city's tragedy. So while stories of local triumph, individual heroism, and communal healing on the Mississippi Gulf Coast were just that, they were also carriers of another narrative informed, consciously or not, by centuries of anti-black ideology and practice.

But the thing is, I can't prove any of this. All I have are hunches, based on an emic, insider perspective colored by decades of living in the area, and on dozens of remembered but unrecorded conversations with the people around me. According to the preface of *Hurricane Katrina: The Mississippi Story*, Smith was asked by the University Press of Mississippi to write the book "lest the Mississippi disaster story be lost." He drew from an archive of 400 oral histories collected from people on the coast, crucial work that is housed in the University of Southern Mississippi's Center for Oral History and Cultural Heritage. These are not *my* collections, though—and oral history is not ethnography. More to the point, I can find no evidence of folklorists going to work in Mississippi in the wake of the storm, or at least, no evidence of folklorists asking big questions about class and race and Katrina's trauma in Mississippi in the wake of the storm.

Groups of people are absent from the national consciousness, and folklorists, too, can succumb to a cultural memory "full of omissions, partial remembering, and purposeful forgetting" (Trethewey 2010: 20). A colleague *in Louisiana* once said to me that she did not realize that Katrina had hit the Mississippi Coast. Take this absence and compound it, over days and years, in the minds of millions of people, and you can imagine the kind of damage such absences can inflict. When we privilege some stories over others because they better fit our disciplinary framework, because they enhance rather than destabilize our received cultural narrative, we lose the opportunity to, in the case of Mississippi's Gulf Coast, give notice to trauma and advocate for healing. Then there is the "us and them" language noted by Trethewey that is often used in discussions of New Orleans (2010: 90). This othering, combined with the rhetoric of self-sufficiency vs. "thuggery," reveals the tenacious grip of Mississippi's (and this country's) structural racism. So we *also* missed a chance to contribute to the study and destabilizing of systems of racial inequality that are upheld in no small part by a white supremacist narrative of self-reliance.

There was and continues to be beautiful work done on the lasting impact of Katrina: by folklorists and anthropologists and historians, by filmmakers and musicians and poets. This work overwhelmingly focuses on people from New Orleans and the surrounding areas.[2] I get it—New Orleans is attractive to culture workers, with its gritty but decadent history, with its music and its food and its dance. The city and its people deserve all of the attention they have received. But we should also admit that New Orleans simply fits folklore's romantic image of itself better than a 76-mile strip of casinos and manmade beaches sometimes called "The Redneck Riviera."

We *know* that we shouldn't have a one-size-fits-all approach to studies of trauma and disaster. The specific set of conditions on the Mississippi Gulf Coast, including its subsequent feelings of invisibility, make for a story that is different from that of New Orleans and Louisiana. And without the kind of sustained fieldwork that takes into account space and performance and context, I ultimately cannot make the argument that I feel in my gut could be true: that the #Landmass meme in 2012, serving as it does as a pivot point between 2005 and 2017, could have a lot to say about racism, poverty, and cultural memory in Mississippi, built as it is on feelings of neglect still festering from Katrina. That it can in fact be read, in hindsight, as a harbinger of the 2016 US presidential election, as evidence of the angry "forgotten" and "invisible" white working class that so many scholars and pundits wrote about in the months leading up to and following to the election. With this meme about *The Weather Channel's* great blunder, the Mississippi Gulf Coast made itself visible, trying to let us know that, despite what the rest of the country may believe, things do, in fact, happen to people on that landmass between New Orleans and Mobile.

NOTES

1. As Gaines Foster, a professor of southern history, once said in a class I took with him while a student at Louisiana State University, "When people talk about 'The South,' they usually mean 'The White South.'" Cf. Thadious Davis, "Reclaiming the South" in *Bridging Southern Cultures* (2005), edited by John Lowe, and the chapter "Real/Black/South" in Scott Romine's *The Real South: Southern Narrative in the Age of Cultural Reproduction* (2008).

2. There are too many to list here. Carl Lindahl's 2006 catalog in *Callalloo* alone discusses fifteen. Instead, I'll list the ones I have read, in no particular order: Patricia Smith *Blood Dazzler* (2008), Chris Rose, *1 Dead in the Attic* (2005), Josh Neufeld, *A.D.: New Orleans After the Deluge* (2009), Tom Piazza, *City of Refuge* (2008), Dan Baum, *Nine Lives* (2009), Douglas Brinkley, *The Great Deluge* (2006), Michael Eric Dyson, *Come Hell or High Water* (2006), Abrahams et. al., *Blues for New Orleans* (2006), Ancelet et al., *Second Line Rescue: Improvised Responses to Katrina and Rita* (2013), Lindahl, "Survivor to Survivor: Katrina Stories from Houston: Recording Katrina: The Survivor Duet" (2006).

REFERENCES CITED

Anderson, Carol. 2016. *White Rage: The Unspoken Truth of Our Racial Divide*. New York: Bloomsbury.

Birmingham News. 2017. "Seattle Times Apologizes for Not Knowing Where Alabama, Mississippi Are Located." AL.com, August 29. http://www.al.com/news/index. ssf/2017/08/ seattle_times_ apologizes_for_n.html.

Brinkley, Douglas. 2006. *The Great Deluge: Hurricane Katrina, New Orleans, and the Mississippi Gulf Coast*. New York: William Morrow.

British Broadcasting Corporation. 2011. "How Hurricane Katrina Shaped Acclaimed Jesmyn Ward Book." BBC.com, December 11. http: //www.bbc.com/news/av/magazine-16296382 /how-hurricane-katrina-shaped-acclaimed-jesmyn-ward-book.

Kspiers. 2012. Amazon.com review of *Hurricane Katrina: The Mississippi Story*, by James Patterson Smith. https: //www.amazon.com/Hurricane-Katrina-James-Patterson-Smith /dp/1617030236.

Lindahl, Carl. 2006. "Publishing Up a Storm: Katrina Book Notes." *Callaloo* 29(4): 1543–48.

MAC (the_ag_fox_1971). 2017. "No worries. . . . .apology accepted #Landmass." pic.twitter. com/ upwW5dvBtb. August 27, 7: 25am. Tweet.

Menken, H. L. [1917] 1977. In *The American Scene: A Reader*, ed. Huntington Cairns, 157–68. New York: Knopf.

Ryden, Wendy. 2012. "The Kitsch of Liberal Whiteness and Bankrupt Discourses of Race." In *Reading, Writing, and the Rhetorics of Whiteness*. Routledge: New York.

Simone, Nina. 1964. "Mississippi Goddam." *Nina Simone in Concert*, Philips.

Smith, James Patterson. 2012. *Hurricane Katrina: The Mississippi Story*. Jackson: University Press of Mississippi.

Strehlow, Andrew (GolferStrehlow). 2017. Thanks Portland! August 26, 8: 54pm. Tweet.

Sun Herald. 2005. Mississippi's Invisible Coast. *Sunherald.com*, December 14. http: //www .sunherald.com/news/local/hurricane-katrina/article36463467.html.

Sun Herald. 2009. Mississippi's STILL Invisible Coast. *Sunherald.com*, September 6.

Trethewey, Natasha. 2010. *Beyond Katrina: A Meditation on the Mississippi Gulf Coast*. Athens and London: University of Georgia Press.

Ward, Jesmyn. 2011. *Salvage the Bones*. New York, Bloomsbury.

FOUR

A Folkloristics of Death: Absence, Sustainability, and Ghosts in the Film *Welcome to Pine Point*

Willow G. Mullins

In graphic design and photography, "memory color" describes the phenomenon of how we remember colors as more vivid and saturated than they were in reality. If we visited Ireland on our vacation, for example, we think of it as greener than it was; the Caribbean more blue. So strong is this belief on our part that Eastman Kodak, who reportedly coined the term, discovered that they had to account for this variation in the processing of their film. Developers had to make our photographs of the places we visited resemble our memories of them. Like nostalgia, or the color sequences from the film *The Wizard of Oz*, memory color makes the past a brighter place. Yet it also makes the past that much more inaccessible, because if we do go back, it will never be or look as good as it does in our memories.

As folklorists, we know this. Dennis Tedlock stands at the head of a long line of scholars who have theorized about the unrepeatability of folkloric events and the futility of our attempts to transcribe them fully before they are gone forever. After all, many cultural products are intended to be fleeting, to be consumed and remembered rather than to endure. Yet there seems to be something in the study of folklore, or perhaps in folklorists themselves, that strives against this kind of obsolescence, naturally occurring or planned—a desire to collect, archive, and preserve. In the last two decades, the conversation in folklore theory has shifted to one of cultural conservation and then cultural sustainability, as efforts have been made to recognize the connection between people and their environment and to root cultural heritage choices in a larger ethical context. All of these conversations, however, are based on the idea that continuance is paramount. But what if the most ethical choice to be made is allowing a community to die? What, in other words, are the ethics of pulling the cultural plug? By our efforts to sustain, do we deny ourselves the potential of memory color—the richness of a past that only exists in memory, the potential of death? Must we as folklorists, like the film developers of Eastman Kodak, make a choice between the vividness of memory and the vivacity of a cultural form, even if it appear more lackluster in the flesh? And must we blind ourselves to the constructedness of those memories, that addition of extra saturated color? As filmmaker Michael Simons asks "Imagine your hometown never changed . . . would it be so bad?"

Welcome to Pine Point is a web-based interactive film, produced by Michael Simons and Paul Shoebridge in 2011 with funding from Canada's National Film Board. Produced by two community outsiders, the film is largely a meditation on memory and the idea of a childhood home. From the perspective of a trained folklorist, the film would seem to offer a perfect introduction to the field: the use of oral history and visual materials to elicit performed narratives about local characters; a clear, geographically situated group; and a community actively maintaining a sense of identity through the conscious continuation of their folklore. From the perspective of a trained folklorist, however, the film also challenges some of the most ingrained assumptions of the field: that folklore *should* be preserved, that groups are organic and natural, and that folklore itself is about cultural presence. I raise these foundational questions not only to probe the assumptions and binaries that the field has inherited but also to suggest ways in which the slippages that occur around the borders, creation, and demise of groups, memories, folklore, and even whole places can themselves be productive, creative, and perhaps even necessary.

ABSENCE MAKES THE HEART GROW FONDER: THE HISTORY OF A COMPANY TOWN NOW GONE

Welcome to Pine Point began as a project on family albums that shifted focus one night when Simons found himself wondering about a town where he had once played hockey as a kid and ran across a website dedicated to its memory. According to its publicity materials, the film "explores the memories of the residents of the former mining community of Pine Point" in the Northwest Territories. Yet in watching it, one feels as though it might be more of a conversation between Simons, the filmmaker, and Richard, one of Pine Point's former residents, as they each attempt to make sense of who they were by visiting the specters of their childhoods. Put together like a scrapbook[1] with individual frames that can be changed by the viewer, the web-based form gives the film a sense of montage, but also of things just out of reach.

Note that the town is former, not the residents. Pine Point was a company town, literally. Cominco mining company built Pine Point in conjunction with the Canadian government to house employees of its nearby lead mine. They set it down complete with schools, shops, and an ice hockey rink in the early 1960s on the site of a tiny, earlier exploration post. At its height, the town boasted a population of roughly 1200 souls. In 1987, the mine closed, following a drop in lead prices, and so did the town. This closure was not a matter of residents shifting to other industries. No other industries existed in Pine Point, nestled between national parklands and Great Slave Lake. While the stark and beautiful landscape could offer tourist potential, Pine Point seemed too remote for any but the most determined escapist and sat amidst hundreds of thousands of hectares of equally stark and beautiful landscape, which did not have the industrial leavings of a lead mine on site. At ninety kilometers from Hay River, population just over 3,500, and seventy kilometers from Fort Resolution, population approximately 500, Pine Point could not become a bedroom community for some other, larger city, as many of the old mill towns of New England and other places have done. Besides, the mine owned the town, and after closing the mine, Cominco liquidated their assets in Pine Point. Buildings and houses were moved, basements bulldozed in. All that remains is the streets and the water tower, and, curiously, a website and a reunion.

As folklorists, we leap to the problematic here—the implications of class struggle, the analogies to homeplaces flooded by the Tennessee Valley Authority and towns dispersed as the result of other political or industrial machinations, the death of a community. We wonder what has been lost with the seeming wholesale murder of a town by a corporate interest, what stories, what local legends, what traditions, however short-lived. Yet *Welcome to Pine Point* suggests an alternative to such despair; as Simons points out, "These people seemed to be holding a decades-long party" (Simons and Shoebridge 2011). Indeed, the film documents a productiveness that follows a death, as if to fill in the hole left by the thing that is now gone that simultaneously references and grows out of that absence. *Welcome to Pine Point* suggests that a town, or anything else, may be more important in its absence than in its continuation—a Derridean specter.

DERRIDA COMES TO PINE POINT: THE POWER OF GHOSTS
AND MEMORY IN RECREATING PINE POINT

Jacques Derrida argues in *The Specters of Marx* that we only understand the present in reference to the past. He probes the idea of mourning as an attempt to "ontologize remains" (1994: 9). For Derrida, in order to mourn we must know that the dead are dead, and further, we must know who those dead were and where they are now. The idea bears out in the particular distress felt by those who must identify victims of tragedy or crime or those for whom the circumstances of death prevent the knowledge of the corpse's whereabouts. The same seems to apply regardless of whether the dead is Hamlet's father and communism, in Derrida's case, or a town and a childhood, in Pine Point's. In the mourning of a childhood, as Simons' superimposed text suggests, we seek an understanding of who we are through an understanding of who we were, and we often seek who we were by returning to the places we used to be. Indeed, the whole impetus for the film came from Simons' own desire to recapture some vaguely remembered experience of his own—living in Yellowknife and once playing a hockey game in Pine Point.

> My family left the North when I was 10. We moved to Regina, and I became . . .
> the guy who didn't look forward to the day things would change, who took it
> hard when they did. (Simons and Shoebridge 2011: "Intro")

Simons seeks to physically locate and people his own past in a similar way to Richard, the central person in the film, who keeps the Pine Point website and legendry alive.

The film highlights four former residents who viewers encounter about halfway through, their pictures set to a quiet cacophony of voices. They appear first as yearbook style archetypes, seen through their high school personae: "The Beauty," "The Brothers," and "The Bully." These flattened images, however, are quickly complicated. The Beauty, Kim, went from small town night club cover artist to social worker. We learn that the two brothers, Wayne and Lyle, had a third, who died and is buried in the town. Most strangely, the Bully, Richard, developed severe multiple sclerosis and now must use a wheelchair. He maintains a website dedicated to the town's memory—its most enduring and determined booster, "the protector" as Simons calls him. Each of these residents acknowledges their own nostalgia for the town, but crucially, they also acknowledge the ability of the town to bear the weight of that nostalgia *because* their memories can never be challenged. For Kim, in particular, Simons notes that the town "became the kind of hometown we see in movies, the place she could leave behind, make her triumphant return to, aspire away from" (Simons and Shoebridge 2011: "Shelf Life"). What the death of the town offers, then, in part, is the potential for memories, which Simons refers to as "specific and vague. Visceral and unreliable. Truth and fiction" (Simons and Shoebridge 2011: "Cosmos 954"), to become stories and specters, a kind of narrative memory color. And in turn, these stories can become legends.

Richard exemplifies this process. We hear several of his stories throughout the film, about fights he won, a toothpick he grabbed out of the air, a day working in the mine after high school when he shoveled so fast steam came off of him, a re-imagined John Henry (Simons and Shoebridge 2011: "Cosmos 954" and "Here to Work"). While it might be easy to dismiss these stories as the grandiose inventions of a man living in his own overwrought glory days, it might also deny the power of that past to act, to be a Derridean ghost. As such, the past may not be Truth with a capital T, singular and undeniable, but it may become story, with all the power that we, as folklorists, know story to possess (cf. Lawless 2001; Shuman 2005). After all, what is a legend if not a story that someone believes could be true?

In a definition that bears close resemblance to memory color and to the process described above, Derrida describes this kind of phantasmic embodiment of the past as a specter. For Derrida, the specter is "virtually more actual than . . . a living presence" (1994: 13). As a specter, the past has a particular hold over the present, which becomes a kind of haunting when the past ceases to exist. Derrida gives the example of the Berlin Wall. For him, communism becomes more relevant following the fall of the Wall, because it is at that moment that the idea of communism becomes a specter, semantically unmoored and thus free to be an object of nostalgia. Indeed, this idea is borne out by the recent surge of what Germans call Ostalgie—nostalgia for the material artifacts of East Germany. Thus, the past's being past frees up people, events, perhaps whole towns to be used as symbols (1994: 32). Simons captures this process, from event to symbol to legend through narrativization, well:

> From the moment an event occurs, it is simplified and purified in memory. We shave off the rough edges and what happened becomes a story or even, over time, a legend. If we're not careful, though, we grind it down to raw superlatives, with none of the banalities or complications that make truth feel true. (Simons and Shoebridge 2011: "Here to Work")

The slippage of death, from being to not being, offers space for creative narration to take place. Kim can only become "The Beauty," an archetype of Western high school culture across North America, once everyone has left high school.

Haunting implies, for Derrida, a kind of waiting or desire for a (lost) embodiment (1994: 4) that seems remarkably literal in the case of *Welcome to Pine Point*. Here, a town that no longer physically is becomes newly embodied through a website and then film memorializing it—virtual ghosts of a physical place. The creator of that website, Richard, who once prided himself on his very physicality, now identifies himself through that virtual world. Richard's narrative of catching a spinning toothpick out of the air can achieve the qualities of legend only when no one is left with a vested interest in calling his bluff. Richard, haunted by specters of himself, seems to relocate himself to the disembodied past when body and town were whole.

EDITING OUR STORIES: IMMANENCE AND EMERGENCE
IN NARRATIONS OF THE PAST

Nonetheless, as Simons points out, the stories that emerge from death must still conform enough to some semblance of past accepted truths to be recognizable. The specter is a thing that comes *into* being following death, persistently repeating the past but always for the first time (Derrida 1994: 10). Playing on the homonym "ontology," Derrida's hauntology, which seeks to describe the specter, seems to encapsulate Barre Toelken's Twin Laws of Folklore (1996: 39–40). If folklore must be both conservative and dynamic, recognizable as a specific folkloric text or performance and yet still able to change to suit the context of its telling, the specter similarly must refer to the original. Hamlet must recognize the ghost as his father, and it must also be original itself, the ghost coming for the first time rather than the father (Derrida 1994: 10). Both specter and folklore are emergent, symbolically not entirely tethered but not totally free to be manipulated either.

As specters, the past can, in fact, become what John Miles Foley referred to as *immanent art*, "indexes of more-than-literal meaning." For Foley, immanent art described how folklore, oral poetry in particular, relied on a "communicative economy," a kind of register that both poets and audiences of a specific culture understand and know so that a performance can take place without additional explanations having to be meted out. Following death, such communicative economy can slip into place, acting not only as a kind of metonymy but also as a move from sign to symbol. "Pine Point" becomes a shorthand not just for the specific childhoods of Richard, Kim, Wayne, and Lyle, but also for Childhood as a concept or for the perfect Small Town. Thus, the specter contains a kind of uncanny doubling (Derrida 1994: 7), as it "encodes traditional meanings" (Foley 2001: 109) like immanent art and inscribes them onto actual things that are no longer, suggesting less what was as what might have been. As Simons points out, "In Richard's memories, he's the undefeated champ" (Simons and Shoebridge 2011: "Cosmos 954"). Richard's story illustrates the uncanny as a return to the self—he cannot rid himself of these ghosts, because they are how he knows himself.

The death of the town allowed the residents a control over their own stories that few of us have. Simons comments on Richard's exaggerations, "I suppose we all want a chance to edit our story, keep the best stuff on top, bury the rest, decide how we'll be remembered by others." While others may have contrasting memories, Kim remains wary of Richard; the inability to return leaves out the possibility of the disappointment of discovering our edited past, our past in memory color, to be untrue. Simons drives home this point in the slide following Richard's story of his day at the mine, asking "And who are you to judge?" Who indeed? We don't know if this is Richard's question or Simons,' nor do we know if it refers to Richard's story, to Richard himself, or to all of the Pine Pointers' investment in their former town. But after all, we weren't there. Who are we to judge?

This is not to say that death is preferable or that nostalgia is not at work. Many Pine Pointers would likely have preferred their town to continue, and both the former residents and Simons have an investment in their nostalgia. Our instincts as folklorists deeply concerned with issues of community do not lead us entirely astray here. The closure of Pine Point *was* difficult for its residents—the government documented increased depression, family break-up, alcohol and drug abuse. The residents received letters that their town would be removed from maps. The mining company produced a video called "Memories of Pine Point" in response (Simons and Shoebridge 2011: "What's Weird"). Make no mistake, death might bring forth new life, but it typically is not an easy process. How does anyone "comprehend the discourse of the end," as Derrida asks (1994: 10). He might be asking how we discuss our own deaths. Perhaps we do so by making that discourse folkloric.

If death can turn memory into legend, it may well generate a genre of its own: stories of what has been, not simply in the nostalgic sense but in a larger memorial way. After all, you can't have the wake, the praise poem, or the lament until the person is gone. Certainly, Pine Point's demise has produced its own folklore. Simons makes a joke out of the number of people who claim to have been the last person to drink a beer in the town bar (Simons and Shoebridge 2011: "What's Weird"). These claims of being "the last" are profoundly tied to ideas of group status. As a culture, such lasts are the bittersweet companion of firsts. To have attended the first year of an event shows a certain stylishness, a sense of being "in" from the start, avant-garde, and thus somehow more of

ABSENCE, SUSTAINABILITY, AND GHOSTS IN *WELCOME TO PINE POINT*

a group member than the average group member. To be there at the end, the last, curiously proves the same point—the last one standing is the most loyal, the epitome of the group. Yet, that idea of group and its structuralist roots lie at the heart of what might trouble folklorists about the story of Pine Point. If the town ceases to exist, what happens to the folk group "Pine Pointers?"

PINE POINTERS, GROUP, AND THE BETRAYAL OF THE STRUCTURALISM

Pine Pointers, as a group in the way we have traditionally thought of it in folkloristics, might seem destined for extinction along with their town. While Alan Dundes defined the folk as "any group of people whatsoever who share at least one common factor" (1965: 2), in practice, we have tended to understand group as locally situated, rooted in a specific place. Ethnic enclaves seem a more natural place for fieldwork than suburbs, family farms and businesses rather than large corporations, the oral and its requisite physical closeness over the written's ability to travel. Certainly, good work has been done in all of these venues and with groups, networks, and communities of wide reaching and ever changing configurations. However, the pages of our journals and texts suggest a constant return to the idea of group as local, organic, and natural. As Katherine Roberts wrote in her essay on land management in West Virginia, "Staying put is an implicit condition in many of the communities that attract the attention of folklorists" (2013: 407).

The connection of the idea of a folk group to a specific place and the importance of group as a marker of folklore carries a long history, and one that has received its fair share of scrutiny. Johann von Herder's interest in folklore, after all, was driven in part by an attempt to uncover how national identity could be found in the folklore of its people (Wilson 1973: 820). This connection has shown profound tenacity into the twenty-first century in spite of critique, notably by Amy Shuman (1993) and Dorothy Noyes (1995). Specifically, Noyes acknowledged that the group as local and natural has become a "habit" within the field (1995: 472).

Indeed, this connection of group to ground would seem to be an article of the "settled law" of folklore theory that Bill Ivey referred to in his 2007 AFS presidential address and has formed the center of many recent debates about folklore and the internet. Ivey's comments sum up both the necessity to reevalute the idea of group as naturalized and the unease with which many folklorists face how technology has changed our world if not our worldview:

> Of course we, as folklorists, study the Internet, and virtual communities, and the ways in which human beings take new devices and make them part of our

impulse to traditionalize. But we know, deep down, that these virtual communities—the nights spent staring at a screen navigating YouTube, MySpace, or SecondLife—are not the same, and not even decent substitutes for, the kind of communities where neighbors and families see and talk to one another. (2007)

That online groups are not "the same" as those rooted in place seems to go without saying, but to say that they are "not even decent substitutes" is a damning judgment. Indeed, in following some of the discussions about the validity and strength of such virtual communities on Publore, a listserv dedicated to the discussion of public sector folklore with a large and varied membership and itself ironically a virtual community, the language used about virtual as opposed to face to face communication profoundly replicates the language used to distinguish high art from low art. The very same language that folklorists have long sought to dismantle. But what holds for ideas about skill, craft, and even authenticity and tradition, does not seem to apply to our ideas about group. Those who study YouTube and Facebook and the folklore of the internet have disagreed, sometimes strenuously (cf. Dorst 1990; Howard 2008; Blank 2009).

For Pine Pointers, this hierarchy of the local over the virtual may be even more troubling, however, for it has real ramifications. For them, to suggest that a group must be rooted in place simultaneously lends credibility to their claims of group status in the past while dismantling them in the present and preemptively negating them in the future. What binds them together as a group is that they all came from the same place; what continues to bind them together is that *that place is no more.* Then, to be a member of the folk group of Pine Point residents was an accident of employment or love or birth. Now, it is a conscious act of commemoration, nostalgia, and identity maintenance. After all, much of Simons' philosophical rumination in the film centers on the idea that we, as adults, are made out of the stuff of our childhood communities, an idea folklorists would likely heartily support. So, why has the field of folklore traditionally preferred groups of circumstance over groups of choice? What is it that bothers some folklorists so very much about these groups that lack a place?

A simple answer may be that because online groups transcend time and place, they seem to take away from more traditional groups that are time and place dependent. As George Lipsitz argues:

Instead of relating to the past through a shared sense of place or ancestry, consumers of electronic mass media can experience a common heritage with people they have never seen; they can acquire memories of a past to which they have no geographic or biological connection. This capacity of electronic mass communication to transcend time and space creates instability by disconnecting people from past traditions, but it also liberates people by making the past less determinate of experiences in the present. (2001: 5)

Such thinking, however, assumes that we interact online in the same way as we do face to face, that people use these two types of interactions for the same reasons, to do the same things, and thus that one form of communication must replace the other. In other words, if one communicative form rises, another falls, an idea somewhat disproven by the advent of other technologies in other eras. While Lipsitz sees the potential benefits of such online groups because of their lack of time and place, he seems to ultimately agree with Ivey that they are *"different"* and that we must choose one or the other as our basis for what constitutes a folk group.

But are the groups different, or is it the way that they perform their folklore that has changed? Pine Pointers remain Pine Pointers, even if they no longer live in Pine Point and have also become Vancouverites or Yellowknifers. Many of the cues of performance derived from oral folklore seem to be missing, and the quantitative and qualitative markers that folklorists have noted, regardless of their focus on text or context, do not appear where we might expect them, if they appear at all. Rosemary Hathaway describes this problem well.

Electronic folklore exchange is seemingly complicated by a lack of contextual elements that can help mediate meaning: recipients cannot rely on nonverbal, visual, or auditory cues to help assess the message's intent. (2005: 36)

Because the cues of performance shift, folklorists cannot necessarily evaluate online folkloric performance the same way that we evaluate face-to-face folkloric performance. And to rephrase Roger Abrahams' definition of group, if a folk group does not seem to have folklore, then perhaps they are not a folk group. But we do recognize that much of what happens online does look and act a lot like folklore, even if the communities themselves seem less stable. Online groups feel notoriously slippery. People come and go, sometimes the same people in multiple personae. Sometimes they appear once and leave forever. Yet, as Bruce Mason argues, "Users create their own locales" (quoted in Hathaway 2005: 35), what Hathaway calls "frameworks" (2005: 36). Few would question that Pine Pointers share a framework, a homeplace, a locale, both real and virtual. The question is whether folkloristic theory can stretch to include them as a group, regardless of how and where they perform their folklore.

This adherence to the concept of the physical locality of the group is likely a moot point. Increasingly, student folklorists seem not to question the validity of online communities and newer texts in the field take the idea of online folklore as a new "settled law," to be questioned again in its time. For them, these communities have always existed, and they engage with them differently but no less strongly than with their local peers. If anything, they seem to feel, like the Pine Pointers, more commonality and more connection with these online folk groups, because they have chosen them based on shared interests and beliefs. If the virtual horse has left the stable, then the tension exists not for the groups, localized or ethereal, but for the folklorists trying to apply ideas developed to fit one paradigm of a communicative world to a radically changed environment. I am reminded of my great grandmother marveling in 1984 that, in the course of her lifetime, women went from being unable to vote to being able to run for vice president of the United States. She commented that the world no longer fit her ability to conceptualize it.

The structuralist heart of the discipline, inherited from our mid-twentieth-century scholarly ancestors and with wider reach than is generally given credit, anticipates the group to be bounded, organic, and relatively clear. Regardless of how folklorists have sought to redefine it, from community to group to network, there remains an implication that a group either exists or does not, that one is either in or out. The both/and state of the Pine Pointers, however, may present one of the most fundamental difficulties with the idea of group as it has been expressed in folklore, because the group represents a seemingly naturalistic binary, a binary that makes structuralist sense. Structuralism studies cultural practices and signs in search of deep structures that stand more or less firm. This approach allows the critic or scholar to sit outside of the system, however, "reading" the signs and divining their meaning. Thus, structuralism creates a series of binaries: signifier/signified, signs/system, culture/critic. The history of folklore as a discipline reveals a desire for exactly such binaries as the field sought to institutionalize itself, at the same time that structuralism was at its zenith in the academy, through careful designations of folk versus mass, folklore versus fakelore (cf. Zumwalt 1988; Bendix 1997; Bronner 1986). These clear markers helped define the field, establish it alongside anthropology and sociology as a critical social science. More than a tool for claiming academic legitimacy, however, the markers also worked to some extent within the science-minded paradigm of the day and remain able to reveal social constructs with particular acuity.

The binaries of structuralism chafe in the face of the multiplicity of lived experience, however, and seem to crumble when confronted with a profoundly post-structuralist situation like Pine Point. For one thing, as Amy Shuman points out regarding the naturalization of the concept of "local culture" (1993: 345), such binaries can ultimately end up essentializing both the people and the category itself, Pine Pointers and the idea of them as a community. As

John Dorst has argued, "as productive and compelling as this critical strategy usually is, its rhetoric preserves a utopian conception of the vernacular (or folk) sphere that can blind us to important aspects of the relatively new conditions of cultural production" (1990: 188). Dorst suggests that the problem lies in the rhetoric of the discipline itself, which, twenty-five years after Dorst's writing, has still not found adequate language to describe the complexities of the cultural constructs that fail to fit the binary, even as the discursive divide between the vernacular and the mass or elite seems to break down. For another, it simply cannot describe a ghost. In the face of a group predicated on a past event, the concept of group turns in on itself and is left mute. If the question is to be or not to be, there remains no place for was.

Our binaries break down both chronologically and environmentally. Folklorists' unease with mediated cultures like those of the internet or Pine Point may also be found in the seeming newness of such virtual groups—we can still see their origins, the trees have yet to grow up and the paint is still wet. Indeed, the trees are not really there at all. The group can no longer be seen as organic, because its construction is apparent. Roland Barthes defines a myth, not as an origin story as in folklore, but as a second-order sign, a sign that has lost the constructedness of its origins (1972: 115). If we agree with the semioticians that all signs are cultural constructs that have largely become naturalized in our minds, then the idea of a sign that has not yet completed that process can be destabilizing. "New traditions" feel ersatz; and "the first annual" like a well-meant pretense (cf. Hobsbawm and Ranger 1983). We have tended to believe our communities to be old, their origins obscured in a distant past, even when we can see the founding date on the town sign. This belief is belied by our own national history, though. Is the emphasis on place-based community then a kind of nostalgia, particularly poignant among a field of scholars who highly value such groups but who readily move for their own careers, who are often themselves displaced? There is either irony or hypocrisy in the tendency of folklorists to physically uproot while insisting those we study and work with remain still; it places folklorists perilously close to claiming their own group's status as "not folk," even while we claim that everyone has folklore. Yet while the newer towns of America have matured over the years, gaining the sediment of history, online communities can only have existed within the last decade or so. They have not yet accrued the weight of obligatory membership; they have not yet obscured their origins, and it remains unclear to what extent they will.

This anxiety also haunts the story of Pine Point. One generation only can call it home. It was a town for less than thirty years, not long enough for large trees to grow or grandchildren to be born. We know the town's birth and death intimately, and the constructedness of the idea of "town" is laid bare for all to see. The film posits the question of how long it takes for a community to form, especially in the kind of rarified, aseptic way that a planned town such as Pine Point had to, as Simons calls it, "a social experiment called 'The Creation of Hometown Memories'":

> After the infrastructure is built and the systems put in place, people move in, go to work, go to school, become best friends, get married, have children, hold funerals.
>
> That planned town becomes a community.
>
> Q. How long does a town have to be around before you make a souvenir spoon with its name on it?
>
> A. Longer than it takes for people to make the spoon rack, apparently. (Simons and Shoebridge 2011: "Ends and Odds")

It turns out—not long. People create communities on the spur of the moment, as festivals amply demonstrate and the internet reiterates every instant. Now, to be a member of that group requires an active allocation of time and interest. That commitment is exemplified by Richard, who painstakingly maintains the Pine Point Revisited website using a voice prompt system. But it also exists among those who attend the almost yearly reunions, some 400 people in 2012.

By some definitions of group, then, Pine Pointers would unquestionably be a folk group. They speak the same language, hold shared experiences and lore. Yet as a group, they are geographically dispersed, even if they once were not, their text exists only in their current memory, and the context of performance now remains only in the occasional reunion. If we view them from traditionally folkloristic perspectives, where do they stand now? Are they a group that has died or is destined to? How do we catalogue their current activities? They seem to have no doubt as to their group status, so the question lies with the folklorists. It is our taxonomy that is in question, not theirs.

But the group itself also now has no way to regenerate, even while their discourse is constantly regenerative. The folklore recreates Pine Pointers anew and proliferates. As folklorists, we should be especially interested in this kind of inversion, a group created and maintained by their folklore. If the folk group, in a structuralist sense, creates folklore and folklife, then the "proper not," to use Susan Stewart's term, of that group may be exemplified by the post-structuralist Pine Pointers. The proper not names the appropriate opposite of a thing, where "every significant feature is inverted" (Stewart 1978: 63). Thus, to repeat Stewart's example, the proper not of "not floor" cannot be "chair" but must be "ceiling." Stewart uses this idea to describe the trickster, who not only breaks taboos but also questions the very inviolateness of taboo itself (1978: 62). Pine Pointers, in their reversal of the more typically documented relationship where living folk group creates folklore, similarly breaks down the organic, localized, and binary construction of group. They can both be and not be, anachronistically, just as Derrida's specter. For Pine Pointers, this ghost state seems especially appropriate, and one curiously marked not by sadness but by joy and creativity. Their town no longer exists on official maps, but Google will still tell you its location. *Was* exactly describes Pine Point as a town, even though Pine Pointers may still exist and *be*. We are left with the question of "for how long?"

FOLKLORE ON LIFE SUPPORT: FOLKLIFE, CULTURAL CONSERVATION, AND THE RHETORIC OF DEATH

The problem for Pine Pointers as a group is one not just of cultural conservation but of cultural continuation. Does "folklife," in some or any of its forms, have a natural lifespan? If so, how do we know, especially as cultural outsiders, when that lifespan is up? This problem of group identities, and how and by whom they may be constituted and articulated, has real ramifications, for it overlaps questions of whether and how a folk group continues to exist. It reveals a conceit in the field of folklore that requires what we study to be "alive," even if only feebly so.

We seem, as a field, to have an unwritten mandate to be conservers of culture, posited as a living entity, which poses particular problems in the case of a place and community like Pine Point. For one thing, they seem to be doing an admirable job of conserving their own culture, insomuch as they feel a need to. For another, as Gertrude Stein wrote disparagingly of Oakland but can be applied quite literally to Pine Point, "There is no there there." If folklore remains predicated on the local, even as the field critiques that idea, then no place implies no folklore. So much for Pine Point. It was good to have known you. If Pine Point is a former folklore site, and perhaps a site of former folklore, how do we folklorists reconcile our desires for folklore to be local with our equally strong desires to conserve folklore—for the folklife to be alive? To look at many of the products of the field suggests that cultural conservation lies at the heart of the discipline, from the Smithsonian Festival of American Folklife to the mission statements of state arts agencies to the language of many of the articles and texts predominantly used by folklorists public and academic. The words "preservation" or "conservation" appear 634 times in the *Journal of American Folklore*, according to a simple database search. Perhaps it is written after all. The intertwining of a desire to preserve and a desire for the local appears at the birth of American folklore studies, features of the newborn, academic babe.

In the inaugural issue of the *Journal of American Folklore*, William Newell sets out the first purpose of the American Folklore Society and its journal as "the collection of the fast-vanishing remains of Folk-Lore in America" (1888: 3). Lest his readers, those early scholars marking the margins of their emergent field, miss that their work must necessarily be preservationist, Newell belabors the point in the pages that follow. On the subject of English lore, he claims, "It is certain that up to a recent date, abundant and interesting collections could everywhere have been made." (1888: 3). Now, it is too late. Ballads, we are told, still may be found in pockets; nursery tales are on their way out (1888: 4). His discussion of the death of Native American culture in the face of civilization may be more alarmist and more familiar:

> A great change is about to take place in the condition of the Indian tribes, and what is to be done must be done quickly. For the sake of the Indians themselves, it is necessary that they should be allowed opportunities for civilization; for our sake and for the future, it is desirable that a complete history should remain of what they have been, since their picturesque and wonderful life will soon be absorbed and lost in the uniformity of the modern world. (1888: 6)

Newell's views on Native Americans, their need for "civilization" and their picturesque cultures, may seem outdated, but the call to arms—record now, cultures are under threat, before we are all the same—bears striking similarities to current discussions about the problematic influences of modern media.

Cultural conservation arose in response to a specific set of problems and contexts: a bureaucratic division between nature, the built environment, and folklife stemming from 1970s legislation aimed at supporting and protecting each, and the pragmatic difficulties of actually separating these three complexly interwoven areas in conservation practice when it came to the practicalities of jurisdiction and grant funding applications (Hufford 1994: 2). Thus, cultural conservation attempted several interlocking actions. It brought together professionals from across a range of disciplines and venues to combine efforts at the nexus of these three protected areas. These professionals then pursued interventions that aimed to include the people whose communities pivoted on, generated, or were otherwise invested in the thing, tangible or intangible, being conserved. Through these joint interventions, both groups, from the institution and the community, hoped to benefit. Hufford puts it more succinctly: "The term, *cultural conservation*, then, applies to advocacy that is ethnographic rather than ethnocentric" (1994: 4).

This idea of conservation shortly followed the rise of the term "folklife" itself to describe what it is folklorists study and was seen at the time as more inclusive than the linguistically oriented "folklore." Conservation, marked by dynamism in contrast to the more static preservation, has had profound effects in the field, as it has come to be part of the driving mission of groups representing folklife at all levels, most notably and iconically the Smithsonian's Folklife Festival. While the Folklife Festival's statement on its publicity materials specifies that "contemporary living cultural traditions" will be presented, the idea of conservation and revitalization runs through the narratives surrounding the festival, most notably here:

> The Festival has strong impacts on policies, scholarship, and folks "back home."
> ... In many cases, the Festival has energized local and regional tradition bearers and their communities and, thus, helped to conserve and create cultural resources. (2014: "Mission and History")

Cultural conservation for the Folklife Festival, then, becomes predicated on a narrative that suggests that if we, predominantly outsiders, represent a cultural form now on a large stage, then those who are most closely culturally associated with the form, presumably insiders, will recognize or re-recognize its value and "save" it, thereby keeping the folklife alive.

While the idea that "saving it" is a major impetus for programs like the Festival may seem secondary here, the metaphor of culture as living being on the verge of death and in need of life support has unfortunate implications for the ghostly Pine Point. If we look to Richard Kurin, the former director of the Center for Folklife and Cultural Heritage, which stages the Folklife Festival, the language of dying cultures in need of intervention moves to the fore:

> There is no one to teach [a cultural form], to transmit its vision of the world, the knowledge and wisdom reposed within, the skills of the generations of people who labored in its bounds. This loss extends beyond the present, for we never know how valuable would have been the contribution of that culture to a larger human future. (1989: 11–12)

Leaving aside the fetishism implied in looking for lost cultures and endowing them with particular wisdom, the narrative of folklorist as interventionist at the deathbed of culture remains almost unchanged from Newell. Robert Cantwell and Patricia Wells both suggest the Faustian bargain here—in order for a cultural form to be conserved, or for a community to get assistance in their own attempts at conservation, they must also be willing to offer up that form for representation, consumption, and commodification to the general public (1991: 149; 2005: 5). Yet for Pine Point, the larger problem is that such a configuration of culture would leave Pine Pointers in a bind. Do they still represent a "living cultural tradition?" And if we say that they do, what constitutes "back home?"

At least some of the difficulty for a group like Pine Pointers lies in that their narrative has always been seemingly at odds with the common (perhaps stereotypical) narratives of a field like folklore, narratives that privilege the organic over the industrial, the folk over the masses, and, indeed, the living over the dead. Cantwell paraphrases Kurin as blaming "industrialism, colonialism, commerce, communication, and the like" for the demise of folk culture (1991: 150)—a popular narrative in folklore discourse, just as it is in mainstream society. Ivey's comments about the difference between internet groups and face-to-face groups sums up this idea well, but one could pull any number of examples. The paradoxes of the discipline's assumptions, that culture is somehow inherently in conflict with technology, which also caused such problems for the idea of group, become insurmountable in the face of a situation like Pine Point. As Cantwell notes, the idea of cultural conservation carries with it a moral imperative that relies on the construction of the "local and traditional" as weak and imperiled by the "technological and commercial" (1991: 149). Pine Point, however, would not have existed in the first place if not for industrialism, commerce, and the like. The town was built by a mining conglomerate and a government. Nor would it be the first of its kind, as company towns form an important part of American history. But if the community and culture of Pine Point are products of commerce and industry, so too is their demise. It makes blaming industrialism for their deaths problematic when we must also acknowledge its role in their creation. Pine Point lived and died by the mine, literally as well as figuratively, at least as a place. Pine Pointers, however, did and do not. Pine Point does not quite square with the typical "technological and commercial" villains of folkloristic writing.

It should be noted that the cultural conservationists have always been acutely aware of the limitations of their work. One difficulty posed by Derrida's specter is that it appears to "disarticulate" time: "Time is out of joint" (1994: 18). The specter is a representation of something that no longer is, and folklorists have long been wary of traditions that are revitalized by seemingly pure academics or well-intentioned outsiders, traditions that died out and were later reinvented, a scenario that does not fit the case of Pine Point. The influence of the past runs the risk of interceding into the present in ways that go against the basic advice given to every fictional time traveler not to meddle in the then lest they muck things up in the now. The authors of the chapters within Mary Hufford's seminal *Conserving Culture* may have sought to keep culture alive and strong but generally not to keep it past its natural lifespan. As Steven Zeitlin points out, "We cannot serve as a life support system to keep dying establishments alive" (1994: 226). In other words, if it is time for a cultural construct to die, then perhaps we should allow it to do so. As anyone who has encountered death firsthand knows, however, deciding to pull the plug is never easy. If anyone should know the multiplicity of ways we seek to ameliorate death, through song, stories, ritual, and other artistic expressions, it should be a folklorist.

If Pine Point has already died, then there would seem nothing left to conserve. Take Zeitlin as our model and let it go. But while the town is gone, the people are not. They have reconstructed their community virtually, which leads to a kind of specter of a cultural community and a living, though dispersed, community in its own right. We are left with an uncanny multiple doubling of Pine Point: Pine Point the place that was; Pine Point the community and its specific culture; Pine Point the website; Pine Point the reunion goers and website readers; and Pine Point the film. On the one hand, Pine Point the website might seem a kind of requiem for Pine Point the place, sung by Pine Point the community. On the other hand, we must acknowledge that Pine Point the website does something that Pine Point the place can no longer do—it provides a venue for Pine Point the community and its culture to continue. And it "begins by coming back," to use Derrida's phrase (1994: 11). Pine Point the website may be a specter; Pine Point the community seems to be alive. One might even call them a "contemporary living cultural tradition," one that could not have existed without not only industrialism but also death. We are left with another inversion, this time of Kurin's concerns voiced in the Folklife Festival's program book from 1989: no, "We [will] never know how valuable would have been the contribution of that culture to a larger human future" (quoted in Cantwell 1991: 150), but we will also never know what cultural creativity, what contributions to a larger human future, might have risen forth from the ashes.

SOVEREIGNTY AND DEATH: A ROMANTIC CALL TO ARMS

Pine Point, in whatever form it takes, presents a puzzle for the orthodox folklorist, particularly one with conservationist leanings. Pine Pointers seem to epitomize "group" in some ways, but they tear at its edges in others, seeming to almost be "not group" and "group" at the same time. The place is dead; the community is alive, but not in a way that we can conserve. No one will present Pine Point at a Canadian version of a Folklife Festival. Indeed, there seems little for a folklorist to do here, which might be the "problem." The Pine Pointers have conserved their own culture, but they have also gone about the rest of their lives, for the most part. The lifespan of the community would seem to be equivalent to the amount of time it remains useful, as a homeplace, a touchstone, a source of identity, a talisman, a memorate, a souvenir. The folklorist can offer no help in documenting it or conserving it further.

At the same time, however, to not document or not look at how Pine Pointers have chosen to document themselves suggests a kind of gatekeeping through definitions. One might cynically ask what the folklorist gains out of maintaining certain definitions of the keywords of the field, much as we have been asking for the last few decades how we might benefit from or benefit the lives of those communities and individuals we document (cf. Behar 1993). Perhaps what is gained is little more than a tenuous ability to keep the magic of the theater in place, to continue to believe that groups are natural, grounded, and organic, and that the language of structuralism can continue to work. Or perhaps this conflict between Pine Point and folklore simply reveals the differences between theory and practice. In the face of that difference, however, it might behoove us as a field to question our own "settled laws" and our investment in them.

In conclusion, I offer two suggestions that might resonate well with the theory of cultural conservation as a kind of advocacy: first, that we consider rethinking the often unwritten limitations on our definitions of group; and second, that we forego "folklife" and consider the potential of absence and death. While locality can and does serve as a basis for community, as it once did for Pine Point, the history of the migrations of humanity, and even more so modern technology, requires a reassessment of those incredibly pesky "settled laws." I am less interested in deciding how the group coheres, who is in or out. Rather, I seek to probe the assumptions of our theoretical framework.

As a starting place, a revision of Benedict Anderson's definition of nationality as "an imagined political community—imagined as both inherently limited and sovereign" (2006) might help. If we think of group as "an imagined cultural community—limited and sovereign," we acknowledge that it has boundaries, however elastic and permeable they may be. By making communities sovereign, we give them the agency and power to imagine themselves in whatever form they choose, tied to place or time, both or neither, even if that must inevitably result in their demise. We agree that they may set their own limitations and definitions. In other words, if we accept that groups limit *who* belongs, often but not always by *where* they are, perhaps we must also accept their right to limit the *when,* even if that means letting go of our commitment as folklorists, researchers, and historians to preservation and sustainability. Not that I am advocating for putting cultural forms out of their misery should they look a bit peaky. Perhaps instead, we must accept that death can be productive in its own right.

The downside of preservation and even sustainability is that you cannot have a folklore of death without the death. It might be helpful to remember the longer history of the field. Herder was, after all, a Romantic, and as such, death was not to be avoided but embraced as the entryway to another kind of being. As F. Scott Fitzgerald wrote in *This Side of Paradise*, "A sentimental person hopes things will last; a romantic person hopes against hope that they won't." Rather than simply trying to keep folklife alive, we can also find ways to eulogize its death and embrace its ghost. On a page all its own, Simons notes, "Absence preserves." He has a point, even if it cannot be seen in the archive, the collection, or the museum.

Ghosts, Derridean or otherwise, are uncomfortable things. That is often their point. They challenge our notions of what we believe we know to be true. They unmoor time and let the past flow into the present, not in ways that seem to conserve or bring new life to tradition or to the past, but rather in ways that seem to question our motives and can influence the future. Specters remind those who see them of past-held ideals and of the inherent messiness of the present, and in doing so, they become incredibly useful, not only in literature and politics, as Derrida describes, but also in folklore. How we deal with our specters determines, in part, how we progress as a field. There is power, after all, in being the last person to drink a beer in the bar.

NOTES

1. Citations of the film used here refer to the chapter headings used in the film that also appear as a kind of navigational menu on the website.

REFERENCES CITED

Anderson, Benedict. 1991. *Imagined Communities: Reflections on the Origin and Spread of Nationalism*. London: Verso.

Barthes, Roland. [1957] 1972. *Mythologies*. New York: Hill and Wang.

Bauman, Richard, and Americo Paredes, eds. 1972. *Toward New Perspectives in Folklore*. Austin: University of Texas Press.

Behar, Ruth. 1993. *Translated Woman*. Boston, Massachusetts: Beacon Press.

Bendix, Regina. 1997. *In Search of Authenticity: The Formation of Folklore Studies*. Madison, WI: University of Wisconsin Press.

Blank, Trevor, ed. 2009. *Folklore and the Internet: Vernacular Expression in a Digital World*. Logan, UT: Utah State University Press.

Bronner, Simon. 1986. *American Folklore Studies: An Intellectual History*. Lawrence, Kansas: University Press of Kansas.

Cantwell, Robert. 1991. "Conjuring Culture: Ideology and Magic in the Festival of American Folklife." *Journal of American Folklore* 104(412): 148–63.

Derrida, Jacques. 1994. *Specters of Marx: The State of the Debt, the Work of Mourning, and the New International.* New York: Routledge.

Dorst, John. 1990. "Tags and Burners, Cycles and Networks: Folklore in the Telectronic Age." *Journal of Folklore Research* 27, 3: 179–90.

Dundes, Alan. 1965. *The Study of Folklore.* Englewood Cliffs, NJ: Prentice-Hall.

Dundes, Alan. 1998. "Bloody Mary in the Mirror: A Ritual Reflection of Pre-Pubescent Anxiety." *Western Folklore* 57 (Summer): 119–35.

Fitzgerald, F. Scott. [1920] 2016. *This Side of Paradise.* Adelaide: ebooks@Adelaide.

Foley, John Miles. 2002. *How to Read an Oral Poem.* Urbana: University of Illinois.

Hathaway, Rosemary. 2005. "Life in the TV: The Visual Nature of 9/11 Lore and Its Impact on Vernacular Response." *Journal of Folklore Research* 42, 1: 33–56.

Hobsbawn, Eric and Terence Ranger. 1983. *The Invention of Tradition.* Cambridge: Cambridge University Press.

Howard, Robert Glenn. 2008. "Electronic Hybridity: The Persistent Processes of the Vernacular Web." *Journal of American Folklore* 121, 480: 192–218.

Hufford, Mary, ed. 1994. *Conserving Culture: A New Discourse on Heritage.* Urbana: University of Illinois Press.

Ivey, Bill. 2011. Values and Value in Folklore (AFS Presidential Plenary Address, 2007). *Journal of American Folklore* 124 (491): 6–18. doi:10.5406/jamerfolk.124.491.0006.

Krohn, Kaarle. 1971. *Folklore Methodology.* Translated by Roger Welsch. Austin: University of Texas Press.

Kurin, Richard. 1989. "Why We Do the Festival." In Smithsonian Festival of American Folklife *Program Book*, ed. Frank Proschan, 8–21. Washington, DC: Smithsonian Institution.

Lawless, Elaine. 2001. *Women Escaping Violence: Empowerment through Narrative.* Columbia, MO: University of Missouri Press.

Lipsitz, George. 2001. *Time Passages: Collective Memory and American Popular Culture.* Minneapolis, MN: University of Minnesota Press.

Newell, William W. 1888. "On the Field and Work of a Journal of American Folk-Lore." *Journal of American Folklore* 1, 1: 3–7.

Noyes, Dorothy. 1995. "Group." *Journal of American Folklore* 108, 430: 449–78.

Roberts, Katherine. 2013. "The Art of Staying Put: Managing Land and Minerals in Rural America." *Journal of American Folklore* 126(502): 407–33.

Shuman, Amy. 1993. "Dismantling Local Culture." *Western Folklore* 52 (April): 345–64.

Shuman, Amy. 2005. Other People's Stories: Entitlement Claims and the Critique of Empathy. Urbana: University of Illinois Press.

Simons, Michael, and Paul Shoebridge, dir. 2011. *Welcome to Pine Point.*

Smithsonian Institution. 2014. "Mission and History." Folklife Festival. SI Websites. Web.

Stewart, Susan. 1989. *Nonsense: Aspects of Intertextuality in Folklore and Literature.* Baltimore: Johns Hopkins University Press.

Tedlock, Dennis. 1972. *Finding the Center: Narrative Poetry of the Zuñi Indians.* New York: Dial Press.

Toelken, Barre. 1996. *The Dynamics of Folklore*, revised. Logan: Utah State University Press.

Wells, Patricia Atkinson. 2006. "Public Folklore in the Twenty-First Century: New Challenges for the Discipline." *Journal of American Folklore* 119 (471).

Wilson, William A. 1973. "Herder, Folklore and Romantic Nationalism." *Journal of Popular Culture,* 6: 819–35.

Zeitlin, Steven J. 1994. "Conserving Our Cities' Endangered Spaces." In *Conserving Culture: A New Discourse on Heritage*, edited by Mary Hufford, 215–28. Urbana: University of Illinois Press.

Zumwalt, Rosemary Levy. 1988. *American Folklore Scholarship*. Bloomington: Indiana University Press.

Check Snopes: Cyborg Folklore in the Internet Age

Willow G. Mullins

When I began teaching folklore courses in the mid-2000s, Snopes.com, the now ubiquitous urban legend and rumor website, was still young enough to not yet be universally known. My students would instead read Jan Brunvand, Patricia Turner, and Gary Alan Fine's work and then be sent out for their first ethnographic collection assignment—record and transcribe an urban legend. It was a tidy little assignment, covering the basics of fieldwork and the troubles of transcribing. Students could get their folkloristic feet wet in a tidal pool of lore they already knew from the slumber party days of their youths, while the depths of the folklore ocean expanded before them. Only then would I point them towards Snopes, the urban legend and rumor verification website named for the family in William Faulkner's novels. Few would have heard of it. They would groan at the realization that they might have cheated the assignment, and then they would come to the next class to relate their evenings spent down the legendary internet rabbit hole.

At the time of this writing, "check Snopes" has become the clarion call of doubters everywhere, from the chalkboard to the chat room. It appears frequently on my own social media feeds at the announcement of any slightly alarmist or suspicious sounding tidbit of information. "Have you checked Snopes?" or "Checked Snopes. It's real!" or "Oops! I should have checked Snopes first." These purveyors of due diligence in internet research, however, are typically not the folklorists on my friends list. Indeed, so common is the "check Snopes" reminder that my students now read Brunvand, Turner, and Fine and then return to class to tell me that they have already "checked Snopes" to learn both the cultural currency of these legends and rumors and their veracity. In other words, they are using Snopes to verify the academics.

Checking Snopes has become a form of folklore itself. Yet Snopes also presents an interesting problem within folklore studies, a problem common to folklore's relationship with the internet. Certainly Snopes demonstrates a breakdown of the clear lines between academic scholarship and popular scholarship, but it points towards other breakdowns as well: between single authorship and community production, between what folklorists study and folklore itself, between human and machine.

Although Snopes may have begun as the hobby of its founders, David and Barbara Mikkelson, it has become one of the best known repositories of folklore on the internet. More importantly, Snopes encapsulates two larger tensions between how folklorists study and think about folklore and how the general population, including folklorists, interact with folklore in daily life. These tensions, writ large in web media, center on interwoven issues of authorship and veracity.

We may all "check Snopes." We don't "check Mikkelson." It has authorship but, in the nature of much on the internet, feels authorless. My students have often been unaware that Snopes had authors. For many, the question never occurred to them to even ask. They should not be taken as unthoughtful, here; they knew that *someone* must have authored it, but if they considered authorship at all, they assumed that Snopes was a crowd-sourced production, like Wikipedia. Not that the Mikkelsons keep their authorship elusive. You can, in fact, find out a bit about them. On Snopes. (The basics of their biographies are also available over on the mass-authored Wikipedia website.) While they founded their local folklore society, partly to give legitimacy to their researches, and cite the legend scholars common to any folklore studies course, they never reveal their own folklore training, if they had any. The terminology employed on the site certainly suggests a broad understanding of folklore scholarship, but they do not use academic certification to authenticate their authentication. Indeed, until 2014[1] when the website changed in design and revealed the recent hiring of a larger support staff of writers and researchers, we knew little more about the founders than that they owned cats (Walker 2016). However, one must ask whether it matters who the Mikkelsons or the newer writers are. For the purposes of good academic research, it does. We must know who said what and what their biases might be. But most of Snopes' users seem less interested in this question than in the site's politics.

The Mikkelsons, in response, have spent more effort in establishing their credibility as apolitical than as experts in the folkloristics of legends and rumors. Yet, this apolitical posturing serves a purpose—Snopes, the verifier of truth, has been accused of purveying untruths. Fears about the Mikkelsons' biases spawned their own category of rumors. Some readers have assumed that because they believe a legend or rumor to be true while Snopes has determined it false, then the fault must lie with Snopes itself. Such rumors have spiraled out, as rumors do, to create a larger conspiracy theory, itself without clear authorship, positing Snopes as a propaganda machine funded by a secret arm of the Democratic party in conjunction with the Soros Foundation (Snopes 2017: "FAQs"). Wonderland-like, the verifier of conspiracies is itself the subject of conspiracies.

Conspiracies aside, without a clear author, it becomes difficult to check the veracity of the stories Snopes verifies, much less of Snopes itself. In an age of "fake news," Americans are warned to be wary of unverified information. Yet Snopes remains trusted. We all seem to believe that Snopes is true first because "checking Snopes" is what you do to verify information: circularly, Snopes must be accurate, because it is Snopes. Snopes the site has replaced Snopes's authors as sites of legitimacy. But it also *feels* true. The quick "true," "false," "mixture" coding of the rumors and legends, and the site as a whole, gives a sense of "truthiness," to use comedian Stephen Colbert's term (2005: "The Word"): it must be true because it simply feels true. The way in which the Mikkelsons fade into the background, superceded by the information they present, gives the information a lack of authorship that peculiarly seems to boost its objectivity. The information moves from being the creation of a single person to an already accepted fact, something we assume to be true. Yet the Mikkelsons and the new writers are there in the wings, should we need them.

Snopes, as we have seen with the Snopes conspiracies, runs into trouble when truth and belief mismatch, but we cannot know for certain that what is on Snopes is true unless we wish to repeat the research, and then what would be the point of Snopes. Instead, we are still stuck taking a leap of faith. Whether we believe it or not, however, the act of checking Snopes (and the calls to do so) is performed ritualistically at specific junctures—after hearing, or more typically reading online, some tidbit whose discursive features feel familiarly legendary or rumor-like; before reposting the same. The verification process of checking Snopes may be an individual one without much ceremony, but it plays out the same over and over, in house and office, among a wide range of people. Checking Snopes becomes a mundane ritual. And intriguingly, it is one that draws attention to the layperson's notion of what makes folklore folklore. Perhaps that Snopes the folklore site has become folklore should not be surprising. As David Nye has argued, "Technologies . . . are social construc-tions with political and social implications" (2006: 597).

In folkloristic terms, the erasure of individual authorship and the ritualistic nature of checking Snopes also move not just the information on Snopes but the site itself into the realm of folklore. In part because of how the information is presented, with straightforward text, plenty of white space, and little extraneous graphics, it feels like a group production centered on "artistic communcation" to deploy Dan Ben-Amos's succinct definition, though we might have to question to what extent that group is "small" (1972). No one would argue whether Snopes's content is folklore. Yet, Snopes itself may also be folklore, functioning like folklore, in a very old school sense.

If we agree with Brunvand, Fine, and Turner that the legends and rumors express the fears that underlie our daily lives (Brunvand 1980: 10–13), however, what do we make of Snopes itself and our relationship to it? Edward Tylor understood much folklore as honest attempts to explain the world around us, to provide origin stories for the natural world. Further, he argued that while people may no longer have faith in the beliefs themselves, they continue to pay homage to them through rituals; thus, folklore becomes "survivals" of early belief systems encoded in rituals (1871: 187). Does Snopes offer a kind of explanation for the modern world—folklore and ritual practice developed on a highly condensed time span? Instead of trying to explain the creation of the universe, the ritual of checking Snopes allows users to navigate their understanding of the recent past and present. Checking Snopes becomes a tiny moment of homage to the Real, a moment when we think we might understand the world we live in and how it came to be this way.

Snopes might also offer something bigger, though. Snopes may be cyborg folklore. Donna Haraway's theory of the cyborg helped challenge rigid and essentializing boundaries between human and machine (1994). As a site for folklore and folklore in itself, Snopes is an amalgam of human and machine, the writers seeming to disappear behind the information. This disappearance is complicated by the relationship between authorship and believability. Snopes is at once both dependent on binaries of truth/falsehood and seems to function outside of that structure: its reason to exist is to mark legends as true or false, but readers also feel Snopes must be true because it is Snopes. And we take what we learn from Snopes about our lived worlds back into those lived worlds, where the rumors again shift and change as folklore does. Yet the technology also demands recognition here—without the kinds of networks, the speed of communication, and the hazy relationship with verification that the internet offers, one must wonder if the legends, rumors, and "fake news" that Snopes seeks to validate, or Snopes itself, could have such currency. Snopes, as a site and a phenomenon, acknowledges that such folklore has always existed, but it also suggests that there is something new afoot. Cyborg folklore slips between the technological and human, the creative project of both.

As such, Snopes and its like may require a different paradigm from traditional folklore and a different methodology for studying it. For cyborg folklore cannot simply be a hunt for the ways in which folklore and its humans engage with the technological or how technology has altered human interaction. Rather as anthropologist and engineer Gary Lee Downey has hypothesized in limning out cyborg anthropology, cyborg folklore must similarly "explore a new alternative by examining the argument that human subjects and subjectivity are crucially as much a function of machines, machine relations, and information transfers as they are machine producers and operators" (1997: 4).

The cyborg may blur the line between human and machine, but there is also a different kind of barrier-blurring taking place, what John Dorst has termed a "collapse of the hierarchy between text and apparatus" (1999: 270). The website has become a folk verification tool for use on the folk's own creation, as Haraway says "a creature of social reality as well as a creature of fiction" (1994). On Snopes, it is possible to lose sight of what is folklore, the rumors, the verification of them, the site itself, its authors, the academics on whose research the site relies, or our rebuttals when we hear those rumors again, and who is acting out a folkloric performance. Snopes folds into a quick search the casual visitor's desire to verify and the professional folklorist's desire to explore how legends comment on society. I use the idea of the cyborg loosely here, but I suggest the term as a way to give us space to be both folk and folklorist. Snopes manages to make it impossible not to.

NOTES

1. Simultaneous with this shift in staffing, Snopes also increased their scope significantly. While the site had always dealt with political stories and recent news, following the "fake news" scandals of 2016, Snopes became more centered on verifying reported news items and rumors.

REFERENCES CITED

Brunvand, Jan Harold. 1980. *The Vanishing Hitchhiker*. New York: W. W. Norton & Co.
The Colbert Report. 2005. Season 1, Episode 1. Directed by Jim Hoskinson. Written by
   Stephen Colbert. Comedy Central, October 17.
Dorst, John D. 1999. "Which Came First, the Chicken Device or the Textual Egg?
   Documentary Film and the Limits of the Hybrid Metaphor." *Journal of American
   Folklore* 112, no. 445: 268–81. doi:10.2307/541362.

Downey, Gary Lee. 1997. "'After Culture': Reflections on the Apparition of Anthropology in Artificial Life, a Science of Simulation." In *Cyborgs and Citadels: Anthropological Interventions in Emerging Sciences, Technologies and Medicines*, edited by Gary Lee Downey and Joseph Dumit. Seattle: SAR/University of Washington Press.

Haraway, Donna. 1994. "A Cyborg Manifesto: Science, Technology, and Socialist-Feminism in the Late Twentieth Century." In *Theorizing Feminism: Parallel Trends in the Humanities and Social Sciences*, edited by Anne C. Hermann and Abigail J. Stewart. Boulder: Westview Press, 1994. 424–57.

Mikkelson, David. 2017. Snopes. http://www.snopes.com. Accessed May 5.

Nye, David E. 2006. "Technology and the Production of Difference." *American Quarterly* 58, no. 3: 597–618. http://www.jstor.org/stable/40068385.

Tylor, Edward B. 1871. *Primitive Culture, Researches into the Development of Mythology, Philosophy, Religion, Art and Custom*. London: J. Murray. In *Peasant Customs and Savage Myths*, edited by Richard Dorson. Chicago: University of Chicago, 1968.

Walker, Rob. 2016. "How the Truth Set Snopes Free." *The Webby Awards*. October 19. http://www.webbyawards.com/lists/how-the-truth-set-snopes-free/.

"Judas!"

Todd Richardson

> Judas' betrayal was not a random act, but predetermined, with its own
> mysterious place in the economy of redemption.
> —Nils Runeberg, *The Secret Savior* (1912)

Bob Dylan won the Nobel Prize for Literature in 2016, and nary a folklorist
was consulted. It should have been a banner moment for the field—a virtuoso
of orality had been awarded the highest literary prize on planet Earth—yet
none of the many high profile stories about Dylan's unexpected honor incorporated a folklorist's perspective. Conventional poets certainly got their say,
whether it was to congratulate a kindred spirit in Dylan or, just as frequently,
lament that so many "real" poets had been passed over in favor of a popular
musician, but not folklorists, despite being uniquely quotable when it comes to
the sophistication of verbal artistry.[1] The response to Dylan's Nobel win made
it clear that even though he is the most accomplished, prolific and insightful
interpreter of traditional material of the last hundred years, Dylan simply isn't
associated with folklore.

That the field of folklore isn't more closely associated with Bob Dylan is
likely due to Dylan's complicated relationship with the American Folk Revival,
a movement that shares a fair bit of its intellectual DNA with American folklore
studies. Both movements crystallized at roughly the same time—The Newport
Folk Festival, shining light of the Folk Music Revival, was founded in 1959,
and the Folklore Institute at Indiana University was made permanent just
three years later in 1962—and both were at least partially inspired by a disil-
lusion with the promises of post-World War II prosperity and consumerism

(Cantwell 1997). Adherents of both sought deeper, more authentic meaning in traditional cultures and expressions that they believed were being threatened by the new national paradigm, and a number of figures—Archie Green, Ellen Stekert, Alan Jabbour and Alan Lomax all come to mind—were influential in both movements. The Folk Revival and folklore studies are, in other words, less than siblings but more than cousins, which means that Bob Dylan's betrayal of the former necessarily affected his association with the latter.

For betrayal to happen—and I mean honest-to-goodness, gut-wrenching betrayal—there must first be trust, and Dylan had earned the trust of the American Folk Revival as an up-and-coming musician in the Greenwich Village folk music scene of the early 1960s. While there were a great many other talented musicians in that scene who hewed more closely to the traditional material at the center of the folk music revival, there was something about the way Dylan embodied the movement's contradictory elements, its oldness *and* its youngness, that made him an easy figure to rally around: perpetually clad in second-hand rags, Dylan knew a large and esoteric catalogue of traditional songs, yet he was notable for working new and topical lyrics into those song structures. In effect, Dylan was new wine in old bottles, making him an ideal figurehead for this new enthusiasm for old music.

Yet he was lying from the start. Bob Dylan was the invention of Robert Zimmerman, who was, himself, the son of an appliance store owner in Hibbing, Minnesota, and this "Bob Dylan" character was really nothing more than a baby-faced facsimile of Woody Guthrie, the most famous figure of the American Folk Music Revival's first wave.[2] The Dylan character that Zimmerman invented heisted his costume, much of his material and at least some of his biography directly from Guthrie—it wasn't until *Newsweek* "exposed" Zimmerman's back story that Dylan gave up claiming he was a roustabout born in Oklahoma (or, alternately, a carnival worker from Gallup, New Mexico, or a ranch hand from South Dakota or whatever else he felt like saying when asked about his origins). In fact, it is entirely accurate to say that there has never been anything authentic about Bob Dylan. Beginning with his early imitation of Guthrie, Bob Dylan has been taking and remaking other people's material for his own gain, and while the songs might be remarkable, the character should never have been trusted in the first place.

The Folk Revival's relationship with Bob Dylan symbolically unraveled when Dylan went electric at the 1965 Newport Folk Festival. Although accounts of what actually happened vary wildly—some insist that it was a simple technical mishap while others recall Pete Seeger trying to disable the sound system with an ax—quite a few boos can be heard in recordings of the performance, proof that in the eyes of many revivalists there, what Dylan was doing was unacceptable. And the acrimony expressed at Newport would accompany

Dylan throughout the year-long world tour that followed, culminating in an anonymous concert-goer yelling "Judas" at him at a show at Free Trade Hall in Manchester, England, on May 17, 1966. Dylan's response: "I don't believe you . . . You're a liar," after which he turned to his backing band and instructed them, "Play fucking loud!"

Nearly fifty years after the fact, Dylan was still stewing over the Judas accusation. In an interview with *Rolling Stone* in September of 2012, Dylan said, "If you think you've been called a bad name, try to work your way out from under that. Yeah, and for what? For playing an electric guitar? As if that is in some kind of way equitable to betraying our Lord and delivering him up to be crucified. All those evil motherfuckers can rot in hell." Dylan's reference to the Judas episode came during his response to a question about his more recent "experiments" in plagiarism, which he defended thus: "I'm not going to limit what I can say. I have to be true to the song. It's a particular art form that has its own rules. It's a different type of thing. All my stuff comes out of the folk tradition—it's not necessarily akin to the pop world." Here, Dylan, who had supposedly turned his back on "the folk tradition" forty-seven years earlier, was invoking "the folk tradition" in defense of his stealing lines from poems by Henry Timrod, "the poet laureate of the Confederacy" (2012).

Dylan never really betrayed anyone or anything, especially not tradition. For one, "Bob Dylan" is a character created by Bobby Zimmerman, and to say that "Bob Dylan" betrayed you is like saying a flawed narrator betrayed you. Nope. You fell for it. More importantly, character or not, Bob Dylan has never not been in the thick of tradition. Consider the first song he played that night at Newport in 1965, "Maggie's Farm." It was a reworking of "Down on Penny's Farm," a song straight out of the canon of American traditional music.[3] Dylan had simply adapted traditional material for a new medium, which is exactly what traditions do to propagate. Far from betraying traditional culture, Dylan was demonstrating its durability.

Dylan has been serving audiences old wine in new bottles throughout his career. Along the way, he's adopted a series of personae to better inhabit the traditions he's working in, becoming a country troubadour, Christian evangelist, drug-addled opportunist and riverboat gambler, among other things, consistently demonstrating an investment in traditional material that would embarrass the most dedicated ethnographic fieldworker. Most recently, he has turned himself into a pop crooner, releasing *Shadows in the Night* and *Triplicate*, both of which consist entirely of pop standards like "These Foolish Things" and "Stormy Weather." Taken as a whole, Dylan's career demonstrates that the only thing he might have betrayed are people's limited conceptions and expectations of tradition. "I have to think of all this as traditional music." Dylan said in an interview a few months after the uproar at Newport, "Traditional music is based on hexagrams. It comes about from legends, Bibles, plagues, and it revolves around vegetables and death. There's nobody that's going to kill traditional music. All these songs about roses growing out of people's brains and lovers who are really geese and swans that turn into angels—they're not going to die. It's all those paranoid people who think that someone's going to come and take away their toilet paper. They're going to die" ([1965] 2006: 98).

• • •

In the late 1960s, Dylan, tired of being the conscience of a generation, retreated to upstate New York, where he dove deeply into American traditional music, producing what has come to be known as *The Basement Tapes*, a motley assortment of traditional and traditional-sounding material that Greil Marcus dubbed the music of "The Old, Weird America" (1997). Between March 1967 and February 1968, Dylan and his backing band The Hawks, better known as The Band, recorded hundreds of hours of material, ranging from blues standards like "See that My Grave is Kept Clean" to contemporary chart-toppers like "If I Were a Carpenter." On their own and without outside expectations, Dylan and The Band were free to explore the possibilities of traditional music. "Those who had left their stages as betrayers of immemorial traditions discovered deeper traditions," Marcus writes of *The Basement Tapes*, "and in a room without mirrors refashioned them. The traditional people, still living, were laid to rest and raised up with new faces" (1997: 223). Whether in spite of or because of his spectacular infidelity on the Newport stage two years earlier, Dylan had been freed, and, in that basement in Woodstock, engaged with traditional music in ways previously unthinkable to the folk establishment.

While the music of *The Basement Tapes* is far less known than early Dylan songs like "Blowin' in the Wind" or "The Time Are A-Changin'," it, too, is a part of the life's work that was awarded the Nobel Prize in 2016. Indeed, all the songs Dylan has written, even the ones on those awful 80s albums, were recognized when Dylan was awarded the Nobel, and every one of those songs, in one way or another, owes its existence to the author's unswerving faith in the durability of tradition. While it may, at times, seem like Dylan is manhandling and manipulating tradition, that's only because he *is* manhandling and manipulating tradition. He knows that tradition can take it. Dylan's respect for tradition is so strong, he refuses to treat it delicately, continually bending and reshaping it to his will. "You don't really serve art, art serves you," Dylan said in an interview to promote *Triplicate*, "and it's only an expression of life anyway; it's not real life. It's tricky, you have to have the right touch and integrity or you could end up with something stupid. Michelangelo's statue of David is not the real David. Some people never get this and they're left outside in the dark. Try to create something original, you're in for a surprise" (2017).

Dylan may not be a folklorist, but he's not entirely ignorant of folklore studies and its history. When asked in that interview for *Triplicate* whether there were national differences between songwriting traditions, he replied, "If I was an anthropologist maybe I could tell you, but I really have no idea. Everybody crosses cultures and time zones and nations now anyway. You know who could probably tell you? Alan Lomax, or maybe Cecil Sharp, one of those guys" (2012). More importantly, Dylan doesn't have to be a folklorist to contribute something crucial to the work of folklorists and the way they treat tradition. Dylan's infidelity, the way in which he is always willing to unsettle accepted notions of propriety in order to uncover new possibilities, provides an idea for how folklorists might be more innovative and take tradition in truly new directions, and all without losing reverence for the subject. Dylan's reverence for tradition, after all, runs so deep, he knows it can survive whatever betrayal you throw at it.

NOTES

1. I may be overstating the case because I was hurt that nobody asked me to say something on the record about Dylan's win. Every Halloween, a reporter from the *Omaha World Herald* interviews me for a story on one local legend or another, but no one there or anywhere thought to contact me about Dylan's Nobel Prize, something I'm far more qualified to talk about than morphing stairs or albino farms on the fringe of town.

2. And it would be even more accurate to say that Bob Dylan was a facsimile of a facsimile, as it turns out he borrowed as much from Ramblin' Jack Elliot, who was, at least originally, Elliot Adnopoz, another middle-class Jewish kid who was doing an impersonation of Woody Guthrie.

3. This is literally true, if one accepts, as many do, that Harry Smith's *Anthology of American Folk Music* is the canon of American traditional music. Also, Dylan had previously reworked the structure of "Down on Penny's Farm" in an even earlier composition, "Hard Times in New York Town."

REFERENCES CITED

Cantwell, Robert. 1997. *When We Were Good*. Cambridge: Harvard University Press.
Dylan, Bob. 2006. *The Essential Interviews*. New York: Wenner.
Dylan, Bob. 2012. Interview with Mikal Gilmore. Bob Dylan Unleashed. *Rolling Stone*, September 27.
Dylan, Bob. 2017. Q & A with Bill Flanagan. *bobdylan.com*. https://www.bobdylan.com/news/qa-with-bill-flanagan/.
Marcus, Greil. 1997. *The Old Weird America*. New York: Picador.
Runeberg, Nils. 1912. "Three Versions of Judas" by Jorge Luis Borges. 1962. *Ficciones*. New York: Grove.

FIVE

White Folks: Literature's Uncanny, Unhomely Folklore of Whiteness

Shelley Ingram

I recently taught Karen Russell's short story "Haunting Olivia" in a course on folklore and literature. It is a story about a young boy tirelessly swimming the waters off the coast of Florida, looking for the ghost of the sister who had disappeared into the ocean months before. The boy ends up in a grotto, staring up to see phosphorescent traces all over the stone, made visible by a pair of enchanted goggles. He only then comes to the realization that Olivia was both everywhere and nowhere. Never one to let a good symbol go unplundered, I asked my students to think about the grotto, the cave, and about what it meant, especially as it related to ghostly absences. What is a cave? A hole in a rock. What makes it a cave, though? The absence of rock. So, you could say that a cave is defined by, given shape by, the place where absence meets presence. One student looked at me and said, "It only exists because something else doesn't exist. It is absence that gives it meaning. I have . . . never thought of it that way." Another, making the appropriate gestures with his hands, said simply "Mind. Blown." We have been so conditioned to see folklore as something obnoxious in its presence that we do not always recognize the epistemological and political forces at work in the construction of its absence. The folklore of "whiteness" is one such construction, and we see the impact of its absence in the ways that we talk about folklore and literature.

Russell Banks's *Affliction* (1990) and Eudora Welty's *Delta Wedding* (1946) are two American novels in which whiteness is inextricably linked to the creation, through acceptance or rejection, of folk groups, to the return of the repressed, and to the uncanniness of the unhomely. These theoretical constructs—the uncanny, the unhomely—are deeply connected to both whiteness and folk culture, and they offer us a way of reading through the constructions of the folklore of *whiteness* as an absence that "begins its presencing." On the surface, these two novels could not be more different. One is set in the American Northeast in late-twentieth century, the other in the early 1920s in Mississippi. One is deeply and carefully concerned with questions of contemporary masculinity, the other with what it meant to be a white woman in the pre-Civil Rights south. And though they each play with the traditional novel form, the shape of their play is profoundly different. What connects them is that they both draw on folklore to test the boundaries of the characters' various whitenesses through the uncanny return of the repressed and through the active hybridity of unhomeliness; moreover, the disrupting characters and spaces within these texts are made visible by traces of the "folk." Banks and Welty both construct a whiteness that has stability and variation, that reacts to the presence of a folk other, and that becomes part of a vernacular language of identity for those inside, outside, and on the borders of their groups. It is a construct, paradoxically absent and present, which inevitably returns.

Whiteness as a concept is often positioned two ways in academic study: as an always invisible default and as a culture defined by lack. It is first the universal standard, the assumptive subject and the seemingly neutral state of being that "silently imposes itself as the standard by which social difference is to be known" (Levine-Rasky 2013: 43). Whiteness thus presents itself as "unmarked, unspecific, universal" (Dyer 1997: 45); as "unremarkable, featureless, common, standard" (Levine-Rasky 2013: 44). Yet whiteness is also figured as *invisible*, because "there is a quality of transparency to whiteness, as if being white means lacking a racial identity" (Stowe 1996: 70), which "allows whites to act as if they had no race" (O'Loughlin 2002: 40). To have no race means to have no racially demarcated traits, so that, as David Roediger has famously asserted, "Whiteness describes, from Little Big Horn to Simi Valley, not a culture but precisely the absence of culture" (1991: 19).[1] Roediger moves from "absence of race" to "absence of culture," and the "absence of culture" inherently implies an absence of *folk* culture.

This perceived absence of a folk culture is intrinsically connected to whiteness, rather than to class or region. Nineteenth-century British anthropologist E. B. Tylor and his cohort suggested that cultures, human societies, "unilaterally" evolved through three distinct stages: savagery to barbarism to civilization.

The sacred myths of savagery, which were the "spoken correlatives" of the rituals of ancient peoples, became folklore among the barbarians—who were "understood to be essentially 'folk' or illiterate peasants"—before deteriorating or dying out or being repressed in civilized society (Dundes 1984: 72). Thus, what survived from the earlier stages into more 'evolved' culture was folklore, most likely to be found in the middle rung of culture. This notion of culture was a useful tool in the project of colonialism, as it situated the "primitive"—almost always dark-skinned people—as less evolved, both culturally and biologically, helping to justify colonialist expansion. This makes the suggestion that whiteness inherently lacks culture all the more troubling, for those who have folklore were historically constructed as less evolved than those who, because of their being situated in the most advanced of cultures, had lost their roots.

Richard Dyer, drawing on David Lloyd's reading of Kant, argues that whiteness involves an aspiration to become a "subject without properties." Kant proposed a teleology that saw progress as a move toward a disinterest in the local, the present. Lloyd renames this disinterest as being a "subject without properties" because the subject, presumed white, would become unmarked by baser instincts and desires. Whiteness is thus the fullest expression of a subject absent of properties, atop the great chain of being and proprietor of the most evolved culture, below only angels and god himself. This propertyless-ness is part of what gives whiteness its perceived neutrality. It is a state of being without locale, without particularity, without folklore; it is non-whites in this paradigm who cannot progress because they will always be local, particular, and marked—in short, objects rather than subjects. While non-whites are always already marked and racialized, and thus perpetually doomed to be 'of' and speak 'for' their race, whites are able to just be human. This 'just humanness' is what allows whiteness to lay claim to the power of representation. Because whiteness has historically been constructed as "absent" of race, white writers can "claim to speak for the commonality of humanity" (Dyer 1997: 2). Claiming whiteness as absence thus constructs an ability to speak of and for other races without being subject to the interests of that race, to be the disinterested ethnographer, the objective observer.[2]

Folklorists have embraced Dundes' notion of a folk group as any group of people with at least one thing in common, displacing race and ethnicity (and class and region) as markers of "folk." But practice has not always followed as quickly. In a statistical study of the rate at which writers of color and white writers are subjected to "folkloric literary criticism," Lucia Pawlowski notices a trend: writers of color are much more likely to be approached through a lens of folkloristics than white writers. She asks, "Why, if folklore is a discipline that by definition explores" the folklore of "*all* people," do "writers of color seem to have a much better chance of having their folklore invoked in literary criticism?" (2015: 49). The answer strains against that which has become one of folklore's most dogmatically repeated tropes, that "we are all the folk": the folklorist "overemphasizes the folkloric influence on writers of color, suggesting that writers of color have more folklore to analyze than white writers" (2015: 51).

But I am not speaking here just of the folklore of people who are white.[3] Instead, I am concerned with the ways that folklore interacts with constructions of whiteness itself, an interaction that the study of folklore and literature in particular has not adequately considered. In this essay, I push back against a critical narrative of whiteness as absence by bringing whiteness into focus as an identity that is guarded and negotiated, present in its absence and critical to the making of meaning and folklore in American literature.

A GHOST LIFE: RUSSELL BANKS'S *AFFLICTION*

Russell Banks is an American writer the *Village Voice* once called "a maestro of loss," a loss he repeatedly connects to questions of race and white identity. For example, his novel Cloudsplitter is a fictionalized oral account of Owen Brown, son of the antebellum hero John Brown. In The Darling, he writes the life of Hannah Musgrave, a white American activist born of wealthy liberal parents who becomes part of the Weather Underground and who ultimately plays a destructive role in the Liberian civil war. Rule of the Bone, Banks's re-visioning of Twain's The Adventures of Huckleberry Finn, follows the young white protagonist Bone as he sets off on a journey that leads him through the Caribbean, accompanied by the Rastafarian I-Man. And Continental Drift sees the white male protagonist Bob Dubois falls in love with a black Caribbean immigrant, and Banks makes it clear that Dubois never comes to understand the racist nature of his obsession. In each of these novels, the white protago-nists' identities are intimately associated with and constructed through their relationship to blackness.

But in the 1989 novel *Affliction*, whiteness is all encompassing, and its force-ful presence leads readers to settle their need for contrast, for the not-white, on Wade Whitehouse. Wade is the sole police officer in the town of Lawford, New Hampshire. The novel is set during the middle of winter, and snow is all around Wade, covering the ground and making the woods "dark and impenetrable behind a white skirt of snow" (Banks 1991: 179). *Affliction* is a murder mystery and a family drama, a story of violence and pain. The narrative follows Wade for several days as he fights his ex-wife Lillian for custody of their daughter Jill, grows suspicious of the business dealings of his employer Gordon LaRiviere, and tries to come to terms with the death of his mother and his abuse at the hands of his father. The narrator, though, is Wade's brother Rolfe, who slips back in forth in time and voice, bringing together stories of the brothers' past and present as he tries to understand what drove Wade to his final destructive and murderous acts. Containing and constricting the story is the ever presence of the cold, the white snow that blankets and "walls in" Wade and the citizens of Lawford.

The novel has a complex structure that begins with Rolfe framing the story as a recollection of his "older brother's strange criminal behavior and his disappearance." Since no one who knew Wade speaks of him now, by telling this story Rolfe is "separating [himself] from the family and from all those who ever loved him" (1). Rolfe begins with a description of the town of Lawford and of the people who live there, "separating" himself even more by his omniscient narration, before he instructs the reader to "imagine that around eight o'clock on this Halloween Eve . . . there comes a pale-green eight-year-old Ford Fairlane with a blue police bubble on top. Let us imagine a dark square-faced man wearing a trooper's cap driving the vehicle" (15). Our first view of Wade, the dark man, is through the imaginative lens not just of the removed narrator, but also through the invited creative imaginings of the reader. Rolfe quickly moves into a relatively straightforward retelling of the portentous Halloween night Wade spent with his daughter Jill, interjecting only occasionally in a first-person voice, such as when the narrator recounts memories of his and Wade's childhood. Only at the end of the novel does the narrative voice shift dramatically, when Rolfe presents the events of Wade's final "strange criminal behavior" through first-person recollections of other people involved, trading in an intrusive authorial voice for the pretense of an ethnographic, objective one.

In the first event Rolfe narrates, Wade is bringing his daughter Jill to the Lawford community Halloween event. They miss the trick-or-treating and are late for the party at the town's community center. Jill eventually calls for her mother and step-father to come rescue her, no longer willing to be a player in Wade's failure as a father. The next morning, in a seemingly unconnected event, Wade's friend Jack Hewitt leads businessman Evan Twombley on a deer hunt in the forests surrounding town, which ends in Twombley being shot in the chest. While the state police and the local townspeople accept Twombley's death as accidental, Wade begins to suspect Jack of being paid by the mob, and consequently Twombley's son-in-law Mel, to kill the man. Wade calls his brother about the shooting, and Rolfe feeds Wade's theory, suggesting additional motives and manipulations that may have led to Twombley's murder. Rolfe imagines "some odd connection" in his mind "between the two stories, between his version of Twombley's death and his version of Lillian's driving up to Lawford and removing Jill from his care. I did not then know how powerful the connection was, of course, but it was there, to be sure, just below the surface of the narrative" (132). We must remember, then, that Rolfe is ultimately controlling the narrative, and the structure of the novel makes it so that it is *his* connection of the two stories that mark them as frames to the last known chapter of Wade's life.

Wade's "strange criminal behavior" ultimately culminates in violence against their father Glen, who had abused Wade, Rolfe, and their mother Sally for years. The final events of the novel are set in motion when Wade finds Sally dead of hypothermia in their old family home, just days after Twombley's death. Glen had neglected to repair the furnace, and Wade and his fiancée Margie find Glen alone in the living room with Sally's body upstairs in bed. As Wade simultaneously fights a custody battle for Jill (which he cannot win) and searches for concrete evidence to substantiate his claims about Twombley's death (which he cannot find), he starts to unravel under his father's watchful eyes. After the town turns on him for his obsessive tracking of Jack, Wade desperately seeks to spend time with his daughter, only to arrive home with her to find Margie moving out. As he begs Margie to stay, Jill, reminded of her father's violence toward her mother, preemptively attacks Wade. Wade then "swung his arms wide, and hit her" (337). This is an act from which Wade cannot recover, for he had finally completed his father's cycle. Margie tells Rolfe, seeing Wade for the last time, that "Wade stood there in the same spot in the snow beside the driveway, staring down at the snow . . . and up on the porch, I saw that Pop had come out—maybe he had been there all along and had seen everything—and he stood there looking at Wade with a smile on his face" (338).

What happens next is a matter of "historical fact," and Margie says to Rolfe, "Well, you know the rest" (339). And he does know, because he says that he has an "uncanny" insight into Wade's life, for "in telling Wade's story here I am telling my own as well" (340). All the police find is a charred body in a barn, but Rolfe is able to confidently narrate the events because "Wade's life, then, and mine, too, is a paradigm, ancient and ongoing, and thus, yes, I do know the rest" (340). As Wade and Glen faced each other for the last time, Wade/ Rolfe saw his father as "huge, an enraged giant from a fairy tale," and he "crouched and twisted away from the colossal figure of his father; he turned like a heretic prepared for stoning." He "clutched the rifle barrel with both hands and . . . smashed it against the side of his father's head, whacked and broke it from jaw to temple: the crack of bone, a puff of air and a groan, *Oh!* And the old man fell in pieces and died at once, eyes wide open—a leathered corpse unearthed from a bog" (342). Banks recreates here the ancient stories of colossuses, heretics, and mummified men, casting the last meeting between Wade (and himself) and Glen in legendary and paradigmatic terms. After Wade burns Glen's body in their barn, he finds Jack Hewitt in the woods and shoots him in the chest, thus bringing closure to all of his stories. Wade leaves in Jack's truck and remains at large, and those who "loved him simply no longer speak of him," absent from the collective conscious of the town (1).

In *Playing in the Dark: Whiteness and the Literary Imagination*, Toni Morrison argues that whiteness is often constructed through an opposition to blackness, where blackness is the way in which whiteness knows itself to be not history-less, not mad, not perverse, used to "reassert class distinctions and otherness as well as to assert privilege and power" (1992: 52). The origins of folklore studies rests on a similar binary, where "the folk" were a way in which the "not-folk" knew themselves to be more evolved, to be more civilized. In literature, as Frank De Caro and Rosan Jordan argue, "Perhaps the simplest use of folklore" is to emphasize "folklore as coming from and marking the realm of the Other," a "perspective or position reflective of a foreign, exotic, bygone, or otherwise different reality" (2004: 16). One of the primary functions of this "poetics of Otherness" is to provide "for oppositional contrasts between Others and moderns" (Bauman and Briggs 2003: 14–15).[4] Banks intentionally conflates these binaries, setting up "folk" and "black" as contrast to "not-folk" and "white" in novels like *Continental Drift, Rule of the Bone*, and *The Darling*, where white protagonists are brought into conflict with black and clearly marked "folk" cultures. In *Affliction*, though, there is no easily identified "folk culture" by which to contrast the novel's whiteness.

The obvious choice would be to equate "white" in *Affliction* with "working class," a position that Banks himself suggests.[5] But noticing the *absence* of "folk" as a marker of whiteness is equally compelling. One reviewer has called the people of Banks's novels "Irish Catholics, French Canadians and deracinated Yankees whose lives and relationships freeze and crack like ponds in winter" (Scott 2000). The "deracinated Yankees" have no "roots," they have been ripped from their home—an act which, according to this reviewer, racializes (presumably) white "Yankees" in a way that equalizes them with other easily identified cultural groups. The lack inherent in whiteness is put on par with the unspoken cultural authenticity of the not-quite-whiteness of the Irish and French Canadians. Their absence becomes their presence, as Rolfe says, because "absence is evidence" (Banks 1991: 350). We see this in the novel when Wade is unable to come to terms with the new neon sign hanging in Lawford's most popular restaurant. He asks, "What was there before? I never saw anything there before." Margie "punched his arm and laughed. 'That's the point.' She patted his hand. '*Nothing* was there before.'" (105). The sign, shiny and new, follows Wade throughout the story, and the amelioration of absence is one of the disconnects that drives Wade.

At one point, Wade is sitting in his truck, waiting for his windshield to defrost. As he sits, the "ice on his windshield melted into a pair of rapidly enlarging circles, like eyes that could look out but also—as if that were the price he had paid for the privilege of looking out—eyes that allowed him to be seen" (58–59). The presence that makes the absence known, as Derrida argues, marks "perhaps the supreme insignia of power: the power to see without being seen" (8). The privilege of seeing and the problems of being seen are also Wade's, and also Rolfe's, whose power allows him to narrate, to transcribe, to be the ethnographer of Wade's life from a seemingly objective space while at the same time opening up his own story to be seen. This is what happens when "the dreaded ethnographic gaze is turned back upon itself, away from the (presumably) nonwhite Other to the (presumably) white subject" (Stowe 1996: 70). The white "impenetrable barrier" melts and reveals that Glen's story *is* Wade's story *is* Rolfe's story. In an uncanny instance of doubling, Rolfe says that Wade's story "is my ghost life, and I want to exorcise it" (Banks 1991: 2)

When Rolfe begins his narration, he is describing the town of Lawford on Halloween Eve. He asks the reader to "think of a village in a medieval German folktale," because "Lawford has no connection to modern life" (2, 5). He calls the citizens of Lawford a "remnant people" who had been left alone by the best and brightest of the younger generation. The results of being a "remnant people" are that they "cling stubbornly as barnacles to the bits and shards of social rites that once invested their lives with meaning" (5). Most importantly,

So that with the family, with the community as a whole, no longer able to unify and organize a people and provide them with a worthy identity, the half-forgot-ten misremembered ceremonies of ancient days become all the more crucial to observe. As in: Halloween. The rites affirm a people's existence, but falsely. And it is this very falsity that most offends those of us who have left. We know better than anyone, precisely because we have fled in such numbers, that those who refused or were unable to leave no longer exist as a family, a tribe, a community. They are no longer a people—if they ever were one. . . . I teach history, I think about these things. (6)

Here Rolfe separates himself immediately from those who remain in the town by his rejection of the "willed conservatism" of these "remnant people." He marks them with otherworldly traces, invoking the trappings of a medieval folktale to guide the reader into well-known narrative grooves, enhancing the imaginative re-creations necessary for the reading of the text. But the type of social cohesion sought by the rites and rituals of "ancient days" in Lawford, according to Rolfe, only leads to a false presence, a degeneracy of authenticity—because they have stayed in Lawford, their folk past is corrupted and thus they no longer exist as a people. Rolfe's rejection of the townspeople's particular atavism, that which looks to ancient ceremonies for identity, places him in a position of epistemological power: he believes that he can see what they cannot, and that he alone recognizes the heights from which Lawford has fallen. He, too, no longer belongs in such a mythic past, but at least he has the decency not to pretend otherwise.

The structure of the novel specifically gives him this power of knowledge, for it is only through his reconstruction of that Halloween weekend that we know the story of Wade and Lawford. Because he is educated and thinks "about these things," Rolfe assumes a representational power that he would lack if he were marked by the particulars of this rural New Hampshire town, a position of privilege afforded to a particular type of whiteness, as he is now a "veritable pillar of a privileged community" and a "welcome guest in the white colonial homes" of Boston (202). Though Rolfe's whiteness is no less present or absent than Wade's, Rolfe is able to leave Lawford and assumes that he has "managed to avoid being afflicted by that man's violence" (277). Indeed, it is Rolfe who survives to tell Wade's tale. He chooses a type of whiteness that is not dependent on folktales and customary ritual, but on knowledge and wealth and colonial homes. And he lives—whereas Wade, who chose the story of the father and the inauthentic life of the remnant "primitive," does not. Rolfe searches out rootlessness as a justification for his success, failing to see that he is substituting one set of folk beliefs for another, subsumed by the "lore of the rich" to believe that he has achieved an ethnographic objectivity by rejecting an unknowing folk inauthenticity for a knowing one.

But Banks does not let this stand. Wade's version of the events had to be "practically invented all over from the beginning," and the invention begins with Rolfe, who gives Wade the seed for the narrative that ultimately destroys him (335). Rolfe, however, is not a metafictional creation, standing in for Banks and speaking to the creation of the novel; instead, he is Rolfe the storyteller, the ethnographer of a ghost and a "ghost life," one that exists for us only because Rolfe writes it into being. This is a crucial distinction, because Rolfe's voice makes sense within the world of the novel if we see Wade not as a wholly separate imaginative creation but instead Rolfe's uncanny double, the return of the repressed. Avery Gordon says that "to write stories concerning exclusions and invisibilities is to write ghost stories" (17). Wade is the ghost, the specter, and his absence from the life of Lawford is profound, made present only after he is gone. *Affliction*, then, is the story of Rolfe's alternate ending, what could have happened if he had chosen a different way of being white, of being folk. The trace of what might have been. *His* absence is evidence.

Rolfe knows that his "life was not different from Wade's," that Wade is "describing my face as much as his" (202, 56). The uncanny double works "so that the one possesses knowledge, feeling and experience in common with the other" (Freud [1919] 1958: 141). This makes Rolfe "uniquely qualified to tell [Wade's] story" (Banks 1991: 2). But the double is also "marked by the fact that the subject identifies himself with someone else, so that he is in doubt as to which his self is, or substitutes the extraneous self for his own" (Freud [1919] 1958: 141). When Wade tells Rolfe a story of his father's abuse as a child, he substitutes Rolfe for himself, and Rolfe corrects him. But if Wade's story is Rolfe's own, then the particular actors in the tale of abuse are not important. The confusion about who suffered in this instance is further deepened when, as Rolfe declares himself lucky to be free of the affliction of his father's violence, Wade says "that's what you think" (277).

Rolfe says that he "remembered how it felt to look at yourself in a mirror and see as stranger looking back," interpreting Wade's confusion as if it were a stranger's reflection. At this moment, though, Wade and Rolfe converge, their stories misremembered and substituted.[6] That a "double" involves "constant recurrence of similar situations, a same face, or character-trait . . . a same crime" (Freud [1919] 1958: 141) makes Rolfe's last words all the more compelling, because he says that "the story will be over. Except that I continue" (Banks 1991: 355). Wade reenacted his father's crimes the moment he hit Jill. His was an ancient act of repetition, making manifest the affliction of "that man's violence." The face in the mirror was not, in fact, a stranger, but an intimate familiar, the father. Wade thus stands as median, the pivot point between Rolfe and their father, the common face of two doubled identities. That Rolfe and Wade (and Wade and his father) are doubled in *Affliction* is in and of itself not singularly compelling until you situate it within the realm of uncanny, by which "whiteness" is embodied and projected onto the body of the other; in this case, it is Wade, othered in both pairs by the degenerate-culture of his folk. This particular convergence—whiteness and the uncanny—is one that is rich with possibility in the study of folklore and literature, as the uncanny makes the familiar menacing because it represents the return of the repressed. For Freud, the return was either of repressed infantile complexes, or, more commonly, "the primitive beliefs" of an animistic, folk society.

Freud's theories of the unconscious were appealing for a time to a certain set of folklorists because he linked, or doubled, the evolution of the individual psyche to the evolution of culture. Ernest Jones argued that "there is a far-reaching parallelism between survivals of primitive life from the racial past and survivals from the individual past" ([1930] 1965: 92). Thus "neurotic symptoms are seen as vestigial remains from infancy just as Tylor's survivals were seen as vestiges from society's primitive past" (Schmaier and Dundes 1961: 143).[7] The folk did not need psychotherapy because they still had folklore, where they worked out, sublimated, expressed the workings of the mind that psychotherapy sought to cure.[8] But civilized society required the repression of this primitive past, to be "hardened" against the "lure of superstition" because "the animistic beliefs of civilized society have been *surmounted*" (Freud [1919] 1958: 157). This class of the uncanny occurs "as soon as something actually happens in our lives which seems to support the old, discarded beliefs" ([1919] 1958: 156). It is familiar because it is part of us, of our cultural past, our *folklore*, but it is threatening because it is something we seek to hide on our way to an evolved civilization, to that privileged community and those white colonial homes. To the power of a whiteness unmarked by the particulars of culture.

In *Affliction*, Wade represents a repressed corrupted atavism, a folk culture that Rolfe divests himself of, and yet when he tells of Glen and Wade's last confrontation Glen is not *like* a "giant from a fairy tale," or a *like* "colossus," he *is* those things. These rites and legends are no longer false affirmations of existence, and the distinction between absent and present culture collapses. The father stands as a mythopoetic figure slain by his son, against which two competing versions of whiteness are set: the inauthentic replication of ancient days in Wade, and Rolfe's own "absent" folk culture. Rolfe has to choose, and he chooses the power of perceived absence over a cheap replica. The ghost story that he wants exorcised is in fact his own uncanny life, the one he would have lived had he not been able to reject this particular construction of a folk identity.

But the absence is not steady, it is not stable—it returns as the abject. The abject "is radically excluded but never banished altogether. It hovers at the periphery of one's' existence, constantly challenging one's own tenuous borders of selfhood" (McAfee 2004: 46). It must be reenacted, the process of its abjection continually repeated if the border is to be maintained. Rolfe is able to co-opt the emptiness of Wade's life, an emptiness made visible by its traces of a degenerative folk culture, and inscribe his story as a way to exert control over the uncanny return of the folk and to keep the abject close at hand. This allows Rolfe to pass as pure white—full of knowledge and reason and white colonial homes, a subject "without properties" who knows himself as not-folk, as civilized. Rolfe created this story so that he could tell it to himself the rest of his life.

AN UNHOMELY LIFE: EUDORA WELTY'S *DELTA WEDDING*

Written over forty years before *Affliction*, *Delta Wedding* is also a novel set in a compressed time and compressed space, and it also follows the play of family conflict as it unfolds in an isolated, rural town. However, *Delta Wedding*'s whiteness is not manifest overtly, it is not marked as significant, it is not offered up, as it is in *Affliction*, as a subject of discourse. The first time I taught the novel, in fact, in a class on race and class in Southern literature, a student raised her hand and asked, "So how is this novel about race? There aren't really any black people in it." I thought about this student a few years later, the first time I lectured about the novel, when an audience member raised his hand and asked, "So how is this novel about folklore? There aren't really any folk in it." Both of these observations are incorrect, on several levels: white *is* race, and regardless there are many black characters in *Delta Wedding*. They are just constructed in a way that serves primarily to make the white characters visible—their presence is read as absence, except when it is not ("there was no one at home, only the negroes," the novel says).

Folklore also pervades the novel, one in which, as Diana Trilling wrote in one of its first reviews, "Nothing happens." The action of *Delta Wedding* takes place over the course of a week as the wealthy white Fairchild family prepares for the wedding of their second oldest daughter Dabney to Troy, the white lower-class overseer of Shellmound, the family plantation. The novel is centered on what many critics at the time called the trivialities of domestic life; what we may, in fact, call folklore. My audience member, though, followed his question by saying, "I see the folklore with Aunt Studney's sack, but that's about it." Aunt Studney is an "ancient" African American woman who worked for the Fairchild family. Her sack is part of her identity, and she strives to keep it hidden from the eyes of the white children of Shellmound, protecting a secret self. Blackness, it would seem, signifies folk-ness.[9] But as folklorists we should know both that "the violence of a racialized society falls most enduringly on the details of life" and that a racialized society depends on the constructions of races and not-races alike (Bhabha [1994] 2006: 13). As folklore certainly comprises a large portion of these "details of life," in a racialized society the folklore of all racial groups, including the "not-race" of white, are implicated in its violence.

Engaging Homi Bhabha's intertwining formulations of hybridity, mimicry, and "the unhomely," then, can help us critically interrogate the folk community boundary-making in *Delta Wedding*. There was a trend in ethnographic studies to privilege the "hybrid" ethnographer—those lucky few who occupy the double position of insider/outsider within the cultural group they are studying by virtue of biological or social belonging, like having parents of different races. From this perspective, "A hybrid form—like an ethnically or otherwise hybrid individual—can 'see' itself because it is more than itself; it is also other," seemingly neutralizing the disparity between seen and not-seen (Kapchan 1993: 305). But this formulates hybridity as a static state of being—a word is a hybrid, a text is hybrid, someone *is* hybrid—rather than as an active negotiation of identity that all participants engage in, even the most privileged. According to Bhabha, hybridity is a complicated and changing phenomenon that, like mimicry, both recognizes and defends against difference, a disruption that "produces its slippages." It is, like folklore, a process and a performance.

The unhomely, linked closely both linguistically and theoretically to Freud's theory of the uncanny, creates a theater for the play of hybridity. Since the conditions of colonialism and oppression have left the subject in a home but without a home, the unhomely troubles the boundaries between the public and private spheres. The unhomely "creeps up on you" and makes you question the almost-familiar (Bhabha [1994] 2006: 13). During moments of unhomeliness we can see the "fuzziness and ambiguity" of the divide between colonized and colonizer, from which "emerge new shifting complex forms of representation that deny binary patterning: "It is *almost, but not quite*, like home, like mimicry is *almost, but not quite* the original (McLeod 2000: 217). The performance of folklore is a method of exchange in such colonial spaces. Hybridity can result from living dynamically in the space of the unhomely, and hybridity very often involves the oppressed's mimicking of the colonial systems and its purveyors in ways that include dress, custom, and speech: folklore is thus used to precipitate hybridity in its most basic sense, to produce slippages at the borders between the oppressed and the oppressor. In some ways, the success or failure of the disruption of the mimicking colonized depends on how well folklore is manipulated by all parties involved. And it is in the third space, that site of hybridity and mimicry, that "something begins its presencing" (Bhabha [1994] 2006: 7).

Delta Wedding is not usually thought about from the anthropological and ethnographic perspective of cultural unhomeliness, as it is a scattered account told from the point of view of white (mostly) upper-middle class wives and daughters of landowners who have seemingly few concerns beyond romance and housekeeping. But we see the ripples of colonialism, the bending and invasion of third spaces, and the ruptures of mimicry—all from the perspective of white women, who are both part of and apart from the dominant ruling class. We can see in this novel Welty's deep understanding of how "the recesses of the domestic space become sites for history's most intricate invasions" (Bhabha [1994] 2006: 13). Welty harnesses the power of hybridity in unhomely interstitial spaces in order to re-make her female characters' identities, within which the violences of modernity and colonialism erupt to make the 'home,' with its connection to tradition and the past, both unfamiliar and menacing.

While there are representations of what we might traditionally call folklore in *Delta Wedding*—like the quilt given to Dabney as a wedding gift, the intricacies of manners, the ceremonial traditions of the wedding—I am more interested here in the process that makes such moments of folklore possible, that is, the process by which the very borders of the folk group are negotiated. In *Delta Wedding* there are specific moments where whiteness recognizes not only blackness but its own whiteness. This particularly striking (and surprisingly ignored) trope of racial recognition offers us a chance to look closely at instances of expulsion and repetition, in which the "center" delineates itself and, consequently, its perimeter: where the folk group is constructed. The perimeter is maintained by constant negotiation of its fluctuations, through its borderguards. Welty recognized, whether consciously or unconsciously, in her border-constructing moments of whiteness the power of hybridity, of unhomeliness and mimicry. What is most compelling is that she notices these ruptures at moments in which her characters are striving to join the protection offered by the closed circle of a folk group, for "sometimes in the circle you longed for the lone outsider to come in—sometimes you couldn't wait to close her out. It was never a good circle unless you were in it. . . . A circle was ugly without you" (Welty [1946] 2001: 95).

This year is 1923, an idyllic one for the Fairchilds, after the war but before the flood. The novel follows the women of the Fairchild family as they prepare for Dabney's wedding, and it is structured around the almost and yet not-quite epiphanies of these female characters. The "almost revelations" in *Delta Wedding* come neither in the home nor in the public sphere—they happen in the third spaces of the text: in the swamp, the hut, the forest, in the telling of the tale. And what makes these moments significantly revelatory is that they happen somewhere "home," *a* home, but not *the* home. For the young, motherless Laura, a Fairchild cousin, this epiphany happens in the swamp while she is visiting her extended family at Shellmound. She and her cousin Roy are exploring Marmion, the closed-up and empty family house that will soon be given to Dabney and Troy. Laura is considered an orphan by the rest of the Fairchilds, though she lives with her father in Jackson, and if there is one plot conflict in the novel to be resolved, it is deciding whether or not Laura will come to live permanently with her aunts and uncles at Shellmound. Laura herself is unsure of what she wants to do, and she spends most of the novel acting as a hybrid ethnographer, if you will; an insider/outsider who is able to recognize, though she had heard from "earliest memory" that the Fairchilds "never seemed to change at all," that she "could see that they changed every moment. The outside did not change but the inside did" (17–18).

Laura is obsessed with the sack carried around by Aunt Studney. As Laura and Roy leave Marmion, Roy pushes Laura into the swampy Yazoo river; it is here in the muck and mire of this swamp that Laura believes she can finally see into Aunt Studney's sack, with "its insides all around her—dark water and fearful fishes" (234). Looking up to see Roy through the dark water, she realizes that she is in danger of losing herself with the Fairchilds, and instead of joining the insular Fairchild community, she decides to leave it. She comes to this decision near the home that is not a home, in a place that is neither land nor water, brought through the darkness of the swamp and the emblem of Aunt Studney's displacement—the sack that is also not a home, but a closely guarded maker of identity. Welty has thus seized a moment of disruptive unhomeliness through the transgression of black-homespace in order to produce the power for Laura to create her own boundary, to reject the allure of the Fairchild's folk group. When it is later revealed that Marmion would probably one day pass to Laura, adding another layer to disorienting disruptiveness of "home," Laura decides to hold close her secret knowledge that she "would go—go from all this, go back to her father" (313).

Shelley, the oldest Fairchild daughter, also transgresses a not-quite-white homespace when she is sent to retrieve Troy from his house for the rehearsal dinner. She walks in on Troy, dressed for the first time all in white, to see him "handling his niggers." The men had been in a fight over Pinchy, the young daughter of the Fairchild's black housekeeper who, as is said throughout the novel, is "coming through," undergoing a period of vague madness that is characterized as an undefined type of spiritual journey. Troy is pulling buckshot out of the "seat" of one of the men; it is knowing how to "handle them" that, according to the Fairchilds, makes a man a planter. Framed by a doorway marked with the fieldhand's blood, Shelley is stunned by the sight of Troy "imitating" a "real Deltan." She is frozen in fear, not of the men in the house, but of having to cross the bloodied threshold. Troy tells her to "jump over it, my darlin.'" It is when she finally does cross the doorway that the "skies opened up a little" for her and she saw the true reason that her sister Dabney could not marry Troy. She couldn't marry a man who had blood on his door, though she knew at the same time that this reason "would not avail," for "she would jump as Troy told her . . . for what was going to happen was going to happen" (258).

The stunning scene of Troy's passing as a "real Deltan" lets us see the ambiguity and the ambivalence of colonial oppression, a complex rendering of the relation between the very real labor of the black workforce on whose backs the Fairchilds' built their plantation, the forces of modernity, the weakening of the Fairchild's power, and the infiltration of their family by the white underclass. The border between the insular family folk group and the rest of the world still holds, but it is showing signs of inevitable change. Because of Troy's "convincing performance" of a planter, his mimicking of their folkways, Shelley starts to ask the question, "What if all Deltans were imitations," what if "the behavior of all *men* were actually no more than this—imitation of other men" (259). She partakes in a customary ritual of folk culture at the request of the mediating mimic man by jumping over the threshold, but she uses the power generated in the liminal space of the ritual to remake the boundaries of her world, even if it is just "a little." It lets the possibility of disorder within the boundaries of her folk group.

These powerful moments of meaning-making are scattered throughout the novel, and they are often closely connected to Ellen: matriarch of the family, mother of eight and pregnant again, married to Battle but nursing a deep and illicit affection for his brother George. Ellen experiences a moment of profound unhomeliness early in the novel while out in the forest searching for a pin she had lost. It is here, where "the chimney to the overseer's [Troy's] house stuck up through the trees," that she meets a young runaway woman. Ellen calls out to the woman in the shadows—when the woman answers, Ellen "all at once . . . cried 'Aren't you a Negro?'" After first assuming the woman is black and thinking she is Pinchy, one of "our people," Ellen discovers that her skin is instead "white to transparency," suggesting an absence of color. With the discovery of her absent whiteness, "A whole mystery of life opened up" (91).

The phallic intrusion of her future son-in-law's house serves as a contrast for the forest, which in this moment felt to Ellen to be an "ancient place," haunted by this woman, a "spirit," a "dark creature, not hiding, but waiting to be seen." She has a freshness made manifest through "the soiled cheek, the leafy hair," linking her to a wood nymph occupying a land outside of time, wandering, in fact, "at the end of the world out here" (90–92). Here we see the suggestion of a mythic folk being used "to suggest remoteness of place or time," to give the woman "a patina of antiquity" (De Caro and Jordan 2004: 16–17). Thus the unhomeliness of the woman, out of place *and* time, marked as such through traces of an ancient folk, renders her unable to be fixed within Ellen's categories of race and gender. She is uncanny, because she is simultaneously dark and folk and white, and this cognitive dissonance destabilizes Ellen's world.

George, the object of Ellen's unstated and unrequited love, later casually claims to have met and had sex with this unnamed woman (103). So it is ultimately patriarchal, and phallic, power that triumphs, bookended by Troy's chimney and George's revelation. But at the end of the novel, the woman's specter, her ghost, returns, a move foreshadowed by her construction as ancient folk. While celebrating Dabney's wedding, Ellen discovers that the young woman had been hit and killed by a train, thrown with her "beauty disfigured before strangers into the blackberry bushes," an image captured by the photographer on his way to the wedding. The image of the woman, a study in contrasts of white and black, is quite literally fixed now in a photograph. The possibility for variation and movement and hybridity gone. Ellen then "all at once" sees "into

[George's] mind as if he had come dancing out of it leaving it unlocked, laughingly inviting her to the unexpected intimacy" (291). Ellen was momentarily destabilized by the unhomeliness of the woman, but her fixity in death puts the world back in order. It is a world, however, that is a little different. Though she is expecting yet another child herself, Ellen finally offers the motherless Laura that which she had been longing for most, a home. In this moment, Ellen secures the circle of the family folk group. Laura, through her rejection, does as well.

It is in moments of the disruption of the seemingly solid white folk group and of the seemingly pure white body that these women Welty writes are able to rethink their gender and class roles. At the moment when the characters are trying to understand what it means to be part of a community, part of a family, and part of a folk culture, we see disruptions of the dominant order of society. The women confront uncanny "folk" others who work in some way to complicate notions of whiteness: Aunt Studney, the woman in the woods, Troy, the absences and presences of Pinchy. These confrontations lead directly to the Fairchild women's re-making of their identities. Welty's white characters are not written as hybrids, but she recognized the power of hybridity generated at these unhomely moments of border-creation and seized it as a site where she could explore gender, motherhood, and sexuality.

Delta Wedding does not advocate for racial equality. It is not overtly political, and Welty does have, as Diana Trilling's criticism of the novel claims, a "rosy poetic" love for her white characters. Welty directs moments of unhomeliness and mimicry away from questions about race and racism in order to address issues of gender and class oppression. The African American characters in the novel are stereotypical, and often written as an absence—as in, "She could hear nothing, except the sounds of the Negroes" (69). Welty draws from stereotypes of folk culture to establish difference, to define communities in the novel, like the juxtaposition of Dabney's white wedding cake with the oily "hoodoo" cake that the servant Partheny gives as a wedding present. Both cakes are products of a folk culture, but only one is marked as such by Welty—the absence of white as folk, the contrast of a folk that marks a civilized whiteness. In another instance, Roxie, an African American servant, yells that "bird in de house mean death," after which "the Negroes simultaneously threw their white aprons over their heads," compelled by their folk tradition to act as one undifferentiated unit (209).[10] And Welty writes the African American part of town as mixed with "smells of darkness," using words like "devious," "invisible," "secret," "hidden," and "shady" to describe their homes (167). This stereotypical imagery of superstition works to position the closed-in life of the Other as unknowable and mysterious.

And yet, in a scene that calls into question all that happened before, Pinchy comes to Dabney's wedding dressed "all in white." Pinchy, as is said throughout the novel, is "coming through," which characterizes her as "for a few days a creature of mystery" (268). "Coming through" constructs Pinchy almost entirely through her connection to the world of superstition and folk belief. Pinchy takes her place at the center of the circle of African American servants who were gathered to watch the wedding, and the flower girl Maureen hands her a red rose from her basket, cementing her place as Dabney's double. This is a folk drama, an expression of the potential subversiveness of folklore, and it enables an act of insurrection, especially if we accept Jan Norby Gretlund's argument that Troy has broken off a sexual relationship with Pinchy in order to marry Dabney. Pinchy, like Wade in *Affliction*, is the uncanny, the representative of the return of a repressed folk culture used to highlight a negotiation of the boundaries of a folk group. Pinchy is at the center of the fight between the fieldhands, which prompted Shelley's recognition of mimicry. She is the figure Ellen thinks she sees in the woods, which prompted her misrecognition of the stranger. And now Pinchy embodies the uncanny, the return of the sins of the Fairchild's particular whiteness, sexual and economic and, above all, racial. Welty surprises the reader with this secret story being negotiated all the way through—a story that was suppressed and oppressed but that still managed to "produce its slippages," whole lives lived just outside the main in the homes absent from white sight, hidden by "shady" vines.

CONCLUSION

Anand Prahlad argues that in folklore studies "whiteness is seldom the subject of analysis in any form," and that such neglect serves "first, the interests of colonization, and subsequently, the maintenance of . . . emerging empires" (2018). To see the moments in these two novels where "the folk" are created, the violence that is enacted through their construction, and the power that such creation generates is to see that whiteness is not an absent identity but one that is compelled and constructed. Furthermore, the tendency that Pawlowski notes in the study of folklore and literature to overlook both literature by white writers and the folkloric nature of whiteness subtly reaffirms, however unconsciously, a hierarchical positioning of white folk as the primary arbiters of reason and enlightenment, naturalizing both dominance and subordination. There is much to be gained by looking at how writers like Banks and Welty, through rejection, abjection, oppression, and acceptance, through their invented folk and invented folkways, use folklore to construct versions of whiteness that are rendered both absent and present by the uncanny and the unhomely. To explore the folklore of whiteness in literature is one way that we can disrupt a narrative that centers whiteness as universal, as ideal, as the only state of being capable of speaking for all of humanity. To analyze whiteness, to mark it in its particularity and in its folklore, is to bring into focus that which has been absent from our scholarship. It lets disorder within our borders and finally helps us to see, as Welty once wrote, "again, but differently."

NOTES

1. This is why we see in the critical study of whiteness scholars seeking to racialize whiteness in order to "de-center" it, to mark it a race so that it can then be removed from the position of default it seems to occupy in Western discourse. Richard Dyer, Ruth Frankenberg, Mike Hill, Marilyn Frye, Cheryl L. Harris, Gary Taylor, and Roediger all argue a version of this. The title of Frankenberg's collection is, in fact, *Displacing Whiteness*.

2. A connected reading of whiteness as propertyless approaches the subject by linking it to postmodernity, particularly the idea that whiteness is equal to mass culture, which is in opposition to the "folk" cultures of Others. This, of course, becomes its property. In Mike Hill's collection *Whiteness: A Critical Reader*, all but two of the twenty-one entries are focused somehow on the connections between whiteness and mass culture, suggesting that whiteness is intimately tied into questions of capitalism—which, with its connections to colonialist tendencies, is often viewed as the destroyer of indigenous culture. This argument is put forth by whiteness, postcolonial, folklore, and ethnic studies scholars alike. This leads to the assumption that whiteness is "rootless" and lacking authenticity. This argument comes out of the work of labor scholars such as Roediger, who essentially argued that immigrants to America traded in their regional identities through things like minstrelsy in order to lay claim to the psychological wage of whiteness. Thus, according to Roediger, whiteness only came into being after industrialization of the immigrant working class and is thus predicated on an erasure of "roots," since "roots" denied full whiteness and thus the full privileges of whiteness.

3. Joanna Bosse's essay "Whiteness and the Performance of Race in American Ballroom" (2007) is a notable example of the kind of analysis this chapter seeks to perform, because it interrogates whiteness directly, rather than treating it as an often minor corollary to other issues of identity like class. She looks explicitly at how "whiteness was made, and perhaps sometimes unmade" in the realm of dance.

4. The debate around folklorists' conceptions of "the folk" has been ongoing for decades. Amy Shuman, as one of many examples, questions the belief in folklore studies that only "peasants, male-risk-taking occupational groups (loggers, whalers, etc.,) or 'native,' tribal, or otherwise authentic others (such as Native American, Afro-Americans, or the elderly)" have folklore (2003: 349). James Clifford suggested that "ethnography in the service of anthropology once looked at clearly defined others, defined as primitive, or tribal, or non-western, or pre-literate, or nonhistorical" (1986: 23). Folklore, Shuman and Charles Briggs argued, developed as the "silent Other of Modernism" grounded in "modernism's binary oppositions" between the authentic and the inauthentic, dominant and minority, global and local. In *Voices of Modernity*, Briggs and Richard Bauman argue that tradition and oral discourse is used as a "mediating force in the alignment of premodernity to modernity," so that "oral tradition became the foundation of a poetics of Otherness, a means of identifying the premodern Others both within modern society (uneducated, rural, poor, female) and outside it (savage, primitive, 'pre-literate')" (2003: 14).

5. Rolfe says, "Wade's body, like my own, is of a[n] ... ancient type, evolved over tens of thousands of years holding the reins of another man's horse in the cold rain while the horseman does business inside by the fire, of climbing rickety ladders with a load of bricks in a hod ... of drawing sticks on a cart from someone else's woods to someone else's fire" (56). Here Wade and Rolfe's bodies are "evolved" not from a racial ancestor, but from one that equates the biology of the (white) body to working-class status. The nature of "poor white" as an identity is complicated in that "it refers not only to poverty and non-ownership of the means of production, but also to a set of behaviors that, in turn, become a signifier of economic status" (Sandell 1997: 219). In such configurations, "poor white" is primarily situated within the realm of the economic and *not* the racial, despite the inclusion of the "white" signifier. Robyn Wiegman argues that many scholars of "poor whiteness" thus racialize class into a minority identity, thus investing in a "white identity formation with no compensatory racial debt to pay" (1999: 147).

6. The Freudian overtones of this scene are heightened when we take into account that the abuse at the hands of the father came after he caught his son (Wade/Rolfe) peering into the window of the bathroom as their mother bathed. At this point, Wade's murder of his father seems inevitable.

7. Jones argued that our "unconscious impulses" represent "relics of the primitive mental state, fragments left over in the process of evolution. In the language of folklore, they would be termed survivals." Furthermore, "There is a far-reaching parallelism between survivals of primitive life from the racial past and survivals from the individual past" (1930: 92)

8. For example, Freud and D. E. Oppenheim, in a long essay entitled "Dreams in Folklore," say that "folklore interprets dream symbols in the same way as psychoanalysis," and that such folklore is not merely "entertainment" but is "to be taken seriously" (65).

9. See Shirley Moody-Turner's *Black Folklore and the Politics of Representation* for a close look at how the institutionalization of folklore studies impacted formulations of "race" in the US. She says simply that early folklorists such as Newell defined "'folk' as synonymous with race, and 'lore' as signifying the 'learning or knowledge peculiar to that race'" (2013: 27).

10. Troy immediately replies, "It does mean that ... my mammy said so" (209). In another instance, Troy says "My nose itches ... company's coming" (197). Troy is linked with darkness throughout the text: he rides a black horse, is likened to "a dark thundercloud," (39) is described as a "dark shouting rider" (41). His participation and knowledge of superstition once again link him to the folk and to blackness, reinforcing the weakening of the family's whiteness and privilege.

REFERENCES CITED

Banks, Russell. 1990. *Affliction*. New York: HarperPerennial.
Banks, Russell. 2005. Interview by Robert Birnbaum. *Identitytheory.com*, January 18. http://www.identitytheory.com/russell-banks/
Banks, Russell. 1998. "The Salon Interview: Russell Banks." Interview by Cynthia Joyce. *Salon.com*. January 5. http://www.salon.com/1998/01/05/cov_si_05int/
Bauman, Richard, and Charles Briggs. 2003. *Voices of Modernity: Language Ideologies and the Politics of Inequality*. Cambridge: Cambridge University Press.
Bhabha, Homi K. [1994] 2006. *The Location of Culture*. 1994. London: Routledge.

Bosse, Joanna. 2007. Whiteness and the Performance of Race in American Ballroom Dance. *Journal of American Folklore* 120(475): 19–47.

Clifford, James. 1986. "Partial Truths." *Writing Culture: The Poetics and Politics of Ethnography.* Berkeley: University of California Press.

De Caro, Frank, and Rosan Augusta Jordan. 2004. *Re-Situating Folklore: Folk Contexts and Twentieth-Century Literature and Art.* Knoxville: University of Tennessee Press.

Dundes, Alan. 1984. *Sacred Narrative, Readings in the Theory of Myth.* Berkeley: University of California Press.

Dyer, Richard. 1997. *White.* London: Routledge.

Frankenberg, Ruth. Ed. 1997. *Displacing Whiteness: Essays in Social and Cultural Criticism.* Durham: Duke University Press.

Freud, Sigmund. [1919] 1958. The "Uncanny." In *On Creativity and the Unconscious: Papers on the Psychology of Art, Literature, Love, Religion.* New York: Harper.

Frye, Marilyn. 1983. *The Politics of Reality: Essays in Feminist Theory.* Trumansburg, NY: Crossing Press.

Harris, Cheryl L. 1993. Whiteness as Property. *Harvard Law Review* 106(8): 1707–91.

Hill, Mike, ed. 1997. *Whiteness: A Critical Reader.* New York: NYU Press.

Jones, Ernest. [1930] 1965. "Psychoanalysis and Folklore." In *The Study of Folklore*, ed. Alan Dundes, 88–102. Englewood Cliffs, NJ: Prentice-Hall, Inc.

Kapchan, Deborah. A. 1993. "Hybridization and the Marketplace." *Theorizing Folklore: Toward New Perspectives on the Politics of Culture*, ed. Amy Shuman and Charles Briggs, special issue, *Western Folklore* 52 (2/4): 303–26.

Levine-Rasky, Cynthia. 2013. *Whiteness Fractured.* Farnham, Surrey: Routledge.

McLeod, John. 2000 *Beginning Postcolonialism.* Manchester: Manchester University Press.

McAfee, Noëlle. 2004. *Julia Kristeva.* New York : Routledge.

Moody-Turner, Shirley. 2013. *Black Folklore and the Politics of Racial Representation.* Jackson: University Press of Mississippi.

Morrison, Toni. 1992. *Playing in the Dark: Whiteness and the Literary Imagination.* Cambridge, MA: Harvard University Press.

O'Loughlin, Jim. 2002. "The Whiteness of Bone: Russell Banks' *Rule of the Bone* and the Contradictory Legacy of *Huckleberry Finn.*" *Modern Language Studies* 32(1): 31–42.

Pawlowski, Lucia. 2015. "What's Wrong with Folklore in Literary Criticism?" *Griot: The Journal of African American Studies.* 34(1): 48–60.

Prahlad, Anand. 2018. African American Folklore and Race. In *The Oxford Handbook of American Folklore and Folklife Studies*, ed. Simon Bronner. Oxford University Press.

Roediger, David. 1991. *The Wages of Whiteness: Race and the Making of the American Working Class.* London: Verso.

Sandell, Jillian. 1997. "Telling Stories of 'Queer White Trash': Race, Class, and Sexuality in the Work of Dorothy Allison." In *White Trash: Race and Class in America*, ed. Matt Wray and Annalee Newitz, 211–30. New York: Routledge.

Schmaier, Maurice D., and Alan Dundes. 1961. "Parallel Paths." *Journal of American Folklore* 74(292): 142–45.

Scott, A. O. 2000. "Cold Comfort." Review of *The Angel on the Roof. NYTimes.com.* June 25.

Shuman, Amy. 1993. "Dismantling Local Culture." *Western Folklore* 52(2/4): 345–64.

Stowe, David. 1996. "Uncolored People: The Rise of Whiteness Studies." *Lingua Franca* 6(6): 68–77.

Taylor, Gary. 2005. *Buying Whiteness: Race, Culture, and Identity from Columbus to Hip Hop.* New York, NY: Palgrave Macmillan.

Trilling, Diana. [1946] 1994. "Fiction in Review." In *The Critical Response to Eudora Welty's Fiction*, ed. Laurie Champion, 103–5. Westport, Conn.: Greenwood Press.

Welty, Eudora. [1946] 2001. *Delta Wedding.* Orlando: Harcourt.

Wiegman, Robyn. 1999. Whiteness Studies and the Paradox of Particularity. *Boundary 2* 26(3): 115–50.

Where Have All the Hoaxes Gone?

Willow G. Mullins

In 1963, German satirist and illustrator Hans Traxler produced what appears to be one of the few folkloric hoaxes. Traxler's book titularly claimed to offer *The Truth about Hansel and Gretel*. The book includes all the hallmarks of both a good tale and a nonfiction account—a teacher, Georg Ossegg, happens to uncover evidence of a Black Forest baker and his wife, Hans and Grete Metzler, who were killed in the 1600s by an old woman over a gingerbread recipe. Traxler embellished his story with Ossegg's folkloristic and historical scholarship, charts, and drawings, a host of details fictionally signifying the nonfictional. Ossegg even indulges in exploring his suspicion that the grown couple could have become the children of the Grimm Brothers' tale (Joosen 2011: 31–32; Zipes 2002: 240–41). The fiction was sufficient to fool many, although no definitive evidence of folklore scholars being taken in could be found. The second edition, published a few years later, was labeled a parody.

As my co-authors and I thought through our approach to this text, the idea of "frauds, quacks, and dilettantes" kept returning to our conversations. Who have been the frauds, quacks, and dilettantes of folklore and folklore study? In a field that during its early years had been the purview of a wealthy elite studying the cultural survivals only extant by virtue of poverty or distance from urban centers, dilettantes were legion. Since the nineteenth century saw a lack of financial motivation as increasing scientific objectivity, the field owes much to the insights of these gentlemen and -women. Nor have quacks been entirely uncommon. Sigmund Freud defined the quack as "anyone who undertakes a treatment without possessing the knowledge and capacities necessary for it" (1959: 230). Between the quick succession of scholarly thought and the tension between the popular and academic definitions of folklore, we all might be in danger of well-meaning quackery.

Outright frauds, however, have been fewer on the ground. As folklorists know, one way to gain understanding of a group is through the folklore they produce. While fraud as a term carries a wide range of meanings that could fold in all manner of nefarious activities and agents, here I wanted to focus specifically on one of the products of frauds—hoaxes. Following Curtis MacDougall's definition, a hoax is "a deliberately concocted untruth made to masquerade as truth" (quoted in Brunvand 2001: 194). A hoax requires both intent to deceive and that the audience be taken in, at least for a while. Generically, hoaxes may act like practical jokes, but they tend to run deeper and be less light hearted. For example, Roger Abrahams perpetrated two "practical jokes," spelling his name backwards in one attribution and writing out a legend in first person only to acknowledge later that he had adapted the tale (1970: 1977). Again, no one in folklore studies appears to have been taken in.

A hoax might be perpetrated for any number of reasons—revenge, jealousy, whimsy, reward. It can be humorous or deadly serious, but a hoax must seem true from the start. What separates the hoax from other forms of humor, if a hoax can be said to have humorous intent, is its framing as serious and its use of the codes associated with non-humorous discourse (Marks and Davis 2014). Hoax can bear a passing resemblance to rumor, which Gordon Allport and Leo Postman define as " a specific proposition for belief, passed along from person to person" (quoted in Turner 1993: 4), and urban legend (cf. Brunvand 2001). There are important differences between these three forms, though. Urban legends and rumors generally cannot be traced to a source, while hoaxes often can. The intent matters as well. Urban legends and rumors are told as true; someone somewhere knows that the hoax is false and intends to deceive (Brunvand 2001: 194). Further, where rumor and urban legend often fail to present concrete evidence or the evidence presented relies on unverifiable and vague references to friends of friends, hoaxes, at least academic hoaxes, tend to have evidence in excess. Traxler, for instance, quotes a large number of both legitimate and ersatz folklore sources, adding validity to his narrative. The hoax's dependence on evidence bears a striking resemblance to academia's, where the evidence makes or breaks the scholar. And academia, the very place where hoaxes *should* be most easily unveiled, has shown a high susceptibility to them.

Anthropologists in particular have been the target of many a hoax. Two, Piltdown Man and the Tasaday tribe, may stand at the apex of hoaxing history. Piltdown Man consisted of a set of remains that seemed to suggest an ancestor to *homo sapiens* other than the Neanderthal, and was found in 1912 by Charles Dawson. Dawson, a lawyer by trade and natural historian by hobby, might be the very dilettante Dundes warned against. The find was not discredited until scientific dating methods improved in the 1950s, and it has yet to be proven who was behind the hoax (Feder 2006: 1171). While Piltdown struck at biological and medical anthropology, evolution and archeology, the Tasaday hoax centered on cultural anthropology and its popular counterpart, *National Geographic* magazine. In a report in a 1971 issue of the magazine, Kenneth MacLeish wrote that the twenty-six remaining Tasaday lived, apparently happily, a stone-age existence devoid of modern technology in the remote caves of Mindinao. The Philippine government moved swiftly to set aside a preserve for the people and a trust fund to ensure that they would be cared for and not further harassed by tourists or scholars. The Tasaday, however, were little more than a money-making scam perpetrated by Manuel Elizalde, an official in Fernando Marcos's government, apparently with Marcos' collusion. When Marcos fell in 1986, Elizalde fled with the assets, and the caves were found to be empty; the twenty-six people had been "recruited" from nearby villages to play the part (Feder 2006: 1174).

Anthropologists should not be taken as particularly gullible, however. Hoaxes abound in other disciplines as well. One of the most famous academic hoaxes occurred in literary criticism. In 1996, the well-respected journal *Social Text* published an article by physicist Alan Sokal entitled "Transgressing the Boundaries: Towards a Transformative Hermeneutics of Quantum Gravity" (1996a). The day the *Social Text* article appeared, Sokal revealed in *Lingua Franca* that it had been a hoax. His stated goal was to see if he could get an essentially nonsensical article published if "it sounded good and it flattered the editors' ideological preconceptions" (1996b). Apparently, he could. In reflection, Sokal asserted that some of his motivation came from the danger of taking postmodern social-construction theory to an extreme, allowing for its misuse by corporations and politicians seeking to bend science to their own ends (2008: xv–xvii). He also clearly disparages the linguistic flights of postmodern criticism, which might have made his hoax less easy to detect. Quality matters, though. A similar hoax targeting *NORMA: International Journal of Masculinity Studies* recently failed. While the academic perpetrators sought to ridicule gender studies as a field, the journal editors quickly dismissed the proposed article as "sheer nonsense" (Graham 2017).

Our hoaxes tell us a lot about our desires and fears. Those things we most want are often the very things that the unscrupulous can offer and that we can accept without too much questioning. As anthropologist Kenneth Feder has commented, all hoaxes require "an audience predisposed to believe the implications of fabricated data" (2006: 1169). These academic hoaxes say as much about what various scholars *want* to believe as they do about the nature of belief itself. The discovery of Piltdown Man in 1912 offered a compelling counternarrative to Darwinian evolution. The archeological data up to that point suggested that the development of modern homo sapiens lay in our bipedalism and our ability to walk upright. The Piltdown remains, however, provided evidence of a "brain-centered paradigm," which hypothesized that it was superior brain power that led to modern humans, reinforcing religious ideas about the primacy of mankind (Feder 2006: 1171). The Tasaday seemed an antidote to much of the technological and social upheaval that plagued Western society in the late 1960s and early '70s, but it also offered the holy grail of anthropological research—the untouched tribe.

The *Social Text* affair suggests a desire for the poetic in theory perhaps, but more tellingly, one of the editors expressed surprise that the journal "was taken seriously enough to be considered a target of a hoax, especially by a physicist" (Robbins and Ross 1996). If folklorists have had concerns that folklore is not well respected in the academy by other humanists (Williams 2017: 136), it seems we are not alone in desiring that scientists like Sokal take the humanities more seriously. The *NORMA* hoax provides a converse relationship: the hoax failed to hit its mark perhaps because gender studies as a discipline seems more firmly situated. Gender studies already fought the battle for their institutional space, and while certain segments of society might continue to attack its utility, few departments have been actually cut. Ultimately, the Tasaday hoax and Sokal's *Social Text* hoax led to some soul searching as to why they had worked so well, and perhaps they made their victim fields more robust as a result (Headland 1992; Robbins and Ross 1996).

If hoaxes reveal our hidden desires, what do folklorists desire enough to be the basis of a hoax? When I first started asking around about hoaxes in folklore studies, most folklorists told me they could not think of any. There have been hoaxes *reported* by folklorists, such as a boy admitting that he was the ghost moving things around his grandparents' house in 1961 (Melnick 1961: 208) or a case of a man claiming that he was a were-crocodile (Cray 1964: 53). Indeed, folklore journals of the early and mid-twentieth century seem to be full of hoax spotting. But folklorists stand largely aloof. In every instance, the reporting folklorists seem to take on the stance of the skeptic, clever or disinterested or perhaps just etic enough to spot the deception.

Yet hoaxes have touched folklore studies, and, like all hoaxes, they reveal a lot about folklore studies itself. While it seems unlikely that folklorists were taken in by Traxler's Hansel and Gretel story, two other possible hoaxes have affected folklorists—*Ossian* and *Aradia*. Like Traxler's book, both center on folkloristic texts gathered from an informant who fades from view in the face of the folklorist himself. Both controversies center on the authenticity of the source material and the informant. Unlike Traxler, neither has been completely laid to rest.

James MacPhearson's *Ossian*, published in 1760, met with almost immediate condemnation. The discussion centered on issues of cultural appropriation and authorship. MacPhearson attributed the poems to a third-century Scottish bard, the eponymous Ossian, and claimed that he had found original manuscripts from this bard; MacPhearson's own role was that of translator. Culturally, MacPhearson's claims caused waves. The Irish claimed the stories as their own and felt that MacPhearson had bastardized and inaccurately reported them (Gaskill 2004). While the two countries share a Celtic origin and culture, in the context of British rule, a native artistic tradition could act as an important cultural commodity, helping foster resistance to colonialism (cf. Fanon). *Ossian* appeared a mere sixteen years after the Battle of Culloden. Thus, the debate about *Ossian*'s cultural origins cannot be separated from the politics of the Scottish Enlightenment and the Europe-wide rise of Romantic nationalism.

But it was not only the cultural origin of the poems that scholars debated— the authenticity of Ossian himself and the existence of the manuscripts was also doubted. None of the original manuscripts have ever been found, and in subsequent centuries, most have agreed that the poems were likely inventions of MacPhearson's. Between the two extremes of faithful translation and wholesale invention, however, lies the middle ground belief that MacPhearson was working from some kind of collected source material, likely stories he heard from Scottish crofters, which he wove into a narrative. Except that MacPhearson himself maintained the veracity of the Ossian manuscript, one might assume he was following the literary trope of ascribing a work to an unknowable bard that dates back to Homer. What the *Ossian* controversy suggests is a more interesting cultural linking among readers between appreciation for MacPhearson's manuscript and belief in its veracity. Throughout the eighteenth and nineteenth centuries, although debate raged about whether Ossian had ever existed, the volume nonetheless was widely read and had a major impact on literature. More recently, however, the "literary worthlessness of MacPhearson's work is all too often taken as read, and the poems themselves left unread" (Glaskill 2004: 2).

Charles Godfrey Leland's *Aradia or the Gospel of Witches* appeared nearly a century and a half after *Ossian*, and yet the discussions about the two texts are strikingly similar. Leland claimed to have acquired the original manuscript on which his text is based from an Italian woman, Maddelena. Unlike Ossian, Maddelena appears to have existed; Leland introduced her to both family members and other folklorists. According to Leland, Maddelena gave him a number of manuscripts that documented the activities of the witches of northern Italy. Leland's work, *Aradia*, purported to be a translation of those manuscripts. Like *Ossian,* however, no trace of the original manuscripts has since been found. Like *Ossian*, too, some have suggested that the manuscripts were an invention of Leland's, the whole story a hoax and Maddelena nonexistent or a paid agent (Mathiesen 1998: 39). Others have suggested that Maddelena is the hoaxer and Leland was the dupe. According to what we believe we know of Maddelena, she was a skilled fortune teller, adept at reading her clients, or in the case of Leland, her patron, and providing what he wanted—evidence of the folklore of Italian witchcraft (Mathiesen 1998: 49). Folklorists since have used *Aradia* mostly for what it tells us about the beliefs *about* witches and witchcraft and the variations of a mythical figure (cf. Magliocco 2002). While MacPhearson's *Ossian* may have been a hoax or a literary practice taken to extremes, Leland's case is less clear.

Taken together, *Ossian, Aradia*, and *The Truth about Hansel and Gretel* provide insight into not only the desires but also the fears of folklorists. The players in the back stories of the three texts are similar: a folklorist collecting in the field; a person with local knowledge and access to previously unstudied texts; the texts themselves, which require translation and interpretation by the folklorist to make them sensible to a wider audience; a disappearing manuscript; and a skeptical scholarly audience. In the debates about these three texts it is possible to see folkloristic desire for an undiscovered set of data and a local guide to provide access and lend authenticity. To find the undiscovered is the goal of much scholarship in a wide range of fields, but the guide, be they bard, local woman, or schoolmaster, suggests that authenticity matters for folklore studies and for folklorists themselves in a way peculiar to folklore studies. But the three back stories also reveal a deep desire for the role of the folklorist as translator and interpreter to be recognized and to be taken seriously. Thus, woven through these desires lie the fears that the guide will prove false, the folklorist themselves will be deceived. As a field reliant on people willing to share their culture, folklore depends on the good will of others to tell the truth. What happens when they do not? The folklorist typically bears the burden of proof for the texts reported, and the gravity of folklore studies suffers.

Three hoaxes in three hundred years does not amount to much, however. Especially when we only know for certain that one, *Hansel and Gretel*, was a true, intentional hoax and only one, *Aradia*, seemed to take in any folklorists. While Traxler certainly wrote a hoax, his work fails to merit a mention in most folklore journals. MacPhearson was challenged immediately, and by the time folklore studies became a field, the text was largely classed as literature rather than a collection of folklore. Leland, or Maddelena, seems the most likely to have perpetrated a lasting hoax, but he, or she, is also the most likely to *not* have committed such a hoax. Is folklore studies oddly immune to hoaxing, then, or is there another reason for the low number of folklore hoaxes?

One could find places, particularly in the presentation of material folk arts, where a hoax could thrive. Folklorists have interests in belief, ritual, ghosts, stories, traditions, things often unproven and unprovable with shifting forms and shifting value. Any of which would seem an easy target for a hoaxer. Further, as many a folklore studies historian has documented, folklorists certainly possess desires—for authenticity (Bendix 1997), for legitimacy (Bronner 1986), for clear institutional positionality (Zumwalt 1988), for clarity of the field (McNeill 2013; Sims and Stephens 2011), for a consistent language that does not reinscribe systematic oppressions (Feintuch 2005; Bauman and Briggs 2003), for empathy (Shuman 2005). But none of these seem to have triggered a hoax aimed specifically at folklorists. Do folklorists desire too many different things to believe blindly in one? Or are folklorists too aware of how hoaxes work or too conscious of our own desires to be hoaxed?

This seeming absence might also be a matter of folklore's deep interest in how people and groups communicate and the workings of belief itself. Whether we believe that Maddelena existed or told Leland the truth might be of less interest to many folklorists than the structures of belief surrounding the narrative. Leland's text, legitimate or not, has fostered the modern American neo-Pagan movement, which is an interesting development in itself (Magliocco 2012). Folklorists may just make terrible dupes, failing to provide the desired response. Of course, there also may have been hoaxes all along that folklorists never figured out. Rather than asking why there haven't been any folklore hoaxes, a better question might be what do folklorists desire so strongly that we would be willing to believe a hoax?

The 1990s television show *The X-Files* featured two FBI agents—the scientifically minded but devout Catholic Scully paired against the seemingly gullible Mulder. Much of the tension of the show rested on their respective willingness or unwillingness to believe in aliens, monsters, god, destiny, life after death, and so on. Adorning Mulder's office wall in the show was a large poster depicting a fuzzy photograph of a UFO and the words "I Want to Believe." The poster and its motto became a signifier of not only Mulder and Scully's quest to reveal the truth but also the show itself and its fandom. Yet the words reveal the central problematic of hoaxes—a desire to believe is not the same thing as believing. Such doubt is bittersweet. It makes folklorists into excellent hoax spotters; it separates folklore studies from being hoaxed. We might want the story of Hansel and Gretel, Schwartzwald bakers, to be true, proof positive of a historical antecedent to at least one folk tale. It answers so many questions, raises so many more. It validates so much of our folkloristic research as more than "just stories," for now we enter the realm of histories and unsolved crimes, legitimizing the field. A desire that might open the field to more hoaxes.

REFERENCES CITED

Abrahams, Roger. 1977. "The Most Embarrassing Thing That Ever Happened: Conversational Stories in a Theory of Enactment." *Folklore Forum* 10(3): 9–15.

Abrahams, Roger. 1970. *A Singer and Her Songs: Almeda Riddle's Book of Ballads*. Baton Rouge: Louisiana State University Press.

Bauman, Richard, and Charles Briggs. 2003. *Voices of Modernity: Language Ideologies and the Politics of Inequality*. Cambridge: Cambridge University Press.

Bendix, Regina. 1997. *In Search of Authenticity: The Formation of Folklore Studies*. Madison: University of Wisconsin Press.

Bronner, Simon. 1986. *American Folklore Studies: An Intellectual History*. Lawrence: University of Kansas.

Brunvand, Jan Harold. 2001. *Encyclopedia of Urban Legends*. Santa Barbara: ABC-CLIO.

Cray, Ed. 1964. Wer-Crocodile Hoax. *Western Folklore* 23(1): 53. doi:10.2307/1520560.

Feder, Kenneth L. 2006. "Hoaxes in Anthropology." *Encyclopedia of Anthropology*, vol. 3, edited by H. James Birx. Thousand Oaks, CA: SAGE Reference: 1169–76.

Feintuch, Burt, ed. 2003. *Eight Words for the Study of Expressive Culture*. Urbana: University of Illinois Press.

Gaskill, Howard, ed. 2004. *The Reception of 'Ossian' in Europe*. London: Thoemmes Continuum.

Graham, Ruth. 2017. "Phallic Anxiety (Probably!) Drives Male Academics to Execute Lame Hoax about Gender Studies." *Slate*. May 25.

Headland, T. N., ed. 1992. *The Tasaday controversy: Assessing the Evidence*. Washington, DC: American Anthropological Association.

Joosen, Vanessa. 2011. *Critical and Creative Perspectives on Fairy Tales: An Intertextual Dialogue between Fairy Tale Texts and Postmodern Retellings*. Detroit: Wayne State University Press.

MacLeish, Kenneth. 1972. "The Tasaday: Stone Age Cavemen of Mindanao." *National Geographic*: 219–48.

Magliocco, Sabina. 2012. "Beyond Belief: Context, Rationality and Participatory Consciousness." *Western Folklore* 71, no. 1: 5–24. http://www.jstor.org.libproxy.wustl.edu/stable/24550769.

Magliocco, Sabina. 2002. Who Was Aradia? The History and Development of a Legend. *Pomegranate: The International Journal of Pagan Studies* 18 (February).

Mathiesen, Robert. 1998. "Charles G. Leland and the Witches of Italy: The Origin of *Aradia*." In Charles G. Leland *Aradia or the Gospel of the Witches*, Mario Pazzaglini, ed. Blaine, WA: Phoenix Publishing, 25–58.

McNeill, Lynn. 2013. *Folklore Rules*. Logan: Utah State University Press.

Melnick, Mimi. 1963. "Ghost Hoax Revealed." *Western Folklore* 22(3): 208. doi:10.2307/1498731.

Robbins, Bruce, and Andrew Ross. 1996. Editorial response to Sokal hoax by editors of Social Text. http://www.physics.nyu.edu/sokal/SocialText_reply_LF.pdf.

Shuman, Amy. 2005. *Other People's Stories: Entitlement Claims and the Critique of Empathy*. Urbana: University of Illinois.

Sims, Martha, and Martine Stephens. 2011. *Living Folklore: An Introduction to the Study of People and Their Traditions*. Logan: Utah State University Press.

Sokal, Alan D. 1996a. Transgressing the Boundaries: Towards a Transformative Hermeneutics of Quantum Gravity. *Social Text* 46/47: 217–52.

Sokal, Alan D. 1996b. "A Physicist Experiments with Cultural Studies." *Lingua Franca*.

Williams, Michael Ann. 2017. After the Revolution: Folklore, History, and the Future of Our Discipline (American Folklore Society Presidential Address, October 2016). *Journal of American Folklore* 130(516): 129–41.

Zipes, Jack. 2002. *The Brothers Grimm: From Enchanted Forests to the Modern World, 2nd ed.* New York: Palgrave Macmillan.

Zumwalt, Rosemary Levy. 1988. *American Folklore Scholarship: A Dialogue of Dissent.* Bloomington: Indiana University.

SIX

Folklore in Vacuo (and Other Disciplinary Predicaments)

Todd Richardson

> I believe that in approaching our subject with the sensibilities of statis-
> ticians and dissectionists, we distance ourselves increasingly from the
> marvelous and spell-binding planet of imagination whose gravity drew
> us to our studies in the first place.
> —Daniel Dreiberg, "Blood from the Shoulder of Pallas." *The Journal of
> the American Ornithological Society* (Fall 1983)

I didn't come to the field of folklore a true believer. Rather, I stumbled into
the field following a drastic change in the University of Missouri's program
in creative nonfiction, which had been my original area of emphasis as a PhD
student.[1] In American folklore studies, I discovered a discipline that was wild-
eyed in concept yet circumspect in practice. Folklore, as an idea, enthralled me,
and I will forever be grateful for the way the concept illuminates the ubiquitous
genius of the everyday. The way folklorists wrote about it, however, bummed
me out. Sure, there were some interesting experiments with ethnographic
methodology going on, but for the most part, folklore research resembled the
same thesis-driven displays of erudition and rigor that had steered me away
from literary criticism and towards creative nonfiction in the first place.

I cannot overstate what a revelation creative nonfiction had been for me. The genre taught me to think less about what writing *ought* to look like and more about what it *might* look like. In practice, creative nonfiction provided the freedom to find formats appropriate for individual ideas rather than having to cram thoughts into industry-standard receptacles (e.g. the scholarly article). For this reason, even though I found folklore, the subject, to be enchanting, I found folklore studies to be humdrum, cautious and predictable, traits that perplexed me until I became more familiar with the curious position of folklore in academe.

I have been participating in the field of folklore for over a decade now, during which time I have been consistently disappointed by the discipline's lack of imagination. Brilliant people populate the field, people with singular insights into the diversity, adaptability and inventiveness of human expression, yet they continue to share their ideas primarily via jargon-heavy scholarly articles published in institutional journals with limited readerships. It doesn't have to be this way. Folklore, both as a subject and as a discipline, overflows with thrilling possibilities, but to get a glimpse of the wide variety of creative avenues open to folklorists requires an honest assessment of how and why the field sees itself the way it does, along with an acknowledgement that the discipline as it is currently construed is but one of folklore studies' possible iterations.[2]

FOLIE À DEUX

Whatever adjectives are attached to it—unofficial, informal, traditional, etc.—the idea of folklore has largely hinged on the conceit that the subject is necessarily imperiled, a belief that gives the subject significance while ennobling corresponding efforts to understand it. For most of the field's existence, this idea was most clearly expressed in the idea of survivals (i.e. antiquated cultural expressions that retain their value despite an ostensible incompatibility with modernity and/or modernization), a concept that did not simply describe the subject, but functioned as the very definition of it. Following the mid-century turn toward performance, the term "survival" lost scholarly value, but the Romantic spirit behind the idea continued to shape the way certain subjects are deemed more worthy or in need of academic study and advocacy. For example, the transitory nature of performance *imperils* folklore, at least in an ontological sense, insofar as the ephemerality of such artistic expressions makes them difficult, often impossible, to commodify and therefore of questionable value in a Capitalist culture.[3] Moreover, the folklore most often addressed within contemporary folklore scholarship belongs to marginalized or disenfranchised groups, people believed to be outside the hegemonic structures of mainstream ideologies. While the artistic expressions of such groups are not necessarily survivals, their deviance from mainstream culture gives them the aura, if not the actuality, of being endangered.

Folklorists, academic folklorists in particular, stretch this imperiled outlook to encompass the discipline as a whole, believing that their work is as precarious as the stuff they study: "If the initial assumption of folklore research is based on the disappearance of its subject matter, there is no way to prevent the science from following the same road," Dan Ben-Amos wrote in the very same article in which he provided the most-commonly cited definition of folklore as *artistic communication in small groups* (1971: 14). This situation has been discussed at length by many folklorists in scholarly works—Richard Dorson captured the situation succinctly when he wrote, "The idea that folklore is dying out is itself a kind of folklore" (1959: 278)—and, I would guess that every folklorist has, at some point, discussed this issue in less formal venues and through less official media.

In practice, this fear of the field's imminent disappearance translates into a fair bit of unflattering navel-gazing. At the 2009 meeting of the American Folklore Society, held in Boise, Idaho, I went to one of the many "Whither Folklore?" sessions included at each AFS meeting, and in the middle of a heated discussion about what needed to be done to save our disappearing discipline, a woman stepped up to a microphone, introduced herself as "an interloping anthropologist," and commented that she was stunned by the disciplinary self-hatred she was hearing. "Anthropologists generally don't like their field," she said, "but I've never heard anything like this from any of my colleagues." From her observation, I unscientifically extrapolate that the professional insecurity that runs throughout American folklore studies is genuinely spectacular, that even though many academics question the value of their work—and, for what it is worth, I would never trust a discipline that did not routinely question why it does what it does—folklorists are especially skilled in self-doubt.

The endemic pessimism of the discipline is, I suspect, at least partially an outgrowth of the Romantic spirit inherent in the very concept of folklore. Folklore's invention was, like Romantic philosophy itself, a response to the violent and unprecedented social changes associated with modernization. Its cause, in other words, has long been lost causes, a sentiment that continues to shape the spirit of the field: "If we have had a predisposition as a whole in folklore," Roger Abrahams (may have) famously said, "it is that we have been brought together through a feeling of cultural loss arising from the onset of modernity" (quoted in Kapchan 1993: 307). This is not to say that folklore studies is, itself, a lost cause, but sharing space with so many lost causes has resulted in a sort of *folie à deux* wherein anxiety for the subject gets transmitted to the discipline as a whole. Living forever in the eleventh hour, folklorists cannot help but see in themselves that which they see in the things they study.[4]

All of which is to suggest that viewing folklore studies as an imperiled field discourages folklorists from taking many expressive chances as doing so would risk pushing the insecure discipline past an imagined tipping point. Occasionally, a well-established scholar will write about a subject that genuinely tests the scope of folkloristic inquiry, and there have been the odd bouts of expressive ingenuity, but on the whole, scholars share their research findings on appropriately folksy subjects through conspicuously rigorous, unimaginative books and articles.

FOLKLORE IN VACUO

There has never been an agreed-upon definition for folklore, which is why much of the discipline's existence has been shaped by a prolonged, ecstatic debate regarding what, exactly, this thing of ours might be. The definitions are multitudinous, so much so that it sometimes feels as if every piece of folklore scholarship expresses an idiosyncratic take on the topic. Certainly, some adjectives appear more frequently than others, yet there has never been anything resembling an official definition. In "Folklore's Crisis," Barbara Kirshenblatt-Gimblett goes so far as to suggest that, ultimately, what unites the discipline is a shared narrative of development, that folklorists are brought together not by a specifically defined subject but by a "distinctive intellectual history" (1998: 320).

As is true in the maintenance of all histories, folklorists have been selective—increasingly so since the academic institutionalization of folklore studies in the middle of the Twentieth Century—about what events and figures get included in the story the field tells about itself. Institutionally trained folklorists have pruned, or at the very least minimized, the work of scholars who do not fit the model of what we think we should be—or perhaps it would be more accurate to say the model of what we believe others think we should be—scholars who often have tremendous influence on folklore as it is imagined by people outside academia. Joseph Campbell, for instance, is one of the most commonly thought-of authorities on folklore in the public imagination, yet his work is rarely mentioned within our field, and, on the rare occasion it is acknowledged, it is mocked as unscientific horsefeathers.[5]

Despite the fact that histories of folklore studies are selectively charted through different events and figures, the origin of the field (or at least the origin of the field's name) is located in a very specific moment: in 1846, William Thoms, a clerk in the secretary's office of Chelsea Hospital in London, proposed

Folk-lore as an alternative term for *popular antiquities*, a designation that had hitherto been used to describe the collection of old and/or unusual cultural materials, a hobby Thoms shared with many gentleman amateurs of the Victorian Era. Considering that Thoms proposed the name as a parenthesis, it is a rather unglamorous origin for the field, yet I have heard many folklorists recount the episode impishly, sort of like *can you believe we made a field out of what started as an aside?* Concealed within the playfulness, however, hides a rather cutthroat abandonment of the field's early years. On the rare occasions that those pre-folklore years, back when what we do was known as popular antiquities, are mentioned, they are treated as an awkward historical genesis that we have outgrown. Simply put, we dismiss our ancestry—a very American thing to do—as incidental, not foundational, to who we are today.

The reason for the amputation of this early history is not all that complicated: wanting to be seen as serious scholars—scientists even—contemporary folklorists do not wish to be affiliated with hobbyists, no matter how visionary or insightful those amateurs may have been. This sort of ivory-tower posturing is not uncommon among academics in general—never invite a literary theorist to your monthly book club, for instance, unless you want a lecture on why everyone is reading the text incorrectly—yet the sentiment is especially pronounced in folklore studies because our academic subject is largely defined through its *un*academic nature (e.g. folk instruction is folklore because it is *not* taught in school). Being a folklorist necessitates questioning the value of institutionalized knowledge, yet we depend so much on the support of institutions for the sustainability of our field that we are forced into doing a Double Dutch: from one direction, we champion informal, extra-institutional learning as being just as sophisticated and meaningful as the education occurring on college campuses, but, from the other direction, we wax academic so that others will not confuse what we are studying with the way we study it. After all, folklorists want their colleagues across campus to see them as folklorists, not as the folk.

American folklore studies' present institutional position was forged by Richard Dorson as he, more than any other individual, fought for a sustainable place for the study of folklore on American campuses. When he took charge of the folklore program at Indiana University, six students were enrolled; when he retired in 1981, there were 150. Virtually every folklore curriculum in North America can be traced back to Dorson's tenure as chair of IU's program and the armada of folklorists he sent forth to realize his vision of a world in which "American folklore [takes its] place alongside American literature, American politics, the history of American ideas, and other studies that illuminate the American mind" (1969: 28). When Dorson ascended to the chair of the IU program, he believed the discipline was "a helter-skelter domain" lacking standardized purpose or form, and he endeavored to legitimize the field by promoting a scientistic approach to the subject. Key to his approach were objective representations of folklore witnessed first-hand, representations that eschewed personal attachment or embellishment. Crucial to Dorson's project, however, was the work of Benjamin Botkin, whom Dorson repeatedly offered as a cautionary counterpoint to the way folklorists ought to conduct themselves. Referring to Botkin's wildly successful folklore treasuries, Dorson wrote, "Some may think that [Botkin] has considerably aided their cause in getting folklore known throughout the country. I say that he has greatly injured it, and lessened the prestige of the study in the eyes of scholars in other disciplines." (1950: 482).

Whereas Dorson was interested in securing scholarly prestige for the field, Benjamin Botkin was interested in something very different. He believed in both "an art as well as a science of folklore." "There is a point where collection and classification break down and creative (including re-creative) interpretation must begin," Botkin wrote, insisting that the folklorist's central concern "is not what is the folk and what is folklore but what can they do for our culture and literature" (1930: 16–18). Botkin used the term Folk-Say, which doubled as the name of the journal he edited at the University of Oklahoma, to describe his subject: "The difference between Folk-Say and folklore," Botkin explained, "is the difference between poetry and history." He continued, "Folk-say is not a substitute or synonym for folklore as some have misconstrued it, but an extension of the older term to include literature about the folk as well as of the folk and to center attention on the oral, story-telling phases of living lore conceived as literary material." (1935: 324–25).

Recollecting an issue of *Folk-Say* he compiled while completing his PhD, Botkin rued that "like my brain, the book was stuffed with facts, dates, references, citations, and arguments. There could be no doubt that *Folk-Say* had sold out to the professors" (1935: 327). As much as Dorson loathed what he deemed "fakelore," Botkin loathed "folklorists talking to themselves, or folklore in vacuo" (1946: 522), evidenced by his belief in the value of accessibility: writing in 1939, eleven years before Dorson's first salvo, "If giving back to the people what we have taken from them and what rightfully belongs to them, in a form in which they can understand and use, is vulgarization, then we need more of it" (1939: 10).

As uncited as Botkin may be in scholarly articles on folklore, he is not without his defenders. Likely his most enduring contribution—at least within the world of institutionally trained folklorists—is applied folklore, a concept Botkin developed while working with the Works Progress Administration.[6]

"Whereas a pure folklorist might tend to think of folklore as an independent discipline," Botkin explained, "the applied folklorist prefers to think of it as ancillary to the study of culture, of history or literature—of people" (1953). In short, Botkin wanted to put the folk back in folklore, to develop an approach that did not simply identify folklore but put it to use. For those folklorists, most often working in the public sector, who are not only documenting and preserving folklore but channeling folklore, using it to unite communities, to undo prejudice, inequality and injustice, Botkin's work is essential.[7]

But another key to Botkin's approach to folklore and something that warrants wider reconsideration among academic folklorists is the creative use of folkloric materials. On the one hand, this means the use of folklore in creative writing, and I must say I am happy to see a wider acceptance of such work within the American Folklore Society. On the other hand, Botkin meant the creative presentation of folklore scholarship, an approach exemplified by his well-ahead-of-its-time journal, *Folk-Say*. This journal was intended for a popular, which is to say not exclusively academic, audience, the sort of publication a non-specialist might pick up and enjoy. Such a publication no longer exists, which means the curious amateur now has to pick up a heavily jargonized scholarly journal to get a sense of this thing we call folklore.

• • •

A spectrum of anxiety-inducing aspects of the field of folklore, ranging from the inherently ephemeral nature of our subject to the idiosyncratic aspirations of Richard Dorson, have led to a hyper-professionalization by folklorists, academic folklorists in particular. Folklorists have worked exceptionally hard to earn the respect of their colleagues from other disciplines and departments through scholarly rigor and sophisticated methodologies, yet these efforts have, concomitantly, alienated them from popular audiences, audiences that, at one point, were the field's strength.

Folklore, the subject, resonates deeply with people as it is a phenomenon most folks intuitively appreciate as belonging to them in some way, connecting individuals to traditions and communities that enlarge their sense of self. Moreover (and more profoundly), the unofficial character of folklore, even one's own, gives such expressions an aura of mystery, a contraband feeling as folklore points to worlds, or least corners of the world, that can't be accounted for using official (i.e. "not folk") approaches. If Modernity (along with its more rambunctious progeny, postmodernity) has instilled in us anything, it is the sense that there is nothing less meaningful than what is obvious, and folklore remains for many the same as it was initially conceived, an alluring alternative to what is apparent. Of course these enigmatic qualities that many people look for in folklore are largely incompatible with the scientific method's emphases on predictability and objectivity, which is why approaching folklore with the scientific method can be a bit like trying to comprehend the outlandishness of a jackalope by analyzing its diet: it may be curious to think about, but it misses the point of what fascinated people in the first place.

I want to make it clear that in no way am I encouraging people to simply seek out weirdness, which too often entails turning other people's traditions into decontextualized decoration. Rather, I think folklorists can do a better job of nourishing the interest that attracts people to the subject in the first place by presenting to audiences the unusual nature of folklore in creative, unexpected, and thoughtful ways, giving back to them, in a way that they can appreciate it, what belongs to them. Doing so, I believe, will increase the field's prominence while lessening the endemic temptation to steal meaning from other people's traditions, a temptation that has too long haunted people's interest in folklore.

Creative writing about folklore is an obvious solution here, and fiction and poetry that deploy folkloristic subjects and strategies are but two ways to go about this. Academic folklorists, it seems, have found much promise in my genre of preference, creative nonfiction, and I must say that the amorphous and renegade qualities of the genre are nicely suited to discussions of folklore. Whether we like it or not, most people hear the word folklore and think the word means *information of questionable veracity that is presented as fact*, a definition that could easily double for creative nonfiction as a genre. Creative nonfiction and folklore are both loose truth. Frank DeCaro's *The Folklore Muse* (2008), a collection of creative writing by folklorists that includes creative nonfiction, fiction, and poetry, provides a solid model for the sort of writing I'm talking about, but much more must be done. I hope to eventually work in a field where collections like DeCaro's aren't novelties, a field where thoughtfully crafted, evocative prose that encourages readers to think for themselves rather than telling them what to think is widespread practice.

I fear, however, that creative writing and especially creative nonfiction within folklore studies is currently viewed as "the other side of ethnography," essentially an opportunity for ethnographers to talk about their fieldwork experiences in a more personal manner. While this approach can be interesting, even illuminating, tales of "the misunderstood folklorist" resonate even less than the scientistic analyses that continue to define the mainstream of folkloristic research. When folklorists write creatively, it behooves them to make the point the folklore, not the folklorist, lest we continue to collapse inward into our own irrelevance.

We ought also to look to our own history for creative inspiration. As maligned as treasuries may now be among institutionally trained folklorists, they were once a staple in American families' libraries. *American Songbag*, compiled by Carl Sandburg, a two-time college dropout and three-time Pulitzer-Prize winner, still ranks as one of the most influential popular books in American history, having inspired thousands of musicians, poets and folklorists throughout its nearly one-hundred-year existence. Likewise, Botkin's many treasuries, despite their poor reputation amongst academically trained folklorists, were once perennial bestsellers—it was not for nothing that Dorson singled these treasuries out for ridicule as they made very large targets.

Of course to expect a book to have the same sort of impact in an increasingly paper-less culture would be foolish.[8] Digital treasuries are more befitting the zeitgeist and might do more to raise the field's profile, particularly digital treasuries that collect and showcase the emergent traditions of post-industrial, mass-mediated consumer cultures.[9] While it is a truism within the discipline that folklore exists everywhere people come together in groups, the general public still thinks of folklore as something from the past. As any folklorist will tell you from personal experience, most people are indifferent to our wise ideas about "old wine in new bottles," an indifference that presents us with a wonderful opportunity to show folks something new. Nevertheless, we have kept ourselves so busy writing jargonized analyses of the performance structures that delineate meaning within traditional expressive customary practices that we have failed to make clear to anyone other than ourselves the staggering grandeur of everyday meaning-making.[10]

There has, of course, been a fair bit of disciplinary attention paid to the ways in which folklore exists on the internet, yet this work has largely amounted to saying, "Hey, there's folklore out there." Using our traditional ideas about traditional culture to understand what's possible online seriously underestimates the potential of folklore in digital culture. Approaching digital expressions ethnographically can be interesting, but there is much more potential in using digital expression *as* ethnography (i.e. the aforementioned digital treasuries), something that is already occurring on sites like Reddit and Tumblr, places where people painstakingly identify, analyze and debate the contours and meanings of folk groups both nascent and long-standing. Folklorists may congratulate the self-awareness of such activities, but we should also acknowledge that that same self-awareness renders us irrelevant. To put it another way, the users of Reddit do not need folklorists to identify and critique the boundaries of their expressive culture because they have already identified and critiqued (and satirized) those boundaries themselves. Frankly, identifying digital culture as folklore is no longer enough because other people are doing it more completely and quickly even if they're not consulting our lexicon when they do so. Instead of writing about such internet communities as "the folk," we ought to consider collaborating with them as fellow folklorists.

• • •

> Work? It's just serious play.
> —Saul Bass

In his plenary address at the 2004 meeting of the American Folklore Society, Alan Dundes identified his thesis thusly: "The combination of the lack of new grand theory and the failure to counter the effective efforts of numerous amateurs and dilettantes who have successfully claimed possession of the field of folklore as their fiefdom has understandably led to a public perception of folkloristics as a weak academic discipline, a perception unfortunately too often shared by college and university administrators" (2005: 393). While Dundes' complete address was far from unifying for our field—a more polarizing speech is hard to imagine—his comment regarding so-called amateurs and dilettantes was one of the few parts of his jeremiad that actually spoke to the field's collective conscience. Whether it is Dorson's ghost speaking to us or something even more ephemeral, folklorists have, since the institutionalization of our field, viewed popular writing about folklore as the amateurish work of frauds, quacks and dilettantes. Might we, instead of simply gainsaying such work, make peace with these amateurs and look to them for examples of how we can better connect to an audience larger than ourselves?

Entering the popular imagination in twenty-first century America won't be easy for folklorists because it will force us to betray many of our longest-held, if often tacit sentiments. From some quarters, this will be seen as selling out, but perhaps the field, as Botkin suggested, sold out long ago in order to curry favor with the professoriate. Either way, I think it's best to reconsider the rhetoric of selling-out, a foolish ethic borne of a sanctimonious naiveté, and reevaluate how and for whom we perform our scholarship. At present, folklorists value scholarship for its exchangeability within the intellectual economy of academia more than for its insightfulness, and very rarely for its lucidity—if anything, a dash of obscurity can help make otherwise dim writing seem rigorously academic. Yet the more intently folklore studies pursues scientism and the scholarly prestige associated with it, the more completely the field fades from the public's imagination. Is it any wonder, then, that there is not wider acknowledgement and appreciation for folklore as a viable and essential mode of expression in American society when those who devote their lives to the study of it dismiss the texts most likely to resonate with a popular audience? Where can curious outsiders go to learn more when the tradition bearers spend their time complicating the subject rather than clarifying it? We ought to stop our scholarly posturing and begin composing works that make our subject interesting and comprehensible to more people, not just our professional kin.

I am certain many professionally trained folklorists find the thought tawdry, and I do not fault them: folklore is serious business. But so is play, and if any folk group can appreciate the essential human need for play, it's folklorists. Instead of lamenting our often self-imposed irrelevance, let us make the endeavor fun again for others and for ourselves by sharing our ideas recklessly and loudly. Not only should we rediscover the artistic temperament that drove Benjamin Botkin, we ought to also resurrect the spirit of weirdness that drove the first folklorists, those quacks, frauds and dilettantes who called themselves popular antiquarians. Frankly, we have become too sober in our approaches, trying to walk a straight line so that we might pass as normal academics. Let us revel in the possibilities of our unique disciplinary presence by sharing our ideas the way we might, not just the way we think we ought to.

NOTES

1. For completely unforeseeable and unavoidable reasons, the University of Missouri's English department lost both of its faculty members in creative nonfiction during my first year in the program. The turnover for creative nonfiction faculty was exceptionally high while I was there, nearly as high as the turnover for Defense against the Dark Arts instructor at Hogwarts, but I am pleased to report that Mizzou has now established a strong and stable faculty in creative nonfiction. Nevertheless, the unpredictability of the program during my time there encouraged me to investigate other fields, which is how I ended up in folklore studies.

2. Although it may act like it at times, this chapter is not intended to be a history of the field of folklore. If that's what one would like, there are scads of more rigorous, insightful texts out there that I recommend highly. I find Regina Bendix's *In Search of Authenticity: The Formation of Folklore Studies* (1997) to be the most critically incisive and useful. In a similar vein, Richard Bauman and Charles Briggs's *Voices of Modernity: Language Ideologies and the Politics of Inequality* (2003) considers the role of folklore in the development of Modernity. As for wider ranging but less critical histories, Simon Bronner's *American Folklore Studies: An Intellectual History* (1986) and Rosemary Zumwalt's *American Folklore Scholarship: A Dialogue of Dissent* (1988) are both helpful. The historical account of folklore studies that most heavily influenced this essay, however, can be found in Chapter Four of Benjamin Filene's *Romancing the Folk: American Roots Music and Public Memory* (2000).

3. In *In Search of Authenticity*, Bendix argues that the emphasis on performance did little to quell the Romantic elements of the field, that, in essence, it shifted the Romantic desire for authenticity from a temporal plane to an experiential one.

4. The arrangement puts folklorists in a curious predicament, one they share with so-called hipsters. Folklorists and hipsters are kindred spirits insofar as both build their

identities, by which I mean their self-perceived social capital, around the scarcity of the information they traffic in. Put another way, hipsters and folklorists generate their sense of importance through having access to and/or familiarity with cultural expressions most folks do not, whether it is independent music or traditional rites and rituals. Ultimately, this engenders an ontological quandary, as once an expression becomes interesting to others, which is what both the hipster and folklorist ostensibly facilitate by sharing it with others, it ceases to interest them. Indeed, there is a fiendish irony to the enterprise, as when a person, be he hipster or folklorist, looks for the overlooked, he undoes what he seeks the moment he finds it. This is all well and good within hipsterism because that ideology is driven by irony—hipsterism strikes me as a deliberate attempt to *not* signify, discussed in the earlier chapter "Misanthropelore"—yet folklorists have always been a sincere bunch. We are ill-equipped to find solace in the irony of such Sisyphean work, which further encourages scholars to see the field as being forever precarious.

5. Alan Dundes did engage the works of Joseph Campbell on multiple occasions, most notably in his 2004 AFS Address, which is discussed later in this essay.

6. For a full account of this, I recommend Jerrold Hirsch's *Portrait of America: A Cultural History of the Federal Writers' Project* (2003).

7. I appreciate that it can be argued that the sort of popular resonance I'm seeking is something best achieved through public folklore programs. Public folklorists have definitely been far more imaginative than academic folklorists when it comes to the representation and sharing of expressive traditions, and I think academic folklorists can learn a lot about how to make their writing more interesting and accessible from public folklorists. Such programs, however, are far less likely to represent folklore that does not exemplify preconceived notions of folklore. In my work with the Nebraska Folklife Network, the expressive traditions put on display and/or supported almost always belonged to appropriately "authentic" populations such as immigrant groups and other marginalized communities. Dependent as they are on public funding, public folklore programs must fulfill conventional definitions of folklore in order to secure their funding. With that in mind, it becomes doubly incumbent on the academic folklorist to manipulate both the form and content of their scholarship to enlarge the public's conception of folklore.

8. I do think there is great potential in books as collectible, fetishizable artifacts, two qualities folklorists are intimately familiar with due to our disciplinary history and subject of study.

9. *Open Folklore* is a fascinating and useful experiment, yet its audience is, again, almost exclusively academic folklorists.

10. As just one example, a website that chronicles the ways in which people creatively express themselves through the things they buy (i.e. the ways people recreate and repurpose mass-produced products to make them their own) would go a long way toward enlarging people's conceptions of folklore.

REFERENCES CITED

Bauman, Richard, and Charles Briggs. 2003. *Voices of Modernity: Language Ideologies and the Politics of Inequality*. Cambridge: Cambridge University Press.

Ben-Amos, Dan. 1971. Toward a Definition of Folklore in Context. *Journal of American Folklore* 84 (331): 3–15.

Bendix, Regina. 1997. *In Search of Authenticity: The Formation of Folklore studies*. Madison: University of Wisconsin Press.

Botkin, B. A. 1930. Introduction to *Folk-Say A Regional Miscellany*. Norman: University of Oklahoma Press.

Botkin, B. A. 1935. Folk-Say and Space: Their Genesis and Exodus. *Southwest Review* 20: 321–29.

Botkin, B. A. 1939. "WPA and Folklore Research: 'Bread and Song.'" *Southern Folklore Quarterly* 3: 7–14.

Botkin, B. A. 1946. "Conference on the Character and State of Studies in Folklore." *Journal of American Folklore* 59 (234): 520–22.

Botkin, B. A. 1953. "Applied Folklore: Creating Understanding through Folklore." *Southern Folklore Quarterly* 17: 199–206.

Bronner, Simon. 1986. *American Folklore Studies: An Intellectual History*. Lawrence: University Press of Kansas.

DeCaro, Frank. 2008. *The Folklore Muse: Poetry, Fiction, and Other Reflections by Folklorists*. Logan: Utah State University Press.

Dorson, Richard. 1959. *American Folklore*. Chicago: University of Chicago Press.

Dorson, Richard. 1950. Review of *A Treasury of Southern Folklore. Journal of American Folklore* 63 (250): 480–82.

Dorson, Richard. 1969. "A Theory for American Folklore." In *American Folklore and the Humanities*, ed. Richard Dorson, 15–48. Chicago: University of Chicago Press.

Dreiberg, Dan. 1983. "Blood on the Shoulder of Pallas." *Journal of the American Ornithological Society*, Fall.

Dundes, Alan. 2005. "Folkloristics in the Twenty-First Century." *Journal of American Folklore* 118 (470): 385–408.

Filene, Benjamin. 2000. *Romancing the Folk: Public Memory and American Roots Music*. Chapel Hill: University of North Carolina Press.

Hirsch, Jerrold. 2003. *Portrait of America: A Cultural History of the Federal Writers' Project*. Chapel Hill: University of North Carolina Press.

Kapchan, Deborah. 1993. "Hybridization and the Marketplace: Emerging Paradigms in Folkloristics." *Western Folklore* 52.2 (4): 303–26.

Kirshenblatt-Gimlet. 1998. "Folklore's Crisis." *Journal of American Folklore* 111.441 (1998): 281–327.

Zumwalt, Rosemary. 1988. *American Folklore Scholarship: A Dialogue of Dissent*. Bloomington: Indiana University Press.

INDEX

abjection, 179, 186

Abrahams, Roger, 35n3, 144, 192, 203

academia, 26, 42, 58, 95, 192, 204, 210

academics, 39, 151, 158, 203, 205, 211; and race, 111–12

Adams, Ryan, 28, 30

adaptation, 119, 122–23; to film, 68, 75

advocacy, 4, 26, 149, 153, 202

Affliction (Banks), 170, 172–79

African American culture, 112–13

African American Literary Studies, 8

agency, 31, 34, 153

alienation, 55, 60, 207

amateurs, 44–46, 48–53, 85, 87, 205, 207, 210

American culture, xi, 7, 11, 41, 115, 146, 197, 209–10; and adolescence, 69, 83n5; and awkwardness, 77; and commercialism, 55, 151; customs, 21, 67, 87, 121; and immigration, 187n2; and loneliness, 76, 81; race, xii (*see also* whiteness); values, 40, 64–65, 76–77, 81, 89, 140, 159, 205

American Folk Revival, 163–64

American Folklore Society, xv, 4, 21, 38, 42, 47, 58, 88, 142, 149, 203, 207, 210

American literature, 12, 172

Anderson, Carol, 130

anthropology, 24, 30, 44, 88, 92, 95, 99, 106, 116n6, 131, 161, 167, 170, 181, 192–94, 203

antiquarians, 50, 211

anxiety, 23, 50, 114, 146, 203, 207

Aradia or the Gospel of Witches (Leland), 194–96

authenticity, x, 8, 11, 13, 14, 21, 41, 96, 105, 109, 143, 164, 177, 194–97; as article of faith, 10, 21, 24–27, 28, 33–35; Bendix, 5, 10, 22, 211n3; creative, 45; desire for, xi, 5; and otherness, 4, 25–27, 41, 175, 187n2, 187n4, 212n7; and representation, 71, 95–98, 101–2

awkwardness, 11, 76–80

Baker Street Irregulars, 48

ballads, 32, 89, 110, 111, 112, 116n5, 149

Banks, Russell, *Affliction*, 170, 172–79

Barthes, Roland, 48, 146

Bascom, William, 88, 89

Bauman, Richard, 5, 8, 10, 22, 29, 30, 49, 60, 175, 197

Behar, Ruth, 20, 153

belief, ix–xi, 19–20, 34, 61–62, 192, 194–97; absence of, 86, 111; and authenticity, 23–24, 27; and language, 7–8; and legend, 104; and the supernatural, 114–15; and truth, 159–60; and the uncanny, 177–79

Bendix, Regina, 5, 10, 15n3, 21–22, 24, 35, 145, 197, 211n2, 211n3

betrayal, 100, 142, 163–64, 167

Bhabha, Homi, 12, 27, 180–81

Boas, Franz, 44, 88, 89

Botkin, Benjamin A., 12, 72, 206–7, 209–11

boundaries, 64–66, 83n3; and discipline building, 14, 21, 29–30, 47, 50; of folk groups, 12, 153, 180–81, 184

Briggs, Charles, 26, 29, 49

Bronner, Simon, 31, 114, 145, 197

Brunvand, Jan, 157, 160, 192

Campbell, Joseph, 50, 204, 212n5

canon, 4, 44, 47, 165, 167n3

Cantwell, Robert, 150–52, 163–64

capitalism, xi, 8, 50, 68, 99, 100, 187n2, 202

Chappell, Louis, 110–12

childhood, 68, 72, 86, 98, 136, 137, 138, 140, 143, 173

classification, 206

Clowes, Daniel, 10, 55–57, 67–82

collection, 75, 109–10, 131, 136, 149, 154, 205–6, 208–9, 212n8

collectivity, 20, 62, 63

colonialism, 4, 151; and folklore studies, 114, 171, 186; and hybridity, 181–83; in reading practices, 109; resistance to, 195; and theory, 21; and whiteness, 187n2

community, xi, 23, 56, 95, 131, 136–37, 152–54; and digital culture, 6, 81, 119, 123, 142–46; as emergent, xi, 66–67, 119, 121–22, 147; and exile, 7, 80; fanfiction as, 45–47; in literature, 86–87, 92, 97–99, 105–6, 115, 176, 185, 207; and network, 62–64; as place, 142, 146; shared values, 34, 56, 60–61

conscience, 166, 210

conservation, 136, 148–51, 153

consumerism, 8, 34, 60, 68, 143, 150, 163, 209

context, 24–27, 30–31, 51n1, 80, 144, 147, 208

Coontz, Stephanie, 74

Cox, John H., 110, 111

creative nonfiction, 201–2, 208

creativity, 62, 118–19, 201–2, 206–11

critical race theory, xii, 12

cyborgs, 157–61

Dawson, Charles, 192

DeCaro, Frank, 175, 208

Deetz, James, 120, 122

Delta Wedding (Welty), 12, 170, 179–86

Derrida, Jacques, 11, 137–42, 151–52, 154, 176

diasporic intimacy, 80

digital folklore, 45, 47, 83n4, 209

dirgewithoutmusic, 48

disaffiliation. *See* misanthropelore

Doble, Jessica, 51n1

domesticity, 91, 180–81

Dorson, Richard, 23, 89, 112, 203, 205–7, 209, 210

Dorst, John, 6–8, 14, 118–19, 143, 146, 161

Dostoevsky, Fyodor, 63

Dundes, Alan, 6, 31–32, 119, 142, 171, 193, 210

Dyer, Richard, 170–71, 187n1

Dylan, Bob, x, 13, 28; *The Basement Tapes*, 166–67; and Folk Revival, 164–65; and Nobel Prize, 163, 168; and plagiarism, 165; and traditional music, 165–67

Eckard, Paula Gallant, 102–3

economics, 28, 29

Eightball (comic), 55–57, 61, 68, 80–82

Ellis, Bill, 6, 7

emergence, 5, 66–67, 106, 140, 209

emptiness, 70, 101, 102, 179

Enlightenment, 29, 114, 195

epistemology, 11, 43, 62, 96, 107, 113, 115, 169, 177

ethnography, 20, 46, 90, 96–101, 107, 131, 176–77, 180–83, 187n4, 201; as writing, 208–9

faith, x, 10, 19–23, 26, 28–35, 159–60, 166

fakelore, 23, 145, 206

fandom, 45–49, 51, 53, 197

fanfiction, 13, 44–48, 50–53, 54

Feder, Kenneth, 193–94

Feintuch, Burt, 21–22, 197

fetishism, 41, 75

fieldwork, 7, 25, 33, 44, 51, 124, 132, 142, 157, 208

folklore: and amateurs, 45, 48–49, 205, 210; "artistic communication in small groups," 42, 56, 203; collections of, 209; and creative writing, 206–8; esoteric and exoteric, 58–60, 64; and ethnicity, 58; festivals, 28, 110–12, 147–48, 150, 152–53; fugitive knowledge, 207; and identity, 56–57, 67–69; as imperiled, 202–4; and

INDEX

the individual, 58, 61–62; and the internet, 44–47, 125–27, 157–62, 209; and literature, 86; as performance, 5, 22, 24, 28–29, 31, 33–34, 60–66, 110, 118, 120–24, 132, 140, 144, 147, 161, 181, 202; popular perceptions of, 204; professionalization of, xi, 4, 12–13, 22, 45–51, 95, 114, 149, 161, 203, 207, 211; as shared belonging, 58, 60–64; as a subject, 202; as survivals, 202; and whiteness, 169–71

folk-say, 206–7

frauds, 4, 13, 45, 47, 86, 89, 191–92, 210–11

Frazer, George, 87–88, 90, 92

Freud, Sigmund, 178–79, 181, 188n6, 191

gender, 36, 49–50, 109, 119, 120, 123–24, 184–85, 193–94, 198

genre, 6, 8, 20–22, 30–35, 45, 47, 58, 108, 119, 122, 141, 202, 208

Ghost World (comic), 67–76, 83n6

Ghost World (film), 75–76

ghosts: and adolescence, 68–69, 83n5; in *Affliction*, 176–79; Derridean, 139–40, 146, 148; as epistemology, 113–15, 154; and folklore studies, 113–14

Glassie, Henry, 26

Goldstein, Diane, 7–8, 22, 29

Hangsaman (Jackson), 90–92

Hansel and Gretel, 191, 194, 196–97

Harris-Lopez, Trudier, 30, 33

Hathaway, Rosemary, 6, 97–98, 144

Hattenhauer, Darryl, 85–86, 90

"Haunting Olivia" (Russell), 169

hauntings. *See* ghosts

hauntology, 11, 140

hipsterism, 69–71, 211n4

Hirsch, Jerrold, 212n6

Howard, Robert Glen, 6, 29–30, 143

Hufford, David, 7, 86

Hurston, Zora Neale, 3, 9, 106, 116n6

hybridity, x, 27, 30–31, 100, 170, 180–85

Hyman, Stanley Edgar, 13, 85–93

inauthenticity, 5, 8, 25–27, 71, 177, 179, 187n4

institutionalization, 29–30, 49; and epistemology, 100–107, 112–15; of folklore studies, 50, 188n9, 204–10; role in hoaxes, 194, 197

invisibility, 4, 13–14, 17, 125–27, 130, 132, 170, 185

Ivey, Bill, 5, 142, 144, 151

Jackson, Shirley, 7, 13, 85–87; *Hangsaman*, 90–92; "The Lottery," 86, 92

Jamison, Anne, 46–47, 49

Jansen, William Hugh, 58–60, 64

Jenkins, Henry, 45–46

John Henry, 105, 109–14, 116–18

John Henry Days (Whitehead), 109–13

Johnson, Guy, 110–13

Journal of American Folklore, 38–42, 87–88

Kenan, Randall, 11, 95–96; "Let the Dead Bury Their Dead," 105–9; *A Visitation of Spirits*, 106–7

keywords, 10, 20–23, 62, 153

Knopf, Alfred, 85

Kotsko, Adam, 77, 79–80

Kurin, Richard, 150–52

Laudun, John, 52n2

Lawless, Elaine, 7, 20, 23, 38, 139

legends, 7–8, 14, 103, 110–13, 139–41; urban, 157–61, 192

Leland, Charles Godfrey, *Aradia or the Gospel of Witches*, 194–96

"Let the Dead Bury Their Dead" (Kenan), 105–9

literary criticism, 91, 98, 111, 171, 172, 193, 201

literary tourism. *See* touristic reading

Lomax, Alan, 27, 164, 167

Lomax, John, 27, 88

"Lottery, The" (Jackson), 86, 92

MacPhearson, James, *Ossian*, 194–96

Maddelena, 195–97

Mama Day (Naylor), 97–101

marketplace, 24–25, 28, 63

mass media, 6–7, 41, 126–30, 143, 209

memes, 7, 13, 125–27, 132

metafiction, 11, 100, 105–10, 177

Mikkelson, David and Barbara, 158

mimicry, 180–82, 185–86

misanthropelore, 10–11, 55–57; and American culture, 76, 83n5; and awkwardness, 76–80; as disaffiliation, 58–67; in *Ghost World*, 67–76; performance of, 62–66, 77; as potential for connection, 80–81

misanthropology. *See* Morson, Gary Saul

misanthropy, 57, 63

Mississippi, 125–32

modernity, 7, 15n2, 75, 102, 114, 121, 181, 183, 187n4, 202–3, 207

Morson, Gary Saul, 63

myth, 23, 87–92, 146, 171

narrative in fanfiction, 45–47; as metafiction, 96–97; and memory, 139–40; as strategy, 119, 123; and untellability, 7–8

Naylor, Gloria, *Mama Day*, 97–105

Nebraska, 38–43, 58–59, 64

New Orleans, 125–32

Newell, William, 149–50, 188n9

nostalgia, x, 11, 27, 72–76, 80, 98, 135, 138–39, 141, 143, 146

Noyes, Dorothy, 62–64, 142

Oral History (Smith), 101–5

Ossian (MacPhearson), 194–96

outsiders, 103–4, 136, 148, 150–51, 182, 211

performance. *See* folklore

Piltdown Man, 192, 193, 194

Pocius, Gerald, 22, 29, 31

popular antiquities, 31, 205

popular culture, 5, 29, 45, 109

postmodernism, 8, 27, 41, 77, 107, 187n2, 193, 207

Prahlad, Anand, 8, 186

presence, 8–10, 80; and folk culture, 97, 104–5; folklore as, 97, 136, 169–70; as privilege, 175–76

preservation, 11, 99, 112, 136, 148–50, 153–54

Primiano, Leonard, 61

professionalization. *See* folklore

racism, 8, 75, 88, 91, 110, 129–32, 172, 185

rituals, 66, 86–87, 89, 92, 98, 152, 159–60, 171, 176–77, 184, 197

Roberts, John, 4, 14

romantic nationalism, 4, 8, 14, 15n2, 115, 195

Routledge, Clay, 74

Russell, Karen, "Haunting Olivia," 169

Sandburg, Carl, 209

Schopenhauer, Arthur, 63–64

self-consciousness, 96–97, 100, 105, 107

Sharp, Cecil, 167

Shuman, Amy, 4–5, 7, 20, 22, 29, 139, 142, 145, 197

Slaven, Amber, 52n3

Smith, John Patterson, 127–29, 131

Smith, Lee, *Oral History*, 101–5

Smith, Moira, 65–66

Snopes, x, 157–62

social media, 7, 83n4, 125–26, 157

Sokal, Adam, 21, 193

Star Trek, 46, 48–49

Stewart, Susan, 8, 30–31, 147

structuralism, 145, 153

sustainability, 11, 135–36, 153–54, 205

Swift, Taylor, 28, 30

Tasaday, 192–94

taxonomy, 30–31, 147

Thompson, Stith, 44, 52n3, 88

Thoms, William, 42, 204–5

Thurschwell, Pamela, 68–69

Toelken, Barre, 31, 33, 140

Toqueville, Alexis de, 76

touristic reading, 96, 98, 103, 109, 115

tradition. *See* folklore

trauma, 8, 75, 114, 130–32

Trethewey, Natasha, 127, 129–31

Turner, Patricia, 157, 160

Tylor, Edward, 160, 170, 178

uncanny, 176–79, 181, 184–86

unhomely, 127, 170, 180–86

unlaughter, 65–66

untellability, 7–8

urban legends. *See* legends: urban

vernacular, 22–23, 27–30, 34–35, 146

Visitation of Spirits, A (Kenan), 106–7

INDEX 219

Ward, Jesmyn, 129
Welsch, Roger: and American Indians, 40–41; and Dannebrog, 38–39; and folklore, 42–43; *Postcards from Nebraska*, 38, 41
Welty, Eudora, *Delta Wedding*, 179–87
Whitehead, Colson, 11; *John Henry Days*, 109–13
whiteness, 169–71, 175, 182–90; and nostalgia, 130; and rage, 133
Williams, Michael Ann, 4, 13
Wilson (comic), 77–80
Workman, Mark, 7–8

Zeitlin, Steven, 151–52